D0225551

Christopher J. Alexander, PhD

Gay and Lesbian Mental Health: A Sourcebook for Practitioners

*Pre-publication
REVIEWS,
COMMENTARIES,
EVALUATIONS . . .*

"**D**r. Alexander's sourcebook fulfills its promises as a resource for clinicians working with the current and complex issues of gay and lesbian clients. Problems once considered esoteric are now common in working with this population, so chapters covering issues such as multiple loss, identity problems of Latino gay men, the misuse of the term narcissism, helping partners of lesbian abuse survivors, and gay youth at risk for suicide are invaluable."

Donald P. McKillop, PhD
*Professor and Clinical Psychologist,
California State University,
Hayward*

More pre-publication
REVIEWS, COMMENTARIES, EVALUATIONS . . .

"This sourcebook is testimony to the need for specialized training in the provision of mental health services to lesbian, gay, and bisexual clients. It serves as an informative, up-to-date clinical reference for practitioners, and is rigorous enough to assist researchers in the field as well. No previous reference has addressed such a range of issues so critical to the lives of lesbian and gay individuals. Research findings from the cutting edge of lesbian and gay mental health such as parenting, aging, and spirituality are addressed with clarity and objectivity.

The writers rigorously review and critique prior research that oftentimes has stigmatized gay and lesbian clients through a heterosexual bias, and they provide practitioners with helpful and specific guidelines for assisting clients with a variety of developmental and relationship concerns.

This sourcebook successfully fills a wide gap in lesbian and gay mental health literature; it should be included in the library of every agency or practitioner serving the counseling needs of lesbian and gay populations."

Jeffrey P. Prince, PhD
Associate Director, Counseling
& Psychological Services,
University Health Service,
University of California at Berkeley

"I loved this book! Chris Alexander's marvelous collection of research and clinical writings defines and clarifies mental health issues for gay/lesbian/bisexual people on the brink of the twenty-first century. It is a refreshingly positive and eminently readable summary of major issues that reflects the maturation of both the gay and lesbian mental health profession and of the gay/lesbian/bisexual community of the 1990s. From the title to the final page, it is insightful, practical, and intellectually rigorous.

The chapters combine thorough, thoughtful reviews of the research and theoretical literature with practical and powerful clinical conceptualizations and recommendations on issues such as youth suicide, aging, sexual objectification and eating disorders, gay families, families of gay people, and more.

It is a joy to have a book on gay and lesbian mental health validate and address the spiritual needs of gay people.

This wonderful book is an excellent addition to the libraries of all psychotherapists, gay and straight. It is a perfect textbook for a course on gay and lesbian mental health."

Thomas F. Merrifield, PhD
Director, Gay & Lesbian Counseling
Program, University Health Service,
University of California at Berkeley

NOTES FOR PROFESSIONAL LIBRARIANS AND LIBRARY USERS

This is an original book title published by Harrington Park Press, an imprint of The Haworth Press, Inc. Unless otherwise noted in specific chapters with attribution, materials in this book have not been previously published elsewhere in any format or language.

CONSERVATION AND PRESERVATION NOTES

All books published by The Haworth Press, Inc. and its imprints are printed on certified ph neutral, acid free book grade paper. This paper meets the minimum requirements of American National Standard for Information Sciences–Permanence of Paper for Printed Material, ANSI Z39.48-1984.

Gay and Lesbian Mental Health
A Sourcebook for Practitioners

HAWORTH Gay & Lesbian Studies
John P. De Cecco, PhD
Editor in Chief

Gay and Lesbian Mental Health
A Sourcebook for Practitioners

Christopher J. Alexander, PhD
Editor

Harrington Park Press
An Imprint of The Haworth Press, Inc.
New York • London

Published by

Harrington Park Press, an imprint of The Haworth Press, Inc., 10 Alice Street, Binghamton, NY 13904-1580

© 1996 by The Haworth Press, Inc. All rights reserved. No part of this work may be reproduced or utilized in any form or by any means, electronic or mechanical, including photocopying, microfilm and recording, or by any information storage and retrieval system, without permission in writing from the publisher. Printed in the United States of America.

Cover photos used with permission from Impact Visuals:
    Photo of male couple (*Gay & Lesbian March*) by Marilyn Humphries.
    Photo of female couple by Carolina Kroon.

Cover designed by Donna M. Brooks.

Library of Congress Cataloging-in-Publication Data

Gay and lesbian mental health: a sourcebook for practitioners/Christopher J. Alexander, editor.
       p.   cm.
    Includes bibliographical references and index.
    ISBN 1-56023-879-8 (alk. paper)
    1. Gays-Mental health. 2. Gays-Psychology. I. Alexander, Christopher J.
RC451.4.G39G39 1996
616.89'008'664-dc20   95-43392
                                                                          CIP

This book is dedicated to my father, for all his love and guidance through the years, and to David, for who you are and all that you do.

CONTENTS

ABOUT THE EDITOR

Christopher J. Alexander, PhD, is a clinical psychologist in private practice in Oakland, California. In his practice, Dr. Alexander offers both individual and couples therapy, as well as psychodiagnostic assessment. In addition, he provides individual and group supervision to clinicians working with sexual minorities. Dr. Alexander holds an adjunct faculty position for the Center for Psychological Studies in Albany, California, and is Editor of the *Gay and Lesbian Quarterly*, a quarterly newsletter that highlights research of interest to those working with sexual minorities.

Contributors

Marcia Iris Baum, LCSW, is a psychotherapist and counselor in private practice in San Francisco. She provides individual, couples, group, and family counseling with specialized training in incest-related issues, eating disorders, and sexual minorities. She has published numerous articles, and has written for *The Healing Woman,* a monthly newsletter for survivors of childhood abuse. She became the legal adoptive parent of Maya, her partner's biological baby, in December 1991.

Anthony R. D'Augelli, PhD, is a professor of Human Development in the Department of Human Development and Family Studies at Pennsylvania State University. A community and clinical psychologist, he received his PhD from the University of Connecticut in 1972. His research has focused on helping processes in community settings, and the development of preventive interventions. Current interests focus on the life circumstances of lesbian, gay, and bisexual youth, especially their experiences of victimization. He is co-editor (with Charlotte J. Patterson) of *Lesbian, Gay, and Bisexual Identities Over the Lifespan,* published by Oxford University Press in 1995.

Miriam Ehrenberg, PhD, is an associate clinical professor at the City University of New York and is in private practice. She also serves as the associate director of the Institute for Human Identity, the first gay and lesbian counseling center in New York. Her publications include *The Psychotherapy Maze, The Intimate Circles: Sexual Dynamics of Family Life,* and *Optimum Brain Power.*

Diana Gray, PhD, is a licensed clinical psychologist living and working in San Francisco. Her work is split between a private practice specializing in women and lesbian/gay issues and being a clinical supervisor for the San Francisco Department of Public Health. Her advocations include wilderness adventure trips. Dr. Gray facilitates workshops and seminars on lesbian and gay couples with Rik Isensee, LCSW.

Scott L. Hershberger, PhD, is an assistant professor of quantitative psychology in the Department of Psychology at the University of Kansas. He received his PhD in psychometrics from Fordham University in 1990. His current research is concerned with genetic and environmental contributions to sexual orientation development. He has published papers in both the quantitative and psychological literature.

Rik Isensee, LCSW, practices psychotherapy with gay men and couples in San Francisco. He is the author of *Love Between Men,* a guide to resolving conflicts in gay relationships, and *Growing Up Gay in a Dysfunctional Family.*

Mark Marion, MFCC, is a psychotherapist in private practice in San Francisco and Berkeley. His interest in reexamining existing models of loss grew out of a specialization in treating depression and anxiety in the gay community. He is currently working on a book to further explore the concepts of global loss.

Vincent J. Nunno, PhD, received his doctorate from the California School of Professional Psychology. Dr. Nunno is licensed as a psychologist, educational psychologist, and marriage, family, and child counselor. He is also a board-certified forensic examiner and a Fellow of the American College of Forensic Examiners. Dr. Nunno is a private practitioner in clinical, educational, and neuropsychological assessment and is on the core faculty and Board of Directors of the San Francisco School of Psychology. Dr. Nunno has published works in the area of Rorschach psychology of the Nazi war criminal and Rorschach studies of thought and affective disorders.

Marcia Perlstein, MFCC, is a marriage and family counselor and has been a practicing psychotherapist in Berkeley, California since 1967. She offers workshops in Self-Acceptance Training in the tradition handed down by the late Richard Olney. She is Director of Psychotherapy Services for North Berkeley Psychiatric Institute and Founder and Director of the East Bay Volunteer Therapist AIDS Project. She consults nationally, is a trainer and supervisor of new and veteran therapists, and has been a lecturer and instructor at various Bay area graduate programs.

Neil W. Pilkington is a PhD candidate in clinical psychology at McGill University in Montreal, Canada. He conducts research on the social psychology of anti-gay prejudice and the mental health consequences of lesbian, gay, and bisexual adolescents' experiences of anti-gay victimization. His work has been published in the social scientific literature and has been presented at conferences of both the American Psychological Association and the American Psychological Society.

Richard A. Rodriguez, PhD, received his doctorate in counseling psychology from the University of Utah in 1991. He is currently a staff psychologist at Counseling and Psychological Services at the University of California at Berkeley. He is also on the adjunct faculty of the California School of Professional Psychology where he teaches a course on counseling lesbians and gay men of color, and the adjunct faculty of California State University at Hayward. His areas of clinical expertise include Chicano/Latino mental health, lesbian and gay identity, HIV and AIDS, and adult survivors of child abuse.

Michael D. Siever, PhD, MEd, obtained his Master's degree in special education and his doctorate in counseling psychology from the University of Washington. He studied with G. Alan Marlatt, PhD, as a Postdoctoral Research Fellow at the the Addictive Behaviors Research Center in the Psychology Department at the University of Washington. He is currently Program Coordinator of Operation Recovery, the substance abuse treatment program of Operation Concern, San Francisco's lesbian and gay mental health center.

Miriam Smolover, MFCC, is a licensed therapist and Certified Expressive Therapist. She is the Clinical Director at the John F. Kennedy University Transpersonal and Holistic Counseling Center in Oakland, California. She also maintains a private psychotherapy practice in Oakland.

Carol A. Thompson, MFT, is a lesbian psychotherapist in private practice in East Lyme, Connecticut. She earned a BFA and an MA in dramatic arts from the University of Connecticut and a Master's degree in family therapy from Southern Connecticut State University. She is the former Bereavement Coordinator for the Hospice of Southeastern Connecticut, and has worked in the areas of trauma and loss. Her chapter is based on an article previously published in *Women and Therapy* by The Haworth Press.

Loris L. Wells-Lurie, ACSW, LCSW, is a social worker and the mother of a lesbian daughter and gay son. She lives and works in Emeryville and San Francisco, California.

Preface

Our understanding of the mental health aspects of being a sexual minority has increased tremendously in recent years. It used to be that popular and scientific notions about who gays and lesbians are, why and how they got that way, and their treatment needs were developed by those who were on the outside looking in. With time, gay and lesbian healthcare professionals started to explore the complexity of sexual orientation by listening to what clients were telling them and developing questionnaires and studies that attempted to ascertain what the experience of being a sexual minority is like. Though we are far from having a universal consensus about the etiology and impact on personal development of being gay or lesbian, we at least have a wealth of research and study with which to understand the diverse issues, needs, and concerns of gay men, lesbians, and those who are our friends and providers.

Books that addressed the topic of homosexuality previously focused on the causes of homosexuality and on ways in which the homosexual could be "cured." The gay man or woman trying to seek some understanding or reality check on his or her feelings would often read such books and feel pathologized and targeted as defective in significant ways. Because many in the healthcare professions further validated these notions, many individuals were left feeling despondent and impaired, and eventually came to distrust the mental health profession's capacity to effectively understand and help them.

Much of the impetus for gays and lesbians to challenge the label of mental disorder stemmed from the classification of homosexuality as a mental disease in the *Diagnostic and Statistical Manual of Psychiatric Disorders* (DSM). In 1973, the American Psychiatric Association (APA) made the decision to remove homosexuality from its official list of mental diseases. This decision resulted in many dissident psychiatrists alleging that the organization gave in to threats and pressure from gay liberation groups, and the issue was eventually brought to vote by the full APA membership. The fact that a significant number of APA members voted to remove homosexuality from its list of mental diseases gave voice to what many already knew to be true: homosexuality is not an illness. There was still the recognition, however, that homosexuals have their own unique mental health concerns, and researchers, many of them gay or lesbian themselves, set out to understand the range of needs and concerns of gays and lesbians.

To this end, books were published for and about gay men and women. Finally, many gays and lesbians had validation, by way of published works about life and emotions they understood too well. As one looks back on many of these books and articles, one sees common themes such as "Coming Out," "Finding a Gay Identity," "History of the Gay Rights Movement," "Finding a Partner," etc. These topics were extremely important to people as they tried to forge for themselves healthy identities, a sense of community, and loving relationships.

Eventually, however, clinicians and researchers began looking at much more complex topics. The subtleties, if you will, of being a sexual minority were begging to be explored, and to that end we started seeing vigorous research and theory on homosexuality. The volume of study eventually warranted specialized journals such as the *Journal of Homosexuality* and the *Journal of Gay and Lesbian Psychotherapy*. Clinicians were afforded the chance to read case studies, as well as quantitative and qualitative research on people they were working with in their practices. Exciting and challenging studies gave us new insight and understanding of such areas as adolescent sexuality, gay teachers, substance use disorders, gay and lesbian sexuality, male sexual dysfunction, homophobia, psychobiological theories of sexual identity development, and eventually, HIV-related topics.

This book is an extension of this progression. It was developed with the idea in mind that clinicians need and require information that reflects many of the recent changes and findings pertinent to gay and lesbian mental health. I author a quarterly newsletter that summarizes recent medical and social science research on gays and lesbians. What I have found in the years that I have published the newsletter is that there is some incredible research being published about sexual minorities, and that most clinicians working with this population rarely read or hear about these studies. This book is an attempt to bridge this gap and bring some of these topics to a wide audience. To that end, four of the chapters included in this volume are extensions of social science research done on gay and lesbian mental health. The remaining chapters focus on topics and issues that are on the cutting edge of our understanding of gay and lesbian mental health.

The authors in this volume each address a specific area of mental health function of gay men and women. The intent of each author is to elaborate on a particular topic area and provide the reader with a practical understanding of how to work with and understand similar issues in the context of professional practice. Each chapter is written in a manner that makes it informative and useful to practicing clinicians. Similarly, the chapters were written to be used as guidelines for study in the social sciences and thus are of interest and relevance to students and interns in the fields of mental health. Our goal is for this book to be an informative and practical guide to further an understanding of the issues and concerns of many in the gay and lesbian community.

OVERVIEW

Each chapter author is a clinician or educator with direct experience working in the areas of which they write. The authors bring to their chapters a combination of clinical experience, and often personal histories that make them well-suited to write about their particular topic areas. An underlying goal for many of the authors is to challenge the stereotypes that others hold about homosexuality and gay and lesbian mental health. Even trained professionals are not beyond carrying misperceptions about what it means to be a sexual minority, and thus we hope to broaden the perspective and comprehension about the lives of gay men and women.

The book begins with an examination of gay male self-image. There has long been a stereotype that gay men are self-centered, narcissistic, and pleasure-seeking. The lay public is guilty of making this association, but clinical theory, too, has been quick to categorize gay men in such terms. Chapter 1 examines self-perceptions of gay men by reviewing a study that utilized psychological testing as a means of ascertaining how gay men perceive themselves. What is discovered is that gay men may be prone to self-examination, and thus present with elements of self-focus, but that narcissistic vulnerability does not necessarily equate with pathology.

In Chapter 2, marriage and family therapist Miriam Smolover writes on the mental health needs of partners of lesbians who are sexual abuse survivors. A great deal of attention has been given to sexual abuse in recent years, but the partners of survivors have often had their own needs gone unnoticed and unaddressed. Smolover, based on her extensive group and individual work with survivors and their partners, outlines steps therapists can take when working with survivors individually or in groups.

In Chapter 3, psychologists Scott L. Hershberger, Neil W. Pilkington, and Anthony R. D'Augelli address the findings of their 1993 research on suicidality among gay, lesbian, and bisexual youth. Of the 194 youths studied, 42 percent had attempted suicide on at least one occasion. Variables that lead to an increase in suicide risk for gay adolescent teenagers are examined, and an attempt to categorize suicide attempters is made. The authors of this study were able to identify a multiplicity of variables that distinguish suicide attempters from nonattempters, including a higher incidence of self-disclosure about their sexuality.

In Chapter 4, San Francisco Bay Area psychotherapist Mark Marion outlines the effects on the gay community of multiple loss to AIDS. He points out that many gay men present clinically with the symptoms of post-traumatic stress disorder, but that the trauma of loss is by no means in their past. Thus, he argues that our current models of understanding grief and trauma are inadequate for comprehending the effects of multiple loss on the gay community, and, in turn, offers a new vocabulary for communicating these effects. A Global Loss Model is presented for helping therapists find ways of assisting clients in recovering the capacity to live a life of self-worth and meaning in the midst of ongoing loss.

In Chapter 5, San Francisco psychotherapists Diana Gray and Rik Isensee address the themes of merging, autonomy, and fear of intimacy in gay and lesbian couples. Practical steps couples can take in their relationships are discussed, and guidelines for clinicians are offered for helping couples foster and develop more effective communication skills.

In Chapter 6, San Francisco psychotherapist Marcia Iris Baum writes on the increase of gays and lesbians choosing to be parents. Acknowledging the dramatic increase in births to gay men and lesbians, Marcia shares with us the decision-making process of one couple and elaborates on the personal, legal, social, and couples issues that are commonly experienced by those making this decision.

In Chapter 7, Berkeley psychologist Richard A. Rodriguez examines the process of identity formation in gay Latino men. Drawing upon his 1991 qualitative study, he presents a social constructivist view of identity development for gay Latino men, examining topics such as religion, family, gender role socialization, sexual abuse, HIV, and coming out. Rodriguez emphasizes that cultural identity development is a process, not a single event, and that counselor/client differences alone do not create barriers to effective counseling with ethnic minorities.

In Chapter 8, social worker and parent of a gay son and lesbian daughter, Loris L. Wells-Lurie, focuses on the needs of parents of gays and lesbians. Acknowledging that when their child comes out of the closet as gay or lesbian, parents often go into the closet, Wells-Lurie emphasizes the need for parents to decrease their isolation. Guidelines for working with and educating parents are suggested, and encouragement for therapists to be aware of parents' needs is addressed.

In Chapter 9, marriage and family therapist Marcia Perlstein writes on the role of religion and spirituality in the lives of gay men and lesbians, and how therapy can provide an avenue for exploring these issues. Many sexual minorities have negative attitudes toward religion and want nothing to do with it. Although Marcia does not ignore such feelings, she does offer that there are alternatives for integrating old or new religion into one's life, and that therapy offers an optimal space for identifying one's spiritual needs and values.

In Chapter 10, psychologist Miriam Ehrenberg looks at gay and lesbian identity over the life span. Dr. Ehrenberg explores research findings in this area which suggest that most older gays and lesbians are psychologically sturdy and content with their lives. The lack of research on less affluent gays and lesbians is noted, however, and thus we may not have a comprehensive understanding of all older gays and lesbians. Dr. Ehrenberg concludes that there needs to be a bridge between younger and older gays and lesbians in order for us all to have a better sense of continuity of the gay and lesbian family.

In Chapter 11, family therapist Carol A. Thompson looks at the development of lesbian identity. By drawing parallels with theories of attachment, grief, and loss, she elaborates on the conditioning of women in our society and how coming out as lesbian often means giving up on what was once a dream or goal of what womanhood should be.

In Chapter 12, Michael D. Siever, PhD, examines the role of body image and eating disorders in populations of heterosexual men and women. Based on his research on body image, Dr. Siever elucidates the ways in which sexual objectification operates within the gay and lesbian subculture. The study found that heightened concern for physical attractiveness and consequent body dissatisfaction led to increased vulnerability to eating disorders for men.

Chapter 1

Narcissism and Egocentricity in Gay Men

Christopher J. Alexander
Vincent J. Nunno

NARCISSISM AND MALE HOMOSEXUALITY

When contacted by a gay man for psychological services, a therapist often notes that invariably one of the desired outcomes expressed is the client's need to feel better about himself. Specifically, to achieve a healthy self-esteem and self-image is a primary goal for many, if not most, sexual minorities. The fact that issues of self-esteem are of such paramount importance to gay men is reflective of the struggle for overall acceptance of oneself by both individuals and society at large. Concerns about self-image are not restricted to the coming-out phase when it is common for there to be ambivalence about identity, role, and object choice. Rather, experience suggests that the attainment of a healthy self-image, confident feelings about one's identity and sexuality, and the self-assurance that one is not inherently damaged because one is gay, is a lifelong struggle with origins deeply rooted in society, family, religion, etc.

Hanley-Hackenbruck (1989) suggests that therapeutic exploration of low self-esteem in gay men and lesbians will uncover internalized homophobia, which has served to cause the individual "severe anxiety, depression, sexual dysfunction, relationship failures, or a feeling of being an impostor" (p. 35). Resolution of internalized homophobia (or "superego modification," as she terms it) is an in-depth process that includes further individuating the person from parental domination (and family perspectives and values concerning homosexuality), defining one's own values and thus defining a sexual identity, and developing an, oftentimes new, social and peer group that is more accepting of the person.

Only in recent years has there been adequate attention given to gay male self-esteem and the self-image gay men maintain of themselves (Voeller, 1980; Cornett, 1993). Clearly, growing up in American society where homosexuality is so ridiculed, condemned, and stereotyped creates an internal struggle for a healthy sense of self. Without sufficient internal and external validation of worth, developing the self-confidence and assuredness that comprises much of self-esteem can be difficult to attain. This carries with it inherent risks for achieving healthy individuation and identity.

An individual who, on the one hand, views his own sexual feelings and identity as natural, yet, on the other hand, receives broad condemnation of such feelings risks developing what Masterson (1988) has identified as a false sense of self. According to Masterson, the false self is defensive in nature, setting out to avoid painful feelings at the expense of mastering reality. Allowing the false self to control one's life results in a severe lack of self-esteem. The false self sends a message to the individual that self-destructive behavior is the only way to deal with the conflict between his feelings and the demands of reality. Masterson writes, "The false self has a highly skilled defensive radar whose purpose is to avoid feelings of rejection although sacrificing the need for intimacy" (1988, p. 66). For Masterson, narcissism is one key manifestation of the false self.

Many gay persons feel shame, guilt, and depression, but mask these feelings to others, often exaggerating the opposite feelings in interpersonal relations. This use of narcissistic defense has led to a stereotyped notion that there may be a higher incidence of narcissism in gay men than in nongay men.

The term *narcissism* was borrowed by Freud from Havelock Ellis, who used the Greek name to describe a form of sexual perversion in which the individual takes himself as a sexual object. Even though narcissism comes from the Greek myth, superficially understood to represent self-love, exactly the opposite is true in the narcissistic style. Rather, the narcissist has buried his true self-expression in response to early injuries and replaced it with a highly developed, compensatory self. Masterson (1988) sees narcissism as an inflated false self, whereby the person seems to have everything including wealth, beauty, health, and power with a strong sense of knowing what they want and how to get it. However, according to Masterson, the individual maintains the defensive false self in order not to feel the underlying rage and depression associated with an inadequate and fragmented sense of self.

Meloy (1988) notes that the narcissistic personality disorder represents personality function and structure at a relatively higher developmental level of borderline personality organization. Kohut (1971) writes that whereas the borderline personality has a less cohesive self, and is thus subject to episodes of fragmentation, the narcissist has more transient episodes of fragmentation and recovers his or her sense of self more readily. Narcissists are therefore able to "snap back" and repair their narcissistic injuries with more ease than the borderline, according to Kohut.

Theories about the etiology of narcissism vary, but most place emphasis on the early, formative years of childhood. Kernberg (1975), for example, suggests that narcissism develops as a consequence of parental rejection or abandonment. His hypothesis is that because of cold and rejecting parents, the child defensively withdraws and comes to believe that only oneself can be trusted and relied on and therefore loved. Millon (1981), on the other hand, offers a social-learning theory of narcissism, where narcissism is seen as a consequence of parental overvaluation. Millon adds that often the child is either the firstborn or an only child, which contributes to the abundance of attention and special treatment received.

That narcissism is a natural process is rarely disputed. Some authors (Masterson, 1981; Stolorow, 1980) write that a normally developed or healthy narcissism is vital to a healthy adaptation. Freud speculated that narcissism might be part of the regular sexual development of human beings. For Freud, pathological outcome results when the child fails to move from the stage of self-love or primary narcissism, to true, other-directed love. For Freud, the function of narcissistic object choice is to regulate self-esteem.

Analytic writers (Ferenczi, 1914; Boehm, 1933; Socarides, 1978) have traditionally agreed upon a close connection between homosexuality and narcissism. Much of this stemmed from the view that homosexuality is a more primitive condition than heterosexuality is because it has not traditionally been viewed as truly object related, it involves impoverished object relations, and its general organization is essentially preoedipal (Lewes, 1988). Cornett (1993) notes that traditional psychoanalytic theory regarding homosexuality has been influenced by the idea that the narcissism characteristic of such disorders as schizophrenia is essentially identical to that of homosexuality, except in terms of relative quantity. Friedman (1988) adds that most behavioral scientists, many psychoanalysts, and most practitioners who have worked with gay men refute the connection between homosexuality and pathological narcissism:

> The personal experience of informed professionals carries special weight in this area because the narcissistic person often appears deceptively normal in social situations. It is virtually impossible, however, to maintain a durable, caring relationship with a narcissist. Many mental health professionals do have lasting friendships with gay men, have shared happiness and sorrow with them, offered support to and received support from them. (p. 183)

Most theories of homophobia (Neisen, 1993) address the issue of shame as an underlying mechanism, and others (Nathanson, 1987) have written extensively about the connection between shame and narcissism. Lewis (1987) sees narcissism as a dangerous defense against the hatred of the self in shame, and adds, " . . . both shame and narcissism so directly involve the self at the center of experience, either being scorned or admired" (p. 97). To this end, there is often a parallel between the narcissistic character and depression, due to the low self-esteem so evident in the narcissistic personality. Shame differs from guilt, even though there is a close association between the two. With guilt, we are punished for something that we did. With shame, we are punished for some quality of who we are. Of shame, Nathanson writes the following:

> The shame experience is one of utter isolation. It is all those moments in which we felt like crawling into a hole and disappearing forever. It involves sudden, unexpected separation; no matter what our age, shame resonates with the worst of our fears of abandonment. And shame can shape a character. We

can live in fearful anticipation of embarrassment, experiencing shame-anxiety; or develop a perfectionistic style to avoid shame. (p. 250)

Thus it is with shame that the person lives in fear of "being found out." Defenses are employed to protect against narcissistic vulnerability and exposure, and by default the development of a healthy sense of self is hindered. We can clearly see how much of the above could account for narcissistic traits in gay men, but the question remains as to whether there really is a connection between male homosexuality and narcissism. Presently, narcissism is assessed by way of clinical interview and psychological testing, and psychological testing has frequently been used to study the personality structure of male homosexuals.

PSYCHOLOGICAL TESTING INDICATORS

Investigations of homosexuality by way of psychological testing is not new. Morin (1977) surveyed the literature for the years 1967 to 1974, and found 27 studies in which the researchers focused on the assessment of homosexual subjects. Reiss (1980) found that the Minnesota Multiphasic Personality Inventory (MMPI) was one of the more popular tests used on homosexual subjects. Hooker (1972) found that blind judges could not distinguish homosexual men's responses on projective tests from those of heterosexual men, leading Friedman (1988) to conclude that this gives indication that the psychodynamic conflicts of the two groups may be similar.

Reiss (1980) found that of the projective tests, the Rorschach Inkblot Test was a popular test administered to homosexual subjects. The Rorschach is considered to be an unstructured test. That is, subjects are given a relatively open-ended set of instructions prior to beginning the test. Subjects are presented with ten cards, one at a time, which show a symmetrical inkblot. Subjects are asked to offer their perceptions of what the blots look like to them, and the responses are recorded by the examiner and then coded and scored according to a standardized scoring system (Exner, 1993). Subjects' responses to the Rorschach inkblots depend on their history of experience, style of perception, preferences for information processing, and modes of self-expression. Rorschach scoring provides data related to each, as well as data pertaining to coping style, thought process, depression, and self-perception.

The first reported study on homosexual signs in the Rorschach included no control group, so it was not known how frequently the findings occur in the protocols of nonhomosexual men. In a later study, Wheeler (1949) compared the frequency of occurrence of 20 signs in the Rorschachs of 100 patients with their therapist's judgments of the homosexual tendencies of these patients. A limitation of his study was that all the men were World War II veterans who were discharged with a neuropsychiatric disability or who were sufficiently disturbed to be accepted by the Veterans Administration clinic where the study was conducted. These studies are examples of the fact that most published studies on homosexuality implementing the Rorschach use hospitalized patients for subjects, and that little research on homosexuality has examined features that the Rorschach is very useful at elucidating.

One set of studies that is still frequently cited in studies of homosexuality using projective tests is that of Exner (1969) and Raychaudhuri and Mukerji (1971). Both studies found significantly more *Reflection* responses given by male homosexuals and male sociopaths compared to populations of depressives and "normal" college students. Reflection responses are those in which mirror images or actual reflections are verbalized during the free association phase of the Rorschach. Exner obtained his homosexual subjects from a hospitalized sample, and Raychaudhuri and Mukerji obtained their homosexual subjects from a prison population. As Reiss (1980) cautions, test results from homosexuals in prison may be at variance with data from an unincarcerated population due to the variables that lead to imprisonment.

Both sets of researchers (Exner, 1969; Raychaudhuri and Mukerji, 1971) also found a higher incidence of male homosexuals offering *Pair* responses to the Rorschach. Pair responses are those in which the symmetry features of the inkblot precipitate the report that "two" of the perceived objects are present (Exner, 1986). In combination, the Reflection and Pair responses make up the *Egocentricity Index* on the Rorschach, a measure of self-image. The offering of even one Reflection response is highly indicative of a narcissistic self-structure. Meloy (1988), for example, points out that Reflection responses suggest an "intensely self-focused, narcissistically disordered individual. It implies a sense of grandiosity and entitlement that are the hallmarks of the psychopathic character" (p. 392).

Exner (1986) refers to a validation study of the Egocentricity Index that examined the length of time subjects spent looking at themselves in a mirror. Twenty-one male subjects were videotaped as they each waited alone in a room with a one-way mirror. The subjects were divided into two groups, based on the amount of time they spent looking in the mirror. Exner reports that the ten protocols in the second half of the group (with an average viewing time of 68.5 seconds) contained six Reflections and 103 Pair responses. The ten protocols in the first half of the group (with an average viewing time of 27.1 seconds) contained no Reflections and 68 Pair responses. The differences were statistically significant.

A STUDY OF NARCISSISM
IN MALE HOMOSEXUALS

To assess whether a group of psychologically healthy gay men would offer more Pair and Reflection responses to the Rorschach than would a group of psychologically healthy heterosexual men, we incorporated the Rorschach into a study on gay male personality. We wanted to find out if, indeed, a noninstitutionalized population of gay men would offer more of these responses, thus having elevated Egocentricity Index scores. Because the assumption behind the presence of Reflection responses in a Rorschach protocol equates with narcissistic personality structure, we decided to include an additional measure of narcissism, the Narcissistic Personality Inventory (NPI). The NPI is a 40-item self-report measure designed to measure individual differences in narcissism as a personality trait.

Trying to attain a representative sample of any population is difficult since people, regardless of the group(s) to which they belong, are rarely homogenous in nature. This was certainly a challenge with this study. We knew that we wanted to assess a group of men who were not incarcerated or under inpatient psychiatric care, but the question remained as to whether everyone else could be classified as *normal* or representative. To control for psychopathology, we decided to make use of the MMPI, a measure of personality and characterologic variables. In general, any score above 70 on a variety of characteristics (i.e., Depression, Hysteria, Schizophrenia, Mania, Psychopathic Deviance, Hypochondriasis, etc.) is considered statistically significant for that classification. Thus, we decided to eliminate from the study all persons who attained two or more MMPI clinical scale scores above 70 (2 standard deviations above the mean of 50). Though not foolproof, this method did provide the best measurable estimate of psychological health, given our intent to look for Pair and Reflection responses in a relatively normal group of gay men.

Results

Forty-five subjects completed test batteries for this research. After excluding those subjects who presented with test indicators of significant pathology, 32 subjects remained. Statistical analysis of the data indicates that our sample did not obtain significantly more Pair responses to the Rorschach when compared to published norms (Exner, 1993). Nor was the overall Egocentricity Index score significantly different, though our study showed more variability in Egocentricity scores comparatively (the range in our sample was 0.00 to 0.82, whereas Exner's normative group had a range of 0.03 to 0.61).

What the results do indicate, however, is that our sample did produce a statistically greater likelihood of offering a Reflection response to the Rorschach, with five of the 32 subjects offering at least one. Interestingly, however, the subjects in this study had a mean NPI score of 14.43. Thus, our sample scored below the mean (which is 16.50) on this measure. When compared to those subjects who were rejected from this study, our sample had a statistically higher MMPI Ego-Strength score (a measure of self-esteem). Other findings revealed that of the subjects we assessed, 31 percent scored positive on the Rorschach Depression Constellation. Further, our sample scored above the expected mean on Rorschach measures of introspection, oppositionality, and emotional control.

Analysis

The central task behind analysis of this study is ascertaining whether we can conclude that gay men as a group are more narcissistic or self-centered than the average male population. It is clear, based on this study, that the probability of a gay male offering a Reflection response is two-and-a-half times greater than nonpatient adult males. Thus, we are left with the question of whether or not the Reflection response is an adequate measure of narcissism, especially in light of the fact that our sample scored below the mean on the Narcissistic Personality Inventory. The question then follows whether the NPI is a better or lesser measure of narcissism than is the Reflection response.

Clinical experience and research on the Reflection response suggest that this Rorschach variable is highly correlated with narcissistic character, primarily the exploitative, entitled, and opportunistic features of the disorder. This is most highly evidenced in the protocols of male sociopaths (Meloy, 1988). One possibility is that the Reflection response is a global measure of narcissistic tendencies, and thus is sensitive to mild and extreme manifestations of the classification. To the extent that this is true, we note that a Reflection response may offer indication of narcissistic vulnerability, vanity, lack of empathy, or any of the extreme manifestations mentioned above.

What is clear, however, is that a trait such as narcissism would not be identified by only one variable in a psychological test battery, rather, there likely would be a convergence of data to offer indication of all or most major features of the disorder. If we assume this line of thinking with the current study, then we see that one aspect of our assessment (i.e., the Rorschach Reflection response) is picking up these features, while other aspects (i.e., the NPI) do not suggest its presence. In psychological assessment theory, a diagnosis of a disorder is rarely, if ever, made on one piece of data alone.

Questions also arise with regard to our particular sample. All of our subjects live in the San Francisco Bay Area of California, and all came forward on their own initiative to volunteer for this study. It has been suggested that there may be more "narcissistic investment" on the part of someone who volunteers to participate in a lengthy series of psychological tests. It is also with great caution that we or any other researcher generalize the results of our study based on the data of so few participants. Thus, we are left with the challenge often encountered in research of how to generate hypotheses and conclusions based on our findings while not making too much of the data we have. This is where we hope that others will build on our study and add further to our understanding of both gay male psychological development and the role of psychodiagnostic testing in this quest.

NARCISSISTIC OR JUST VULNERABLE?

In our introduction to this study, we spoke of the unique challenges that sexual minorities must confront along the way to developing a cohesive sense of self. Societal homophobia, selective acceptance, and the necessity, on the part of the homosexual, to size up an individual or situation before letting down one's guard all contribute to a hypersensitivity of one's role vis-à-vis others. Confronted with circumstances such as these, one can argue that the self-focus used by homosexual men is not to affirm a sense of grandiosity and entitlement, nor is the need of tribute from others (Kernberg, 1975) about self-idealization. Rather, a focus on the self may be adaptive as the individual looks within to formulate his own view of self compared to what he senses from others. That guilt and shame are major components of the person who feels inferior and inadequate are themes we often see in clients. Thus, perhaps the etiology of this familiar struggle is, as Lewis (1987) points out, consistent with what psychoanalysts have long believed: that being in a chronic state of guilt is a defense against forbidden grandiosity or narcissism. Further, the need for recognition from others is likely a very primal desire for affirmation and acceptance, rather than some attempt to have others collude in one's feelings of greatness.

It is curious that the men in our study scored significantly higher on indicators of oppositionality, introspection, and emotional control than would be expected. Using the MMPI as a gauge, we can ascertain that the oppositionality seen in this sample is not of the severity to warrant a diagnosis of antisocial personality disorder. Otherwise, the MMPI would have disqualified the subjects. But when these variables are looked at collectively, in light of the gay male's life experience, their presence makes sense.

By *oppositionality* it is meant that the individual has a somewhat defiant, somewhat adolescent, approach to life. It does not necessarily equate with getting into trouble and disobeying major societal rules, but rather indicates that the person may be more guarded in their participation in normative behavior. To the extent that we interpret being gay as going against the mainstream, this type of defiance is probably healthy and adaptive for these men. The alternative is total conformity, and thus disowning a very significant piece of one's identity. More simplistically, it may represent caution on the subjects' part with regard to participating in psychological research, given historic concerns regarding confidentiality.

Introspection refers to the process of turning inward, of examining one's identity, motives, goals, and attributes. Introspection is not inherently narcissistic. Rather, it is a normal, healthy process, and constitutes the foundation of much of psychotherapy. That test indicators show a high incidence of introspection in this sample is illuminating given our quest to determine whether or not gay men are overly self-focused and self-identified. It should be noted that over half of our sample is or has been in some form of psychotherapy. Thus, the foundation for introspection had been established for many of them. Still, it warrants our attention as to whether or not gay men as a group are more inclined to "look within," again to assess if they are as damaged or inferior as much of society would suggest.

In light of this, we remind the reader that 31 percent of our sample scored positive on the Rorschach Depression Constellation, a highly sensitive measure to features consistent with depressive affect. This finding is recognized in addition to the finding that this group of men had lost an average of seven people to AIDS, some their lovers of many years. The likelihood of depression in the gay community cannot be underestimated, though its prevalence is undocumented, and clinicians are encouraged to be sensitive to issues of depression and mood with their gay clients.

Finally, a word about emotional control. Rorschach indicators suggest that this sample of men may be sacrificing an element of individuality in order to maintain control. If generalized to the broader gay male community, one interpretation of this finding is that gay men, because of the need to evaluate an individual or situation, may hinder spontaneous and genuine expression. Thus, the external appearance is not so much the grandiose persona of a narcissistic character, but rather a "best-foot-forward" approach that will hopefully result in less grief or critique.

CONCLUSION

Again, our hope is that future research will tackle the complexities of gay male personality structure. Our study is one indication that gay men may be in a process of introspection and self-awareness, some of which may contain a narcissistic component. Yet, narcissistic vulnerability and the periodic reliance upon narcissistic defense does not equate with pathology. Rather, its use may be adaptive given the assaultiveness of being gay in our society.

REFERENCES

Boehm, F. (1933). Beitraege zur Psychologie der Homosexualitaet IV: Ueber zwei Typen von maennlichen Homosexuellen. *Int Z Psa* 19:499-506.

Cornett, C. (1993). *Affirmative Dynamic Psychotherapy with Gay Men*. Northvale, New Jersey: Aronson.

Exner, J. E., Jr. (1969). Rorschach responses as an index of narcissism. *Journal of Projective Techniques and Personality Assessment*. 33:324-330.

Exner, J. E., Jr. (1974). *The Rorschach: A Comprehensive System*. New York: John Wiley and Sons.

Exner, J. E., Jr. (1986). *The Rorschach: A Comprehensive System*. Volume 1. *Basic Foundations*. New York: John Wiley and Sons.

Exner, J. E., Jr. (1990). *A Rorschach Workbook for the Comprehensive System*. North Carolina: Rorschach Workshops.

Exner, J. E., Jr. (1993). *The Rorschach: A Comprehensive System*. New York: John Wiley and Sons.

Ferenczi, S. (1914). The nosology of male homosexuality. In *Sex in Psycho-Analysis*. Boston: Gorham Press.

Friedman, R. C. (1988). *Male Homosexuality: A Contemporary Psychoanalytic Perspective*. New Haven, CT: Yale University Press.

Hanley-Hackenbruck, P. (1988). Psychotherapy and the coming out process. *Journal of Gay and Lesbian Psychotherapy*. 1:21-39.

Hooker, E. (1972). *Homosexuality*. In Department of Health, Education, and Welfare, NIMH Task Force on Homosexuality: Final Report and Background Papers. Pub. no. HSM72-9116, pp. 11-22. Washington, DC: Government Printing Office.

Kernberg, O. (1975). *Borderline Conditions and Pathological Narcissism*. New York: Jason Aronson.

Kohut, H. (1971). *The Analysis of the Self.* New York: International Universities Press.

Lewes, K. (1988). *The Psychoanalytic Theory of Male Homosexuality.* New York: Meridian.

Lewis, H. B. (1987). Shame and the Narcissistic Personality. In D.L. Nathanson (ed.) *The Many Faces of Shame.* New York: Guilford Press.

Masterson, J. F. (1981). The Narcissistic and Borderline Disorders: An Integrated Developmental Approach. New York: Brunner/Mazel.

Masterson, J. F. (1988). *The Search for the Real Self.* New York: Free Press.

Meloy, R. (1988). *The Psychopathic Mind: Origins, Dynamics, and Treatment.* New Jersey: Jason Aronson.

Millon, T. (1981). *Disorders of Personality.* New York: Wiley.

Morin, S. F. (1977). Heterosexual bias in psychological research on lesbianism and male homosexuality. *American Psychologist.* 32:629-637.

Nathanson, D. L. (1987). *The Many Faces of Shame.* New York: Guilford Press.

Neisen, J.H. (1993). Healing from a culture of victimization: Recovery from shame due to heterosexism. *Journal of Gay and Lesbian Psychotherapy.* Vol. 2, No. 1, 49-63.

Raychaudhuri, M. and Mukerji, K. (1971). Homosexual and narcissistic reflections in the Rorscach: An examination of Exner's diagnostic Rorschach signs. *Rorschachiana Japonica.* 12:119-126.

Reiss, B. F. (1980). Psychological tests in homosexuality. In J. Marmor (ed.) *Homosexual Behavior: A Modern Reappraisal.* New York: Basic Books.

Socarides, C. W. (1978). *Homosexuality.* New York: Jason Aronson.

Stolorow, R. and Lachman, F. (1980). Psychoanalysis of developmental arrests. New York: International Universities Press. (1986).

Voeller, B. (1980). Society and the gay movement. In J. Marmor (ed.). *Homosexual Behavior: A Modern Reappraisal.* New York: Basic Books.

Wheeler, W.M. (1949). An analysis of Rorschach indices of male homosexuality. *Rorschach Research Exchange,* 13, 97-126.

Chapter 2

What About My Needs?
Working with Lesbian Partners
of Childhood Sexual Abuse Survivors:
Using Expressive Arts Therapy

Miriam Smolover

INTRODUCTION

Being partners with someone healing from incest or childhood sexual abuse can be confusing, frustrating, painful, and overwhelming. The hurts the survivor suffered and the agony of her healing process can often take precedence over the partner's needs, experiences, and process of change. This focus on the survivor's needs is often encouraged by either one or both of the people in the relationship, their support network, and therapists.

Many books, groups, and workshops are available for survivors, while almost none exist for their partners. The resources that do exist are mainly geared toward a heterosexual population. Many of the common survivor/partner dynamics are similarly experienced by couples of any gender combination. However, lesbian couples have their own unique dynamics that arise from both members having been socialized as women. These may include training to be a caretaker, difficulties in establishing boundaries and expressing anger, the desire to merge, and internalized homophobia. Because the inci-

I would like to gratefully acknowledge the contributions of Meryl Lieberman, PhD, with whom I began this work in 1985.

dence rate of sexual abuse of girls is so high, it is also not uncommon that both members of a lesbian relationship are survivors. When this is the case, the healing path can be convoluted indeed.

I began offering one-day workshops for lesbian partners of incest survivors in 1985 called "What About My Needs?" Each workshop provided an environment in which women could, often for the first time, share their experiences with others who understood. The relief was palpable. I have since also offered both time-limited and ongoing groups for this population. Although I work with survivors and partners both individually and in couples, group work for partners is vital. It is the most powerful way to break the isolation and share coping strategies. The incorporation of expressive arts therapy into this work is one of the most exciting and effective ways I have found to be most useful for these women.

The literature available for either partners or the couple is often framed as a guide that enables partners to be a better support for the survivors, thus helping them to understand what the survivor is experiencing. Clients I have worked with feel that this focus on supporting the survivor once again ignores the depth of their own pain. This chapter will cover the common partner/survivor dynamics, and present a healing cycle that many partners go through. Special attention will be paid to those areas that affect lesbian relationships in particular. Various expressive arts techniques will be suggested for working through particular healing tasks, and a self-care list for partners will be provided. All quotes cited are generalized comments from composite partners, with three exceptions. "Zoe" and "Honora" are pseudonyms for group members who have graciously allowed me to use direct quotes from their writings, and Susan Schulman is the real author of the poem.

The timing of when each member of the couple is aware of the sexual abuse varies from couple to couple. The survivor may have always known about her abuse; she may have remembered the abuse prior to this relationship; or she may remember it after this relationship has begun. If she were aware of the abuse ahead of time, she may or may not have revealed it to her partner. She may or may not have worked on resolving the trauma prior to this relationship. Each of these scenarios affects the partner/survivor dynamics differently. The impact on the relationship seems to be most severe when the memories emerge after a relationship has begun, and the survivor is thrown into the whirlpool of early trauma recovery. This is the circumstance that I will generally be describing. For clarity, I will work with the assumption of one sexual abuse survivor in these descriptions.

HEY, I'M HERE, TOO!

In many of these relationships, the balance of attention is heavily weighted toward the survivor. While healing from her abuse, the impact of her memories, the release of long-suppressed feelings, and the recognition of how the abuse has affected her as an adult can all combine in a sometimes overwhelming barrage that can deplete her storehouse of attention for anyone else's needs. Because of the immensity of the healing task, the survivor may need to be more or less totally self-absorbed. The partner can be left feeling that she is not getting the attention she wants and requires. At the same time, she may believe that it is her role to be totally supportive, and may feel guilty for even being aware of her own needs, much less expecting her mate to respond to them. As the survivor attunes to her inner process, she may or may not be aware of her partner's attempts at caretaking, or she may reject them. Alternately, she may verbally or nonverbally ask for or demand constant attunement and nurturing, without being able to respond in kind. If she is aware of this imbalance, she may feel guilty as well as incapable, adding to the self-hatred that is often a part of early recovery. This creates more distance between the mates.

WHAT CAN I DO?

Partners often feel a tremendous desire or obligation to "make it all better." They may develop a "savior mentality," often expressed by overidentification with the survivor. Partners assume the role of protector via *fusion* and *isolation.* Fusion entails a blurring of boundaries and a subsequent loss of autonomous perspective. For example, a couple may spend all their unstructured time together or exert pressure to possess the other's attention and energy. Both may collude in a "you and me against the world" posture, thereby isolating themselves from the "unsafe" world outside. In her desperate need to be the most helpful one in the survivor's healing process, a partner may inadvertently sabotage the healing with her own fear of change.

Sometimes survivors have an unusually low tolerance for gentle nurturing and even nonsexual touch. A partner's typical lament is, "How can I give if she won't receive?" Or there will be contradictory statements about how the survivor wants to be taken care of. She could as easily want undivided attention as she wants to be left completely alone. So partners risk being "wrong" no matter what they offer. They may overcompensate for this by withholding or deferring. Or, to equalize their lack of control in some aspects of the relationship, such as sex, partners may become overly controlling in others, such as how much time to spend together or where they will go when they go out. Partners may find themselves setting boundaries that are incongruent with their real desires.

For the partner, the desire to be a caretaker in the relationship may have a "shadow" side. Women are generally raised to put others' needs above their own, to the point where they may not even know what theirs are. The obvious nature of the survivor's pain and dysfunctional family patterns may act as a screen to obscure the partner's focusing on her own issues. She may consciously or unconsciously use the seriousness of the survivor's situation to avoid looking at her own, past and present.

The survivor's healing process includes gaining a whole new perspective on her right to establish personal boundaries and set limits. As with the acquisition of any new skill, the survivor may go to extremes before learning a comfortable middle ground. The partner may end up feeling rejected, locked out of her lover's world. This is particularly painful if the couple previously had highly valued merging, which many lesbian couples do. Partners report experiencing that behaviors which were once an accepted part of the relationship are now unacceptable, sometimes inexplicably so. This creates confusion and frustration. A cycle of mistrust may start which seems to keep growing.

If the survivor has told others about her abuse, she may receive a lot of attention and sympathy from the couple's support system. The difficulties of being a partner may go unnoticed or not be seen as valid, and she may be considered selfish if she talks about how hard her mate's healing is being for her.

Because the healing cycle usually takes at least several years, the partner may feel trapped in a relationship she did not expect. Although loving the survivor, she may feel angry that the surfacing of the abuse has significantly altered their prior relationship. She may sometimes want to leave, and feel guilty for even considering the idea.

WHAT CAN I SAY?

Many difficulties arise in even knowing how to talk about the abuse, both with the survivor and other people. While brimming with reactions, partners often feel afraid to show their horror, sadness, or disgust, not wishing their lovers to feel any worse about themselves. The survivor sometimes may feel safe only if her partner says nothing, while at other times she may be hurt or angered by her partner's silence. The survivor also will often give double messages about hearing anger directed at her abusing or nonprotecting family. Sometimes she defends them and gets angry if the partner challenges her stance. Other times she expects an immediate supportive anger, thus leaving the partner confused once again. Partners have a right to their own responses, while acknowledging and supporting whatever feelings their lover is currently having.

It is very hard to be the (often sole) recipient of all of the survivor's revelations and feelings. Partners have a legitimate need to talk with other people about what it is like to hear this, reactions that may not even be useful for the survivor to hear. At the same time, survivors often have rigid rules about maintaining total secrecy. Her degree of flexibility around disclosure is usually linked to her own processes of denial and self-forgiveness. The more she accepts what happened and believes in her own innocence, the more room there generally is for her partner to talk with others. The couple can negotiate what can be shared and with whom as her healing progresses. A support group made up of other lesbian partners is the best place to share this.

Partners can also experience shame when considering sharing what they are experiencing in their relationship. Many women have been engaging in self-examination regarding their socialized roles as caretakers. There is much confusion about the difference between caring and codependency. Partners may feel caught between different models of commitment: the fairy-tale romance of the 1950s, wherein you stay no matter what, which is equated with maturity versus the "stay as long as we both shall love" ethic of the 1960s. It is often seen as bad self-care or low self-esteem if you stay when your needs are not being met. Many partners report being criticized for staying in their relationships when seeking support for persevering.

A partner may also feel shame as it relates to blame. If the partner is uneducated about the dynamics of childhood sexual abuse, she may parallel the survivor's holding of self-blame. She may somehow see the survivor as being responsible for her abuse and damaged by it. She can blame the survivor for not working hard enough to heal, or not understand why she cannot "just get over it." This shame/blame duet can move the partner to collude in the secrecy of not wanting others to know.

Homophobia affects the possibility of sharing the reality of the partner's life with others. If she is not out to certain people in her life, such as coworkers, some friends, or family members, then the likelihood of her being able to share this level of personal information is slight. Even if she is out, the fear of others' stereotypes and prejudices about lesbians being sick, perverted, or damaged man-haters may keep a partner silent about the sexual abuse and the struggles of the relationship.

I DIDN'T AUDITION FOR THIS ROLE

Partners of women healing from incest and sexual abuse are victims of abuse by default. As in all relationships, unresolved material from family-of-origin dynamics are projected into the present, hopefully to work them through to a healthy resolution. Partners therefore participate in an incestuous family dynamic, often playing out a script they had no conscious part in creating. Sometimes they are responded to as the abuser/perpetrator. Any gestures of affection may be misinterpreted as an act of violation. Nothing is consistent or predictable. What appears acceptable and mutual in one encounter is construed as a blatant offense at some other time.

A survivor's healing process may include compulsive reenactment of the abuse. Sometimes there will be an unconscious attempt to rebuild an incestuous family by sexualizing within her chosen family network. This may involve sleeping with either her lover's best friend or best friend's lover or participating in some other inappropriate relationship. A belief in nonmonogamy may be avowed, which can actually be a rationalization of the unconscious incest dynamic. The distinction between sex and intimacy is amorphous—the expression of each is distorted by unclear boundaries. As in the family of origin, these types of incestuous relationships have a devastating impact on the couple.

SEXUALITY

It is a rare sexual relationship with a survivor that is not affected by the sexual abuse history. This is perhaps the most painful adjustment that partners have to make, often for several years. It is the area that may cause the most arguments, power struggles, and alienation between the mates. Some survivors feel a sense of imminent danger if someone so much as finds them sexually attractive. Others believe that no one who truly loves them would tarnish that love with sexual desire. The more emotionally close the couple is and the more "like family" they feel to each other, the more threatening sexuality in the relationship can be. Partners often get these and other myths projected onto them. This is particularly painful and confusing if the relationship began with a period of easy, passionate, mutual (or seemingly mutual) lovemaking, as is often the case.

As memories and feelings surface, the survivor may lose all interest in sex or be actively repulsed by it. Memories often first surface when the survivor is recovering from substance abuse. In addition to the abuse-related psychological diminished interest in sex, she will often go through a period of lack of sexual interest, sensation, and activity as her body is detoxifying. Whatever the source, the partner ends up having to curb her own sexual needs. *Ann: "I never get a chance to feel and express my own sexuality." Connie: "I don't have the chance to work on my own sexual development with her."*

This can lead to the partner feeling that she had better take advantage of any sexual opportunity offered by the survivor, even if she herself is not feeling sexual at the time. The partner may lose her assertiveness and ability to initiate sex out of fear or tiredness of being rejected. In an attempt to superficially address the power imbalance regarding sexual availability and assertiveness, the survivor may make advances to the partner at a time when she knows the partner is unavailable, thus setting up being rejected. She can then accuse the partner of being the one who is controlling the sexual relationship.

Alternately, because the survivor may have learned to experience sexuality as the only time or way she received physical nurturing, the partner may feel pressured to be sexual all the time. No other way of nurturing or affection may seem to count or be satisfying to the survivor. This pattern happens less frequently, but is as equally destructive to the rhythms of the partner's sexuality and the couple's cycle of mutual desire as is the sexual withdrawal.

Sometimes it is the partner who loses interest in sex. If she has been told the details of the sexual abuse, she may be filled with feelings of dismay, horror, or disgust as the images enter her consciousness. These images and feelings can intrude into her awareness when she looks at her lover in a sexual way. *Tina: "Even when my partner is willing to try to have sex, I see all the disgusting things she was made to do, and I just can't touch her."*

Once a sexual interaction has begun, it may be interrupted by a flashback of the abuse. Often, the survivor confuses her partner with the abuser. The more dissociated she is, the more likely this is to happen. (This is most complex when the survivor has a Dissociative Identity Disorder, which is beyond the scope of this chapter to address.) This is very distressing to the partner, and may bring up feelings of helplessness and anger. The interruption of the lovemaking is frustrating for both lovers. Once again, the attention is turned to nurturing the survivor. It may appear that the sexual and emotional feelings of the partner have no place to go. The option of being angry at someone who is now effectively two, five, ten, or fourteen years old seems mean and unfair. These are all factors that can contribute to lessening the partner's own interest in lovemaking.

The abuse dynamics may be reinvoked by the survivor. Having been taught to use sex to placate the abuser, she may offer to have sex to appease the partner. On the one hand, the partner may end up feeling used or as though she were set up to use the survivor; on the other hand, the survivor may not say no when she wants to. Whether she later tells her partner or not, the abuser/victim roles are being played out. The survivor may participate in sex using the same dissociative coping methods she learned as a child to help her through the molestation. This can be confusing and frightening to the partner. *Emanuela: "It's scary to make love with someone who looks like she's there, but she's really dissociated."*

Specific sexual activities may be controlled by the abuse as well. Certain things that the partner likes to do may be rejected by the survivor because they remind her of the abuse. Alternately, the survivor may want the partner to do certain things that are connected to the abuse that she finds arousing.

The partner either may not like these activities or may not want to replicate the abuse. The survivor may want to perform certain acts on the partner that were done to her. *Samantha: "I'm afraid of her. Sometimes it feels like she's being her abuser and I'm the victim."*

Of course, learning to define her own sexuality and owning the right to invite someone else to share that with her permission and in safety is an essential part of a survivor's recovery. While she welcomes this regaining of her lover's sexual pleasure and boundary-making, the partner again usually has to proceed at her lover's pace. This pace is often necessarily very slow, with many sudden halts along the way. While the survivor may be feeling delight in having both pleasure and control, the partner may be experiencing repeated frustration.

Both members of the couple may have questions, usually silent, about the survivor's sexual identity. These questions are rooted in internalized homophobia. Similar questions do not usually come up in heterosexual couples. Each may wonder if the survivor is a lesbian because she was abused. If her abuser(s) were male, then is she now in retreat from men, and will she return to them once she is healed? If her abuser(s) were female, then her partner may fear that she is just repeating the abuse in her current relationship, and will leave for a man when she feels better about herself. If we did not live in a homophobic society, these questions would not occur.

TRAUMATIC AFTEREFFECTS

One of the most painful roles partners are asked to fulfill is that of witness to and perhaps rescuer from the self-harming behaviors of the survivors. Many survivors learned to use alcohol and drugs as a way of coping with or blocking out the abuse. A survivor may or may not be in recovery from her substance dependence while she is grappling with the sexual abuse. Partners have to be very careful of being codependent in this area. It is also a good opportunity for partners to focus on their own possible substance or process addictions and examine if they are using any unhealthy behaviors to cope with the stress they are experiencing in their relationship.

Self-mutilation is another behavior that many survivors turn to. It may accelerate during the intensity of early abuse recovery (and can linger on for quite a long time). Partners experience a multitude of responses to discovering fresh bloody wounds on their lover's bodies, including horror, anger, disgust, compassion, and overwhelming helplessness. *Honora: "Being a partner has meant watching the smooth skin of the one I love become jagged with scars from self-inflicted cuts and scratches. It means laying next to her, gently tracing the outlines of the scars with my fingers, wondering if all my love can even make a difference in the face of her pain."* Partners may become involved in desperate attempts to keep their mates from harming themselves, only to learn over and over again that they are not in control of what the survivor does. *Josie: "It is almost intolerable for me to witness her suffering and self-abuse."*

This extends into the realm of threatened or attempted suicide. The specter of suicide may float in the air, always hovering around. Partners may experience an ongoing sense of dread and uncertainty. *Marnie: "I'm never sure what I'll find when I walk in the door, when she's been talking about suicide. I start to get a stomachache when I'm halfway home."* Honora (after her partner's suicide attempt): *"Being a partner has meant . . . laying with her in the hospital bed feeling the most profound gratitude that she was alive, and then feeling the surges of rage, fear, and abandonment over what had happened."* A partner may start orienting her schedule and her life around trying to prevent her mate from killing herself. This may be welcomed or demanded or rejected by the survivor, and is ultimately both useless and unhealthy for each person. With repeated threats or attempts at suicide, partners feel increasingly abandoned and that the trust in the relationship has been broken over and over again. Partners must face questioning their spiritual beliefs and learn to grapple with their own depths of despair, abandonment, and powerlessness.

Because sexual abuse has a generational legacy, some survivors have passed on their abuse by harming others. It is possible that within every abuser is an undiscovered and/or unrecovered victim. It is usually quite a shock for a partner to learn that her mate, whom she has regarded with tenderness and compassion for her suffering, and whose molesters she hates, has inflicted a similar wound onto someone else. This will often create a distance between the partners for some time, and may be the breaking point in the relationship for some partners.

If the effects of the trauma have been extreme, then the partner may be called upon to interact with the legal, mental health, or welfare systems as her lover's ally and advocate (or occasionally as a victim of her abuse). The legitimacy of her position as the mate of the survivor can be challenged, as it would not be in a heterosexual couple. She may be ignored, ridiculed, or discriminated against. The partner's life can become oriented around responding to multiple crises. She may be the only one working and have enormous financial burdens to carry.

Partners dealing with these consequences can feel that they are no longer in a relationship with another adult. Rather, they may feel that they are being called upon to be the mother. (This is most complicated when the survivor has a Dissociative Identity Disorder with child alters.) Both mates may collude in infantalizing the survivor. It is a steady challenge to maintain the relationship on a peer level.

FAMILIES OF ORIGIN

The relationship that each member of the couple has with her family of origin and her "in-laws" is affected by the abuse. As part of her recovery, a survivor may decide to limit or eliminate contact with her own family. A partner will often be asked to be the liaison between the survivor and her family, relaying messages to and from. Or she may be asked to run interference, such as lying to the family about the survivor's availability or whereabouts. Depending on when the abuse was remembered, a partner may have an already-established relationship with her "in-laws," perhaps many years old. As the survivor's relationship with her family keeps changing, often moment by moment in her thinking, partners may be confused as to whether or not they can have an independent relationship with members of that family. They may experience similar feelings of betrayal and loss.

Survivors may have ambivalent feelings about their own and their mate's relationships with the partner's family. Sometimes the survivor adopts the partner's family as a replacement for her own. Or she may challenge the partner as to the level of dysfunction present in that family. When her relationship to her family of origin shifts, the survivor may change how she relates to the partner's family as well. *Frances: "When she cuts off from her own family, she can't tolerate any closeness with mine, either. She tries to control my relationship with my family, or she just vanishes. I'm left having to explain her sudden disappearance, which is pretty damn hard when the incest is a secret."*

Probably the hardest feature of the survivor's relationship with her family for the partner to tolerate is the survivor's continued contact, cordiality, and especially affection with her abuser or nonprotecting parents. *Nancy: "I'm the one who's up with her all night while she screams and sobs through her nightmares. I can't stand it when she talks with them the next day as though nothing has happened. It makes my skin crawl to watch her hug her mother after all she did to her."* A partner may choose not to attend events with the survivor and her family, though she may be asked or pressured to do so by the survivor, for protection. She may be experienced as the nonprotecting parent if she refuses to go. It is another area in which the partner gets to practice establishing appropriate boundaries for herself.

PARENTING

When children are part of the survivor/partner family, fear of the abuse being repeated arises. This fear may be experienced as an underground current, or actual abuse may be suspected or occurring. Because she was raised in a family with inappropriate sexual or affectional boundaries, a survivor may not understand what healthy, loving family touch may be. Her own worries about touching the children improperly may be projected onto her partner. The partner may be concerned that the survivor will be inappropriate, especially if the survivor ever abused anyone. An uneasy watchfulness may develop that will intensify when the children are at the ages when the abuse occurred. The issue of appropriate touch will also be affected by the cultural mores of each mate. Volatile arguments may take place.

This is an opportunity for the partner, relying on the survivor's exquisite sensitivity, to take a closer look at whether there were any boundary violations in her own family's physical expression. It is also an opportunity for the survivor to expand her repertoire of healthy, loving touch. At the same time, snuggling and hugging the children may be the only affectional contact that feels safe to the survivor. Partners may feel jealous and left out. *Rhonda: "Whatever nurturing is available goes to the children, not me. I need to be held, too, and I don't want to turn to the children to get it."* Couples need to be aware not to channel their adult needs for giving and receiving nurturance through the children.

During periods of immersion in her healing process, the survivor may experience mood variations that make it hard for her to parent effectively. She may need to withdraw into isolation; she may experience upwellings of rage, irrationality, and terror; she may become deeply depressed. The partner may end up functioning as a single parent, when previously that role had been shared. She may feel the need to protect the children from the most extreme emotional behaviors of the survivor, if the survivor is unable to contain her process.

Children, too, will be scared and confused by observing their mother in such turmoil. The couple must decide together where to establish appropriate boundaries between no family secrets and privacy, and between no secrets and what would be overwhelming knowledge for the children.

The couple also has to decide what kind of contact, if any, the children may have with the abusing family. Depending on her level of denial, resolution, or vacillating ambivalence, the survivor may vary in her wish for the children to be part of her family of origin. If the abuse was recalled after relationships with the extended family had already been established, then it will be harder to explain to the children why they can no longer visit (although many children will be relieved, if the abusive energy or behavior is still being enacted).

One dubious advantage of being a lesbian couple is that the couple and their children may never have been accepted by the families of origin in the first place, particularly if the partner is the biological parent. Because the partner is generally free of emotional attachment to the abusing family, she can be clearer about not exposing the children to them. The survivor will often have conflicting feelings about that choice.

THERAPY

The central place that therapy may assume in a survivor's life, and consequently in her partner's life, can be a contentious one. The therapy relationship can feel as though it has become the primary one. Although appreciating that the survivor has an outside person with whom she can work through her abuse, the partner may feel jealous or resentful. She may be angry at the amount of time, money, and energy going into the therapy rather than directly into the relationship, especially when individual therapy is augmented with group, bodywork, and/or 12-step meetings. Partners may be frustrated and angry at the direction the therapy is taking, such as when therapists are encouraging the survivor's regression, while the partner is struggling to maintain an adult relationship. If the survivor is in the hospital, the lesbian partner may not be granted equal visitation rights as would be given to a heterosexual mate. Partners must make sure that their own needs for support and for working through their own issues are being met.

SPIRITUAL CRISIS

Many partners experience the appearance of sexual abuse in their lives as a profound spiritual crisis. Core beliefs about the nature of the world are threatened and torn to shreds. *Zoe: "I once felt the world, in spite of its wars and suffering, was a good place, a place where evil was beaten down by the goodness in people. That trust has been shaken, and I no longer believe in the innate good in any person. My morals have been challenged, and I have come away from this much more cynical, less trusting, fragile, and often very sad."*

The Chinese definition of *crisis* as opportunity pertains as well. Having been plunged into a spiritual abyss, partners often emerge stronger and more grounded. *Zoe: "I have become a more spiritual person because of this. I have learned to practice a daily program of blessing that which is around me that is good." Honora: "Being a partner has taught me more about letting go than anything I have ever been through . . . . It has meant learning to live in the moment, because when you're with an incest survivor, reality can be snatched away in a second, from a sound, a smell, a touch, a breath."*

THE HEALING CYCLE

Partners may go through several common stages of healing. In this section, I will address these stages and briefly describe a sample of various expressive arts techniques that help partners work through their issues. Although an exercise may be described in one modality, such as drama or writing, I actually use them intermodally, which provides the deepest experience (e.g., going from a drawing into movement based on the drawing). They are especially effective when used in a group context, but can be adapted for other treatment settings. As with any healing cycle, it is a cyclical rather than linear progression. Each step may be revisited at different times and depths. A partner can experience them in a different order and be in more than one at a time.

Protecting

Denying the impact on both of you; preserving and protecting the couple/family; maintaining the false front; colluding in secrecy.

Exercises: From Protecting to Expressing

- Have the participants draw a picture of why they are there. Have them include themselves and the survivor in it. It may be abstract, symbolic, or representational. Have the participants introduce themselves by way of the picture. Invite others to share their observations, if welcomed. Note disparities in size, color, orientation of the characters to each other, missing features, degree of groundedness, etc.
- Build a script: Denote every other person as a composite survivor character, and the others as a composite partner. Ask for a line to be volunteered from a typical interaction that seems to have something to do with the sexual abuse. Create a script by going around the circle. This is a very quick and powerful way to break isolation and build rapport, as the participants rapidly discover they all pretty well know the coming line.
- Generate a list of common issues from each of the participants.

Blaming the Victim

Blaming her for having been abused in the first place; believing the survivor created or willingly participated in the abuse; blaming her for everything that is difficult in the relationship.

Exercises: From Blaming to Aiming the Anger at the Abuser

- Guided meditation focusing on the anger which has been directed at the survivor. Redirect it to the abuser(s).
- Clay sculpture of the abuser/abusive system. Tell the survivor's story. Transform the sculpture by changing or destroying it.
- Writing or speaking around the circle: "I will hold onto my anger until . . . . "
- Make masks of the shadow self. Explore with movement and dialogue.

Controlling

How the survivor heals (e.g., suggesting groups, books, etc.); dominating other aspects of the relationship to compensate for the survivor controlling the sex and/or intimacy; weighing all actions and speech in order to influence the survivor's responses and feelings.

Exercises: Establishing Boundaries and Limits

- Boundary exercises: Feeling and filling your personal boundaries and space through imagery and movement. In pairs, have one person stand still while another walks toward her. Have participants practice recognizing when their boundary has been crossed. Process how each person handles these feelings.
- Sitting in pairs, have both people close their eyes. At a signal, have them open their eyes and determine where in the space between them their gaze falls. Have them practice extending and retracting their gaze.
- Standing in pairs, with hands up and pushing against each other, one person says, "No," while the other says, "Yes." Have them switch roles.
- Writing. Have participants write, beginning with the sentence, "I know I've gone too far away from myself when . . . "
- Psychodrama. Have everyone in the group arrive in the character of their martyr parent. Role-play these parts as a group. Afterward, have participants discuss how they are similar to the martyr parent and how they bring these aspects of themselves into their relationship.
- Ritual. Have participants bring an object that symbolizes what belongs to their partner that they, themselves, have been holding onto. Role-play having each person give the object back to the partner. Similarly, role-play taking back an object that symbolizes a part of themselves that they have given away.

Exercises: From Controlling to Focusing on the Self

- Using clay, have the participants sculpt the impact the incest has on them, their self-esteem, sexuality, body image, etc. Use movement to give the sculpture a different form and meaning for the person. For example, *LaVonne's* sculpture was of a woman with an empty space in place of her genitals, an oversized heart, three sets of arms, and empty eye sockets. A small ball of fire representing her sexual energy was off to the side. In her movement, *LaVonne* sought her missing sexual energy and restored it to her body. She let her hands drop to her sides and looked into a mirror to see her own reflection.

- Writing. Have participants write, beginning with the sentence, "If I were not in this relationship, I'd be focusing on . . . "
- Writing. Have participants write about what, in their mind, constitutes a healthy relationship. Have them write a list of their needs in a relationship, including three minimum requirements. Have them discuss their current relationship in light of what they have written.
- Have participants make a list of self-nurturing activities. Have group members discuss what they have written, and encourage participants to actively schedule these activities.

Grieving

Breaking one's own denial and feeling the grief, including loss (of the preabuse-focused relationship, beliefs in a safe morality-based world, spontaneity, sexuality, money, planned future, predictability, power, etc.); rage (at the abuse, the perpetrators, the "system," the loss, the survivor); sorrow (for the loss, the effects of the abuse on the beloved); and despair (losing hope of recovery, being stuck in the belief that it will never get better, fearing that the couple will not be able to bear and heal this wound together).

Exercises: Grieving the Loss

- Guided imagery on what the relationship was like before the abuse consciously entered, and then how it changed.
- After the guided imagery, have participants make a collage of the pre- and poststates.
- Have participants draw a picture of what they are "storing away," thus encouraging them to say good-bye to it for now.

- Have participants write poems about sexuality. For example, *Susan Schulman* wrote the following:

Ten months since you first allowed me
to touch your body, dark hairs
surrounding your brown nipple, healed
scar buried in the rolls of your belly.
Nights we spent laughing
until you fell asleep, my arms
still wrapped around you, fingers nestled
among downy hairs growing
in the small of your back.
I would hold you, even after
my limbs became stiff, just to feel
the weight of your body, smell
the clean scent of your hair.
And the nights you rolled away from my kiss,
your father's hands reaching out
from childhood beds to drag you from me,
your body suddenly rigid and cold.
The very air between us felt chill.
I would lie lonely next to you,
touch your hand—
the tight muscles of your back,
try to hold you in the present.
But you could not stay with me—
and I could not wait.

Exercises: From Despair to Empowerment

- **Masks.** Using the inner and outer surfaces of a paper bag or plate, have participants represent the face they show the world and their partner, as well as the face they do not reveal. Have them walk around the group, wearing the outer mask. Encourage feedback from other group members. Have participants share and discuss the inner mask, asking them, "Why do you hide it? What do you imagine would happen if you showed it to the group or to your partner?"

- Have participants write or speak to the group, completing the sentence, "What I'm scared to say to you is . . . "
- Movement. In pairs, holding a twisted towel, have participants engage in a tug-of-war between the power of the abuse and themselves. This exercise can be very intense, as the participants confront their feelings of fear, helplessness, despair, and rage. Ultimately, the partner may experience a victorious sense of empowerment.
- Have participants sculpt in clay or with their bodies, themselves in relationship to the abuse and/or their partner. Physically transform it.
- Movement. Have participants walk around and interact in a state of mistrust, then of trust. Have them write a dialogue, using the dominant hand to ask questions and the nondominant hand to provide answers from the trust and mistrust subpersonalities.
- Have participants sculpt clay images of their healing sources.
- Have participants fashion costumes of their healing sources and interact in a group ritual.
- Writing and movement: Have participants create personal affirmations and enact them in movement.

Understanding

Living in the present, accepting that this may be the most you can hope for; recognizing that you are both doing the best you can; accepting that the survivor's history and pain belong to her and that neither of you is the original source of the fallout.

Forgiveness

Ask this of both of you for the mistakes each has made; yourself for not being able to compensate for everything that happened to her; and the survivor for not being healed sooner. Be as powerful in yourselves and in your commitment to loving as the abuse has been.

Exercises

- Writing and speaking circle. Have participants name and discuss the gifts the struggle with the abuse has brought each of them.
- Ritual. In the survivor/partner relationship, honoring the stages of recovery is necessary. Part of this is learning to say good-

bye to the anger and despair. Participants can be encouraged to create an image of a protective container for the relationship that allows for a feeling of safety, but is also open to the outside world.

STRENGTHENING PERSONAL BOUNDARIES

The task that partners have to accomplish over and over again is learning how to keep their focus on their own lives and issues, including grieving, while determining appropriate boundaries for caregiving. This is particularly crucial in a lesbian relationship where the values of merging and mothering are strong. The following list contains suggestions that lesbian partners of childhood sexual abuse survivors have found useful in focusing on themselves.

1. Know that your needs are valid.
2. Ask yourself what you would be focusing on if you were not in this relationship.
3. Recognize that, in effect, you have entered into an abusive family and direct your anger toward the abuser, not the victim. For example, when flashbacks occur during sex, both mates can yell together at the abuser to get out of their bed.
4. Recognize your limits as to how much you can give her and how much a part of her healing process you can be. Use your bodily cues as a barometer. Ask for specifics of what is needed at a given time, and do not play mind reader or "twenty questions."
5. Ask yourself what would happen if you did not fill her need(s) for yourself and her. Does not "abandoning" her mean abandoning yourself?
6. Ask yourself what you are gaining and what you are losing by being in this relationship.
7. Think about your minimum requirements for being in a committed relationship and whether or not you are getting them met over the long haul. Think about redefining or leaving the relationship. Beware of making deadlines that keep getting extended.

8. Look at your own issues of abuse, deprivation, problems with intimacy, trust, and sex. Do not hide behind hers.
9. Get support from other people. Clarify and negotiate specifics with her of what can and cannot be shared. Renegotiate as each of your needs change.
10. Consider being in a group with other partners and doing couples counseling with your lover.
11. Make a list of self-nurturing activities apart from your relationship. Do them.
12. Discuss other ways of getting your needs met. Include in this discussion your needs for nurturing, intimacy, and sex.
13. Know that you will make mistakes. Do not let that prevent you from taking chances. Do not give up too soon. Forgive yourself for past mistakes.
14. Deal with your own desire to deny the reality of her abuse, whether or not she has specific memories or is currently in a phase of denial.
15. Finally, expect her to be powerful. Do not expect her to be a victim. Each of you should strive to hold the attitude that she is a whole human being, going through a difficult recovery, and is not permanently damaged.

There are several basic premises to guide therapists working with this population. Be sure not to collude with focusing on the survivor's story, pain, or understandable reasons for not being able to meet the partner's needs. Provide a container for the safe expression of all feelings, especially those that the partner feels she should not have. Work with partners to become aware of and respect their boundaries. Facilitate partners working on their own unresolved issues. Help partners determine areas in which they can assert themselves with their mates, and work with any reluctance to do so. Finally, explore with partners the possibility of getting support from other people in their lives.

SUMMARY

A relationship that successfully struggles with sexual abuse recovery has bonds that have been truly forged like steel. The profound love, courage, and commitment that each mate brings is an awe-inspiring force. There are positive aspects that counter the depths of despair. The partner's issues of pain and growth are catalyzed by the intense focus on the dynamics of the relationship and her own part in it. If she is not also a survivor, she has the opportunity to learn more about life beyond her own experience, broadening her understanding and compassion. Being a part of such a serious healing is a beautiful affirmation of both people. One's capacity to love and be a healing force expands, becoming part of each forever. On a spiritual level, turning mistrust to love puts positive energy into the world, which is part of healing our planet. Finally, working through such an intense transformative healing brings the partners closer together and strengthens their bond.

Chapter 3

Categorization of Lesbian, Gay, and Bisexual Suicide Attempters

Scott L. Hershberger
Neil W. Pilkington
Anthony R. D'Augelli

Suicide is now recognized to be a major health problem for adolescents in the United States, accounting for approximately 5,000 (13.3 percent) of the 37,000 annual deaths in the 15- to 24-year-old age category (National Center for Health Statistics, 1993). The rate of youth suicide has increased by over 200 percent since 1950, compared to a rise of only 17 percent in the general population (National Center for Health Statistics, 1986). For example, there were 2.7 suicides for every 100,000 adolescents between the ages of 15 and 19 in 1950; in 1993, the number was 9.3 suicides per 100,000. In addition, as many as 8 to 13 percent of adolescents have attempted suicide on at least one occasion (Friedman et al., 1987; Mehan et al., 1992; Schneider, Farberow, and Kruks, 1989; Smith and Crawford, 1986), with over 10 percent of these ultimately committing suicide successfully (Diekstra, 1989).

Numerous risk factors for suicide attempt have been suggested. One recent review (Lewinsohn, Rohde, and Seeley, 1994) identified externalizing problem behaviors (e.g., attention deficit hyperactivity, conduct, and oppositional disorders); suicide ideation; a perceived lack of control over one's life; a tendency toward the self-attribution of negative life events; high self-consciousness; low self-esteem; poor coping skills; the perception of inadequate family support (including the death of a parent); past suicide attempts; and problems with appetite. Other recent reviews (e.g., Garland and

Zigler, 1993; Pfeffer et al., 1991) have found similar correlates of suicide attempt in adolescence.

The apparent multicausal pathways for suicide attempt by sexual-minority youths emphasizes the need to identify the different types of suicide attempters. One goal of this chapter is to empirically derive such a classification of sexual-minority suicide attempters. This classification is based on the responses of lesbian, gay, and bisexual youths, ages 15 to 21, from community-based groups, to a questionnaire concerned with their social and sexual lives. Other purposes of this chapter include a description of the mental health status of the youths, as well as the identification of those factors that differentiate suicide attempters from nonattempters.

BACKGROUND ON GAY AND LESBIAN SUICIDE

Few researchers would dispute the high prevalence of suicide attempt among adolescents in general. More controversial is the proposal that suicide attempts among sexual-minority (lesbian/gay/bisexual) youths occur at an even greater rate than for the general adolescent population. Evidence for this elevated prevalence has been obtained from a number of sources: clinical observation (e.g., Kourany, 1987); lesbian and gay adults' retrospective accounts of adolescent suicidality (Bell and Weinberg, 1978; Bradford, Ryan, and Rothblum, 1994; Harry, 1983; Jay and Young, 1977; Saghir and Robins, 1973); interviews conducted with lesbian, gay, and bisexual youths in clinical, rehabilitative, or crisis settings (Hunter, 1990; Martin and Hetrick, 1988; Roesler and Deisher, 1972; Rotheram-Borus, Rosario, and Koopman, 1991; Rotheram-Borus, Hunter, and Rosario, 1994); and interviews conducted with lesbian, gay, and bisexual youths in nonclinical or community settings (D'Augelli and Hershberger, 1993; Hammelman, 1993; Herdt and Boxer, 1993; Hershberger and D'Augelli, 1995; Hershberger, Pilkington, and D'Augelli, 1995; Remafedi, 1987a and b; Remafedi, Farrow, and Deisher, 1991; Schneider, Farberow, and Kruks, 1989; Schneider, 1991). Estimates of suicide attempt vary among these studies, ranging from 21 percent among a predominantly minority sample of lesbian, gay, and bisexual youths 14 to 21 years of age at a community agency in New York (Martin and Hetrick, 1988) to 42 percent among a white majority sample of youths 15 to 21 years of age from 14 community centers across the United States (D'Augelli and Hershberger, 1993). Gibson (1989), as part of a federal report, concluded that sexual-minority youths may account for nearly 30 percent of all youth suicides. The basis of Gibson's estimate were an assumed 10 percent rate of homosexuality in the population and the risk of suicide in adolescence.

Many of these studies have been criticized as being methodologically unsound, and consequently, providing highly inflated estimates of suicide attempt. Suicide attempt estimates derived from samples obtained from clinical settings may be nonrepresentative of the sexual-minority population in terms of overall mental health and troubled lives, and estimates derived from retrospective accounts may suffer from the memory biases so often encountered in such studies. More confidence may be placed in estimates obtained from nonclinical or community settings, often involving youth groups, but even here, a question remains as to how comparable sexual-minority youths who participate in youth groups are to those who do not.

Not all epidemiological studies of adolescent suicide find an elevated rate for sexual-minority youth. Perhaps the strongest evidence against an elevated suicide attempt rate among sexual-minority youth comes from systematically conducted psychological autopsy studies, examining the lives of youths who have recently committed suicide. Shaffer (1988) found that only 2.5 percent of adolescent suicide completers were lesbian or gay, whereas Rich et al. (1986) identified a rate of 7 percent. Yet estimates of obtained psychological autopsies may be attenuated because of their dependence on interviews with relatives and close friends, who may be reluctant to identify the suicide completer as homosexual or who may simply be unaware of the person's sexual orientation. Disagreement concerning the prevalence of suicidal behavior among sexual-minority youths has occasionally been contentious as seen by Shaffer's (1993) assertion that lesbian and gay researchers and advocates have deliberately inflated suicide estimates for political gain.

Only additional, empirical research with representative samples will ultimately resolve the issue as to whether sexual-minority youths engage in more suicidal behavior. Yet information from other sources would lead us to predict elevated rates of suicidality among sexual-minority youths. As adolescents, lesbian, gay, and bisexual youths are vulnerable to all the stressors commonly encountered by adolescents. As sexual minorities, lesbian, gay, and bisexual youths encounter a host of stressors related to their stigmatized sexual orientation beyond those encountered by heterosexual youths (Boxer and Cohler, 1989; Cwayna, Remafedi, and Treadway, 1991; Gonsiorek, 1988; Martin, 1982).

Negative family reactions to the adolescent's disclosure of sexual orientation or the adolescent's fear of the consequences of disclosure are a major stress experienced by sexual-minority youths (Boxer, Cook, and Herdt, 1991). Based on the youths used in the D'Augelli and Hershberger (1993) study, more than half feared the prospect of disclosure of sexual orientation to families, with nearly a quarter reporting disclosure to be extremely troubling. Furthermore, of the mothers aware of their children's sexual orientation, 8 percent were seen as intolerant but not rejecting, and 12 percent were rejecting; of the fathers who knew, 10 percent were intolerant and 18 percent rejecting. Rejection by families also extends to rejection by friends. D'Augelli and Hershberger (1993) reported that one third of their sample feared losing friends on disclosure, and 46 percent reported they had lost friends. Remafedi (1987c) found that 41 percent of sexual-minority youths reported strong negative reactions from friends.

Another source of stress experienced by sexual-minority youths is verbal and physical abuse. Pilkington and D'Augelli (1995) found that, based on their sexual orientation, 80 percent of the sample had experienced verbal insults; 44 percent had experienced physical threats of violence; 33 percent had objects thrown at them; 31 percent had been chased or followed; 13 percent reported being spat on; 20 percent had been physically assaulted; and 22 percent reported at least one sexual assault. These results are consistent with the results of other studies that have found a high frequency of verbal and physical abuse of sexual-minority youths (e.g., Berrill, 1990; Dean, Wu, and Martin 1992; Gross, Aurand, and Adessa, 1988; Hunter, 1990; Remafedi, 1987a and c; Remafedi, Farrow, and Deisher, 1991).

As with straight youth, suicidality among sexual-minority youth is not caused by one factor but by a multitude of factors, highlighting the individual differences that exist among sexual-minority youth suicide attempters. The most consistently identified risk factors include precocity of sexual orientation awareness (Hershberger, Pilkington, and D'Augelli, 1995; Schneider, Farberow, and Kruks, 1989); substance abuse (Hershberger, Pilkington, and D'Augelli, 1995; Remafedi, Farrow, and Deisher, 1991); gender nonconformity (Harry, 1983; Remafedi, Farrow, and Deisher, 1991); family conflict (Remafedi, 1987a; Rotheram-Borus, Hunter, and Rosario, 1994); sexual abuse (Hershberger, Pilkington, and D'Augelli, 1995; Remafedi, Farrow, and Deisher, 1991); and physical abuse (Hershberger, Pilkington, and D'Augelli, 1995; Hunter, 1990). Numerous other risk factors (e.g., low religiosity) have been identified by individual studies.

CATEGORIZING TYPES OF MINORITY YOUTH SUICIDE ATTEMPTERS

In an effort to identify the different types of minority youth suicide attempters, we recruited study participants from 14 organized youth groups in metropolitan lesbian/gay centers from across the United States: Atlanta, Baltimore, Boston, Chicago, Cleveland, Dallas, Denver, Detroit, Indianapolis, Los Angeles, Pittsburgh, San Diego, San Francisco, and Washington, DC. We contacted an adult human services professional located in each of the centers, who elicited the cooperation of the youths in completing the study's survey instrument. On completion of the surveys, the centers returned them to the researchers. No youth who was given a survey declined participation.

The final sample consisted of 194 participants. Of these, 73 percent (142) were men, and 27 percent (52) were women. The participants' ages ranged from 15 to 21 years, with an average age of 18.86. Male youths were significantly older than female youths. Sixty-six percent of the respondents were white, 15 percent were African American, 5 percent were Asian American, 5 percent Hispanic American, and 4 percent Native American. Additional details concerning the study's procedures, inclusionary criteria for participants, and participant characteristics may be found in D'Augelli and Hershberger (1993).

The instrument's questions may be placed into six domains as follows:

1. *Participant Background.* Background variables included age, sex, socioeconomic status (measured by parental education and occupation), ethnicity, residence status (living alone or with someone), place of residence (city or elsewhere), financial independence of respondent, religiosity, and sexual orientation status in the past and now.

2. *Sexual Orientation and Behavior.* The ages at which several sexual milestones occurred were ascertained: ages of first awareness, first labeling self as lesbian or gay, first disclosure to someone else, first disclosure to friend or acquaintance, first disclosure to a parent, first disclosure to another family member, first same-sex sexual experience, and first opposite-sex sexual experience. The number of past same- and opposite-sex sexual partners was also determined.

3. *Social Aspects of Sexual Orientation.* Items in this domain were concerned with the participants' openness about their sexual orientation, their identifiability to others as a sexual minority, their own and other's perceptions of their gender conformity, their involvement in lesbian/gay social networks (including having many lesbian/gay friends, participating in organized events, going to bars, being politically involved), and if they had lost friends because of their sexual orientation.

4. *Disclosure of Sexual Orientation Within the Family.* In this domain, the questions were concerned with the overall relationship between the respondents and their families, including to whom lesbians and gays had disclosed their sexual orientation (mother, father, siblings, other relatives) and how accepting these relatives were of the participants' sexual orientation.

5. *Victimization.* Respondents were asked how often they had experienced various kinds of victimization based on their sexual orientation. Four categories of victimization events were assessed: (a) verbal insults and threats of physical violence; (b) personal property damage, objects thrown at them,

and being chased, followed, or spat upon; (c) physical assault and assault with a weapon; and (d) sexual assault. Violence specific to the family was ascertained, as determined from the number of relatives who had verbally insulted, threatened, or physically assaulted the respondent. The respondents were also asked to identify whether certain types of individuals (e.g., roommate, counselor, etc.) had harmed them in any way.

6. *Mental Health Problems.* Distress regarding 12 personal problems and concerns representing fairly common stressors in the lives of sexual minorities was obtained. The participants were also asked if personal worry overwhelms them, and about their comfort with being lesbian or gay. Self-esteem was measured with the Rosenberg Self-Esteem Inventory (Rosenberg, 1979). Also included as part of the study instrument was a standardized measure of psychiatric symptoms, the Brief Symptom Inventory (BSI) (Derogatis and Spencer, 1982), consisting of nine subscales (Somatization, Obsessive-Compulsiveness, Interpersonal Sensitivity, Depression, Anxiety, Hostility, Phobic Anxiety, Paranoid Ideation, and Psychoticism), as well as an overall measure of psychopathology, the Global Severity Index (GSI). Participants were also asked about current suicidal thinking, past suicide attempts, the number of attempts, and the methods used. Response options for methods were drug overdose, alcohol, a gun, a knife, a razor blade, gas, a car, fire, or other. For purposes of analysis, drug overdose was classified as a "nonviolent" method of suicide, while other methods were designated as "violent."

FINDINGS

Suicidality and Other Mental Health Characteristics

As shown in Table 3.1, 58 percent of the sample had never attempted suicide, whereas 42 percent had tried on at least one occasion. For attempters, the number of occasions ranged from 1 to 15. Methods of suicide attempt varied, and included drug overdose

TABLE 3.1. Distribution of Suicide Attempts (n = 194)

Number of Attempts	Frequency	
	Men (n = 142)	Women (n = 52)
0	85 (60%)	30 (57%)
1	21 (15%)	14 (27%)
2	10 (7%)	3 (6%)
3	9 (6%)	1 (2%)
4	3 (2%)	1 (2%)
5	5 (3%)	1 (2%)
7	3 (2%)	0
8	1 (1%)	0
10	4 (3%)	0
12	1 (1%)	0
13	0	1 (2%)
15	0	1 (2%)

(44 percent), alcohol abuse (17 percent), use of gun (13 percent), razor blade (8 percent), knife (5 percent), car (4 percent), and fire (1 percent). Multiple-occasion attempters selected violent methods of suicide more frequently (23 percent) than did single-occasion attempters (3 percent). No significant differences were found between men and women.

Clearly, suicidal behavior is common among these youths. Not surprisingly, current suicidal ideation is also common, as shown in Figure 3.1. A majority of the respondents (60 percent) have thoughts about killing themselves, with 8 percent having such thoughts "often."

Participants' evaluations of 12 personal problems appear in Table 3.2. Men reported more dissatisfaction with their sex lives, more depression, more anxiety, and more worry about AIDS. The prob-

FIGURE 3.1. Distribution of Suicidal Ideation Among Sexual Minority Youth

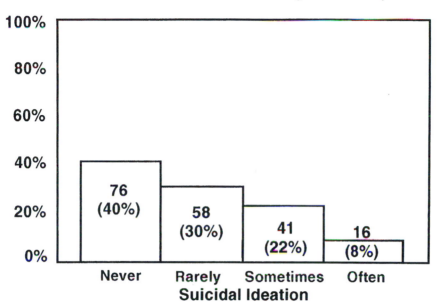

lem of most concern ("extremely troubling") to the sample was worry about AIDS; of least concern was developing close relationships with lesbians or gay men. Interestingly, these results were applicable to both men and women: for men and women, respectively, worry about AIDS (29 percent, 23 percent); developing close relationships (3 percent, 0 percent). Further, no significant differences were found between men and women for self-esteem, personal worry, or comfort with sexual orientation.

In order to evaluate the representativeness of the youths in this study, an important consideration is the degree of psychopathology in this sample of sexual-minority youths, as compared to a normative sample of youths. According to Table 3.3, sexual-minority youths differ significantly from a normative sample on two of the nine BSI dimensions: the sexual-minority youths show less somatization but more depression. Whereas the overall BSI score did not differ between men and women, statistical analysis found that women scored higher than men on somatization and hostility.

TABLE 3.2. Personal Concerns of Lesbian and Gay Male Youths

Concern	No problem		Somewhat troubling		Very troubling		Extremely troubling		t
	M	W	M	W	M	W	M	W	
Developing close relationships with lesbians or gay men	73	81	18	17	6	2	3	2	1.61
Telling family about sexual orientation	31	39	30	25	16	14	23	22	0.73
Telling co-workers about sexual orientation	32	41	30	31	19	10	19	18	0.99
Excessive alcohol use	63	75	16	14	9	0	11	12	1.12
Dissatisfaction with sex life	41	52	35	36	10	6	14	6	1.98*
Problems in close relationship	33	40	40	42	15	11	12	6	1.58
Excessive drug use	76	78	5	8	4	2	14	12	0.50
Depression	23	38	36	33	21	13	20	15	1.92*
Telling friends about sexual orientation	41	50	35	35	11	18	12	8	1.33
Anxiety	27	47	46	33	17	14	10	6	2.07*
Religious issues about sexual orientation	66	56	18	25	5	12	10	8	0.76
Worry about AIDS	10	38	34	31	27	8	29	23	3.51**
AIDS/HIV (I am HIV+)	76	91	7	2	6	0	11	7	1.90

Note: Men: n = 142; women: n = 52. Numbers (except for t values) are percentages.
*p < .05. **p < .001.

TABLE 3.3. Brief Symptom Inventory Responses from Normative Sample and Lesbian/Gay Youth Sample

Dimension	Normative[a] (n = 2408)		Lesbian/Gay Youth (n = 191)		
	M	*SD*	*M*	*SD*	*t*
Somatization	.63	.64	.51	.68	−2.37*
Obsessive-compulsiveness	.93	.75	.95	.93	.29
Interpersonal sensitivity	.99	.85	1.20	1.27	.23
Depression	.82	.79	1.13	1.10	4.02**
Anxiety	.78	.68	.89	.96	1.57
Hostility	1.02	.86	.96	.92	−1.46
Phobic anxiety	.54	.64	.50	.73	−.74
Paranoid ideation	1.13	.82	1.05	.93	−1.12
Psychoticism	.73	.73	.87	.89	.60

[a]Source: Derogatis and Spencer (1982), p. 34.

*$p < .05$. **$p < .001$.

Comparisons Between Suicide Attempters and Nonattempters

Attempter youth (ATT) were more precocious in recognizing their sexual orientation and disclosing their orientation to others. ATT youth also had greater numbers of same-sex sexual experiences than did nonattempters (NATT). ATT were also generally more open about their sexual orientation, engaging in more social activities and having more lesbian/gay friends, but also losing more friends due to their sexual orientation. Furthermore, female ATT frequented bars more often than did female NATT, but male ATT did not differ from male NATT. ATT (both male and female alike) had better overall relations with their families than did nonattempters, with both attempter mothers and fathers more knowledgeable about their child's sexual orientation. Without exception, attempter's experienced more victimization of all types and had greater psychopathology than did nonattempters.

Types of Suicide Attempters

As revealed above, a number of significant differences are identifiable between those sexual-minority youths who have attempted suicide and those who have not. A global comparison of these two groups should not imply, however, that all suicide attempters are the same. Indeed, those variables that distinguish attempters from nonattempters may differ from those variables that differentiate among attempters. Thus, an effort was made to identify different types of suicide attempters among minority youth.

An analysis of results was made on the 79 youths who had carried out at least one suicide attempt, using those variables considered to be most representative of the six categories of variables; 45 variables were used in all. Our analysis factored people instead of variables, assigning people who are most similar to each other on the set of variables to the same factor. A person's membership in a category, or factor, is based on the person's pattern of factor loadings, with the person designated as belonging to the category (factor) for which the largest loading appears. Following the assignment of individuals to their respective categories, mean differences across the variables used in the analysis were tested among the categories, as well as between the categories of suicide attempters and nonattempters.

Comparisons among the attempter types and between the attempters and nonattempters are shown in Table 3.4. Of the attempters, 33 percent were allocated to category one, 48 percent to category two, and 19 percent to category three. Numbers that have been underlined within a category represent variables that are particularly definitive in interpreting the characteristics of the category, based on a significant mean difference between the category and the others.

Category one includes those youths who became aware of their same-sex sexual attractions at younger ages, and engaged in same-sex sexual behaviors at younger ages. Perhaps as a necessary consequence of earlier experimentation, these youths also engaged in opposite-sex sexual relations at younger ages. Greater financial independence and less substance abuse are also associated with this category. Category two consists of youths who, although they were aware of their

TABLE 3.4. Differences Among Suicide Attempter Types and Between Suicide Attempters and Nonattempters

Variable	Attempter Types			Nonattempters
	1 (n = 26)	2 (n = 38)	3 (n = 15)	4 (n = 115)
Background				
Age	18.58	19.13	19.00	18.82
% Male	65%	79%	67%	74%
SES	5.11	4.86	4.64	5.24
% White	58%	63%	80%	68%
% Live alone	0%	11%	7%	8%
% Live in city	0%	5%	7%	1%
% Financially independent[b,f]	<u>33%</u>	58%	73%	74%
Sexual orientation throughout most of life	5.08	4.62	5.00	4.89
% Homosexual now	81%	76%	73%	46%
% Multiple attempters	50%	53%	73%	—
Religiosity	2.17	2.16	2.33	2.30
Sexual orientation and behavior				
Age of first awareness[b,d]	<u>6.44</u>	10.35	10.83	10.86
Age of first self-labeling[a,c,e]	12.40	<u>16.03</u>	13.80	14.96
Age of first disclosure[a,c,e]	14.92	<u>17.05</u>	15.67	16.77
Age for first same-sex sexual experience[a,d]	<u>11.89</u>	14.79	14.72	15.19
Age of first opposite-sex sexual experience[a,b,d]	<u>10.24</u>	15.71	13.84	14.74
Number of same-sex sexual partners[c,d,f]	5.15	4.64	6.67	3.91

TABLE 3.4 (continued)

Variable	Attempter Types			Nonattempters
	1 (n=26)	2 (n=38)	3 (n=15)	4 (n=115)
Social aspects of sexual orientation				
Number of opposite-sex sexual partners	2.54	2.42	2.53	2.34
Open about sexual orientation[b,c,d,f]	.27*	.08	.76	−.19
Fear of openness	.21*	−.24	−.36	.08
Perception of masculinity	5.88	5.61	5.45	5.58
% Participate in gay/bisexual groups[c]	96%	82%	100%	93%
Friends lost due to sexual orientation[b,e,f]	1.46	1.42	1.07	1.66
Have many close gay and lesbian friends	5.77	5.58	5.33	5.81
Sexual orientation within the family				
Mother's knowledge of sexual orientation	1.44	1.50	1.21	1.83
Mother's reaction to sexual orientation[b,c]	1.83	1.82	2.57	1.99
Father's knowledge of sexual orientation[c,f]	2.09	2.03	1.21	2.41
Father's reaction to sexual orientation	2.29	2.33	2.42	2.41
Victimization				
Verbal insults[b,c,d,f]	2.24	1.30	6.00	1.40
Property damage; chased[b,c,f]	1.20	1.03	9.67	1.23
Physical assaults[b,c,f]	.68	.18	3.93	.29
Sexual assaults[c,d,f]	.72	.29	1.20	.19
Family violence[b,c,f]	1.81	1.24	3.43	1.12

TABLE 3.4 (continued)

Variable	Attempter Types 1 (n=26)	2 (n=38)	3 (n=15)	Nonattempters 4 (n=115)
Mental health problems				
Self-esteem[a,e]	33.62	<u>27.80</u>	31.67	33.47
Personal worry[b,f]	2.62	2.95	<u>3.27</u>	2.61
% Always used violent methods	8%	16%	20%	—
Suicidal ideation[d,e,f]	2.42	2.66	2.53	1.58
Comfort with sexual orientation	2.42	2.03	2.67	2.19
Problems with alcohol use[a,b,e,f]	<u>.76</u>	1.06	1.06	.39
Problems with sex life[e]	1.16	1.45	1.13	.80
Problems developing close relationships[e]	1.16	1.45	1.13	.80
Problems with drug use	.48	.83	1.07	.38
Problems with AIDS fears	1.48	1.76	1.80	1.53
Problems with depression[a,e]	1.36	<u>2.03</u>	1.53	1.01
Global Severity Index[e,f]	.93	1.04	1.27	.65

*means given in standard deviation units from zero.
[a] Group 1 vs. Group 2, $p < .05$.
[b] Group 1 vs. Group 3, $p < .05$.
[c] Group 2 vs. Group 3, $p < .05$.
[d] Group 1 vs. Group 4, $p < .05$.
[e] Group 2 vs. Group 4, $p < .05$.
[f] Group 3 vs. Group 4, $p < .05$.

same-sex sexual attraction and engaged in sexual behaviors at typical ages, label themselves lesbian, gay, or bisexual, and subsequently disclose those identities to others at significantly later ages. These youths are also lower in self-esteem and participate less frequently in lesbian and/or gay groups. Within category three are those youths who are significantly more open about their sexual orientation and engage in significantly more same-sex sexual encounters. In fact, father's knowledge of the youth's sexual orientation is largest within this category. This greater openness appears to have come at a high price, in that these youth have lost more friends due to their sexual orientation, perceive their mothers as more rejecting, and have experienced greater victimization of all kinds. Most dramatically, while the incidence of sexual assault is 36 percent for category one, 21% for category two, and 14% for category four (nonattempters), it is 60 percent for category three. Personal worry is also significantly associated with this category.

DISCUSSION

Several results reported in this chapter deserve special emphasis. First, 42 percent of the sexual-minority youths in this sample (n= 194) had attempted suicide on at least one occasion. This is the highest estimate reported to date; the closest to this based on empirical data was the rate of 29 percent reported by Hammelman (1993) and Herdt and Boxer (1993). As in this study, both studies used youths obtained from community groups.

Although it could be argued that using a community-based sample to estimate the rate of suicidality among sexual-minority youths is preferable to using clinically based samples or retrospective reports from adults due to the greater representativeness of the youths who attend community groups, an equally strong argument could be made that community groups are often nominally preferable. In fact, youths who attend lesbian/gay/bisexual groups may differ in any number of ways from sexual-minority youths in the population. One way in which they may differ is by having more psychopathology (Shaffer, 1993). Yet clearly this is not the case in this sample, where the only significant differences on the Brief Symptom Inventory we found between it and a normative group were on depression (more) and somatization (less). These two differences, one indicating more psychopathology, one indicating less, cancel each other, resulting in a Global Severity Index that does not differ significantly between the groups. Still, this does not completely settle the question as to whether this sample of sexual-minority youths has a greater than average tendency for attempting suicide, in part due to the high association between depression and suicide in the general population (Sainsbury, 1986). Yet if one can assess how much a community-based sample differs from the population, and this difference is small, then confidence can be placed in the results found from that sample.

The suicide attempt rate of 42 percent found in this study should alert both researchers and practitioners that a great deal more needs to be done in the area of detection and prevention. Minimally, in the future, questions concerning sexual orientation should be incorporated into population-based adolescent health surveys, thus bypassing a reliance on volunteer samples, and perhaps, obtaining information of vital importance to the detection and prevention of suicide in all sexual-minority youths.

A second finding of importance in this study was the multiplicity of variables that distinguished suicide attempters from nonattempters. Suicide attempters were more precocious in their sexual orientation identity formation, lost more friends due to others' knowledge of their sexual orientation, had lower self-esteem, reported more current suicidal ideation, were more open about their sexual orientation with others, had experienced greater victimization, and acknowledged more mental health problems. The identification of these predictors of suicide attempt both confirms and extends the results of previous studies of the predictors of suicidality among sexual-minority youths and many of these predictors are specific to such youths. Therefore, even if the rate of suicidality does not differ significantly between sexual-minority and -majority adolescents, suicidality among sexual-minority adolescents merits study in its own right; certainly it does not deserve the almost complete neglect it has received from a large part of the community of suicidology researchers and the federal government (Remafedi, 1994).

A third finding of significance in this chapter was the existence of three categories of sexual-minority youth suicide attempters (Table 3.4). One category consisted of those youth who became aware of their same-sex sexual attractions and engaged in same-sex/opposite-sex behavior earlier than did other suicide attempters. A second category consisted of youths with lower self-esteem, less participation in lesbian/gay social activities, and most importantly, youths who identified themselves as sexual minorities at significantly older ages. A third category consisted of relatively open but extremely victimized and socially rejected youths. A statistical analysis confirmed that the three categories could be used to correctly classify 100 percent of the suicide attempters.

A classification scheme such as the one derived in this study is of value because it informs us of two lessons. The first lesson has to do with the correlation between two variables: although two variables may be highly correlated within a sample of suicide attempters, it does not follow that both are equally predictive of suicidality for everyone. Take, for example, the correlation between age of first awareness of same-sex sexual attraction and age of first self-labeling. Despite the larger than modest correlation between these two variables, one variable (early awareness) serves to predict suicidality among sexually precocious suicide attempters (category one), and the other variable (late self-labeling) serves to predict suicidality among suicide attempters with lower self-esteem (category two). A second lesson, related to the first, is not to assume that because a variable is a strong and consistently replicable predictor of suicidality, it will be equally relevant or even relevant at all to all suicide attempters. Conversely, it should not be assumed that if a variable fails to predict suicidality using the entire sample, it predicts suicidality for no one in the sample. Again, take, for example, awareness and self-labeling. Awareness has been found to significantly predict suicide attempt in several studies (e.g., Remafedi, Farrow, and Deisher, 1991), as in this study (e.g., for every year decrease in age, the probability of a suicide attempt increases by 10 percent; Hershberger and D'Augelli, 1995). On the other hand, using the entire current sample, self-labeling was found not to predict suicide attempt; that is, for every single-year change in age, the probability of a suicide attempt remains constant (Hershberger and D'Augelli, 1995). Yet awareness is most relevant to those youths of category one, and self-labeling, most relevant to those youths of category two.

Not all sexual-minority suicide attempters become aware of

same-sex sexual attractions at an early age. Lesbian, gay, and bisexual suicide attempters are not all alike, and therapists and researchers should acknowledge and respect these individual differences. In order to most effectively reduce the prevalence of suicidality, therapists and researchers will have to respect such differences. Only then can those insidious factors in an individual youth's life leading to suicide be removed.

REFERENCES

Bell, A. and Weinberg, M. (1978). *Homosexualities: A study of diversity among gay men and women*. New York: Simon & Schuster.

Berrill, K. (1990). Anti-gay violence and victimization in the United States: An overview. *Journal of Interpersonal Violence*, 5:274-294.

Boxer, A. M. and Cohler, B. J. (1989). The life course of gay and lesbian youth: An immodest proposal for the study of lives. *Journal of Homosexuality*, 17:315-355.

Boxer, A. M., Cook, J. A., and Herdt, G. (1991). Double jeopardy: Identity transitions and parent-child relations among gay and lesbian youth. In K. Pillemer and K. McCartney (eds.) *Parent-child relations throughout life*, pp. 59-92. Hillsdale, NJ: Erlbaum.

Bradford, J., Ryan, C., and Rothblum, E. D. (1994). National lesbian health care survey: Implications for mental health care. *Journal of Consulting and Clinical Psychology*, 62:228-242.

Cwayna, K., Remafedi, G., and Treadway, L. (1991). Caring for gay and lesbian youth. *Medical Aspects of Human Sexuality*, 25:50-57.

D'Augelli, A. R. and Herschberger, S. L. (1993). Lesbian, gay, and bisexual youth in community settings: Personal challenges and mental health problems. *American Journal of Community Psychology*, 21:1-28.

Dean, L., Wu, S., and Martin, J. L. (1992). Trends in violence and discrimination against gay men in New York City: 1984 to 1990. In G. M. Herek and K. T. Berrill (eds.) *Hate crimes: Confronting violence against lesbians and gay men*, pp. 46-64. Newbury Park, CA: Sage.

Derogatis, L. R. and Spencer, P. M. (1982). *The Brief Symptom Inventory: Administration scoring, and procedures manual*. Towson, MD: Clinical Psychometric Research.

Diekstra, R. F. (1989). Suicidal behavior in adolescents and young adults: The international picture. *Crisis*, 10:16-35.

Friedman, J. M., Asnis, G. M., Boeck, M., and DiFiore, J. (1987). Prevalence of specific suicidal behaviors in a high school sample. *American Journal of Psychiatry*, 144:1203-1206.

Garland, A. F. and Zigler, E. (1993). Adolescent suicide prevention: Current research and social policy implications. *American Psychologist*, 48:169-182.

Gibson, P. (1989). Gay male and lesbian youth suicide. In *Report to the secretary's task force on youth suicide, volume 3: Prevention and intervention in youth suicide*, pp. 110-142. Washington, DC: U.S. Department of Health and Human Services.

Gonsiorek, J. C. (1988). Mental health issues of gay and lesbian adolescents. *Journal of Adolescent Health Care*, 9:114-122.

Gross, L., Aurand, S., and Adessa, R. (1988). *Violence and discrimination against lesbian and gay people in Philadelphia and the Commonwealth of Pennsylvania*. Unpublished report, Philadelphia Lesbian and Gay Task Force.

Hammelman, T. L. (1993). Gay and lesbian youth: Contributing factors to serious attempts or considerations of suicide. *Journal of Gay and Lesbian Psychotherapy*, 2:77-89.

Harry, J. (1983). Parasuicide, gender, and gender deviance. *Journal of Health and Social Behavior*, 24:350-361.

Herdt, G. and Boxer, A. M. (1993). *Children of horizons: How gay and lesbian teens are leading a new way out of the closet*. Boston: Beacon.

Herschberger, S. L. and D'Augelli, A. R. (1995). The impact of victimization on the mental health and suicidality of lesbian, gay, and bisexual youths. *Developmental Psychology*, 31:65-74.

Herschberger, S. L., Pilkington, N. W., and D'Augelli, A. R. (1995). *Predictors of suicidality in gay, lesbian, and bisexual youths*. Unpublished manuscript.

Hunter, J. (1990). Violence against lesbian and gay male youths. *Journal of Interpersonal Violence*, 5:295-300.

Jay, K. and Young, A. (eds.). (1977). *The gay report: Lesbians and gay men speak out about their sexual experiences and lifestyles*. New York: Summit.

Kournay, R. F. C. (1987). Suicide among homosexual adolescents. *Journal of Homosexuality*, 13:111-117.

Lewinsohn, P. M., Rohde, P., and Seeley, J. R. (1994). Psychosocial risk factors for future adolescent suicide attempts. *Journal of Consulting and Clinical Psychology*, 62:297-305.

Martin, A. D. (1982). Learning to hide: Socialization of the gay adolescent. *Adolescent Psychiatry*, 10:52-65.

Martin, A. D. and Hetrick, E. S. (1988). The stigmatization of the gay and lesbian adolescent. *Journal of Homosexuality*, 15:163-184.

Mehan, P. J., Lamb, J. A., Saltzman, L. E., and O'Carroll, P. W. (1992). Attempted suicide among young adults: Progress toward a meaningful estimate of prevalence. *American Journal of Psychiatry*, 149:41-44.

National Center for Health Statistics. (1986). *Vital statistics of the United States, Volume 2. Mortality*, Part A. Hyattsville, MD: U.S. Public Health Service.

National Center for Health Statistics. (1993). *Advance report of final mortality statistics, 1990*. Monthly Vital Statistics Report, Volume 41, No. 7, Suppl. Jan. 7, 1993. Hyattsville, MD: U.S. Public Health Service.

Pfeffer, C. R., Klerman, G. L., Hurt, S. W., Lesser, M., Peskin, J. R., and Sieffker, C. A. (1991). Suicidal children growing up: Demographics and clinical risk factors for adolescent suicide attempts. *Journal of the Academy of Child and Adolescent Psychiatry*, 30:609-616.

Pilkington, N. W. and D'Augelli, A. R. (1995). Victimization of lesbian, gay, and bisexual youth in community settings. *Journal of Community Psychology*, 23:33-56.

Remafedi, G. (1987a). Adolescent homosexuality: Psychosocial and medical implications. *Pediatrics*, 79:331-337.

Remafedi, G. (1987b). Homosexual youth: A challenge to contemporary society. *JAMA*, 258:222-225.

Remafedi, G. (1987c). Male homosexuality: The adolescent's perspective. *Pediatrics*, 79:326-330.

Remafedi, G. (ed.). (1994). *Death by denial: Studies of suicide in gay and lesbian teenagers*. Boston: Alyson Publications, Inc.

Remafedi, G., Farrow, J. A., and Deisher, R. W. (1991). Risk factors for attempted suicide in gay and bisexual youth. *Pediatrics*, 87:869-875.

Rich, C. L., Fowler, R. C., Young, D., and Blenkush, M. (1986). San Diego suicide study: Comparison of gay to straight males. *Suicide and Life-Threatening Behavior*, 16:448-457.

Roesler, T. and Deisher, R. W. (1972). Youthful male homosexuality. *JAMA*, 219:1018-1023.

Rosenberg, M. (1979). *Conceiving the self*. New York: Basic Books.

Rotheram-Borus, M. J., Hunter, J., and Rosario, M. (1994). Suicidal behavior and gay-related stress among gay and bisexual male adolescents. *Journal of Adolescent Research*, 9:498-508.

Rotheram-Borus, M. J., Rosario, M., and Koopman, C. (1991). Minority youths and high risk: Gay males and runaways. In M. E. Colton and S. Gore (eds.) *Adolescent stress: Causes and consequences*, pp. 181-200. New York: Aldine.

Saghir, M. and Robins, E. (1973). *Male and female homosexuality*. Baltimore: Williams & Wilkins.

Sainsbury, P. (1986). The epidemiology of suicide. In A. Roy (ed.) *Suicide*, pp. 17-40. Baltimore: Williams & Wilkins.

Schneider, M. (1991). Developing services for lesbian and gay adolescents. *Canadian Journal of Community Mental Health*, 10:133-151.

Schneider, S. G., Fareberow, N. L., and Kruks, G. N. (1989). Suicidal behavior in adolescent and young adult gay men. *Suicide and Life-Threatening Behavior*, 19:381-394.

Shaffer, D. (1988). The epidemiology of teen suicide: An examination of risk factors. *Journal of Clinical Psychiatry*, 27:36-41.

Shaffer, D. (1993). Political science. *The New Yorker*, May 3, p. 116.

Smith, K. and Crawford, S. (1986). Suicidal behavior among "normal" high school students. *Suicide and Life-Threatening Behavior*, 16:313-325.

Chapter 4

Living in an Era of Multiple Loss and Trauma: Understanding Global Loss in the Gay Community

Mark Marion

Multiple loss has increasingly defined the gay male experience since the advent of the AIDS pandemic. With more than a decade of ongoing loss already past, and with no cure in sight, it is essential to continue examining the issue of psychological survival in the face of catastrophic and continuing loss. This chapter explores the concepts of multiple loss and loss-related trauma in the gay community, and offers approaches for helping gay men sustain a quality of life in the face of continued loss. Guidelines are offered toward the goal of helping clients rebuild or enhance the capacity to live a meaningful and passionate life in an environment where the only certainty may seem to be more loss. The first section of this chapter defines different degrees of severity in the human experience of loss, and explains their impact on the survivor. The second section examines loss within the gay community and the symptoms of AIDS global loss. The third section develops the idea of a vocabulary or language for global loss, and introduces a Global Loss Model. The Global Loss Model is analyzed as part of the language of global loss and serves as a road map for survival in ongoing, global loss that allows for recovery of the capacity to live fully, while sustaining self-worth and personal meaning.

In order to understand the experience of loss for gay men in the AIDS epidemic, it is essential to briefly define different degrees of severity in the human experience of loss. From what has come to be called *normal* grief, to the added dimensions of loss experienced in multiple loss, and, finally, the devastation of global loss, there is an exponential increase in the impact on the survivor. Furthermore, the psychology of grief and bereavement becomes more complex with each step in the severity of loss, specifically that grief is complicated by the experience of trauma. For the purposes of understanding the gay male experience of living in an era defined by loss, these terms will be defined. The foundations of the discussion of multiple loss in AIDS, and its comparison with historical precedents were introduced by Jeremy Hollinger, MFCC and Gail Bigelow, MFCC out of Visiting Nurses and Hospice in San Francisco. Jeremy's insight and expertise on multiple loss and trauma in the gay community provided invaluable support in further defining and developing the loss concepts presented here.

INDIVIDUAL LOSS COMPARED TO MULTIPLE LOSS

Much has been written about normal grief in individual loss and the process of bereavement related to the death of a significant other. Sigmund Freud, Elisabeth Kübler-Ross, and others have defined the experience of loss and the tasks and stages of grieving that typically follow. These models define an acute stage of shock (denial), followed by the process of grieving (anger, sadness, depression, etc.), and, finally, acceptance of the reality of the loss with a withdrawal of psychic energy away from the lost person that is then reinvested in life.

Multiple loss refers to more extensive losses happening in or around the same period of time. Examples include losing one's family in a car accident or being a survivor of a plane crash. Multiple loss often includes not only the deaths of loved ones, but it also impacts other aspects of a survivor's life such as home or work. In natural disasters, such as floods or earthquakes, and in criminal acts, such as the Oklahoma City bombing or the 1000 California Street massacre in San Francisco, loss encompasses violation or destruction of homes and places of employment. In all these examples, survivors experience not only grief, but also *trauma*. Here, the experience of shock (a brief, initial phase of most normal loss) becomes a part of a much longer process of bereavement.

Before examining how trauma is experienced in multiple loss, it is important to make a distinction within the category of multiple loss between *single-event* and *progressive* multiple loss. With single-event multiple loss, the event of traumatic loss, however horrific, is relatively time-limited and has a defined end, typically when the horror stops. Afterward, the extent of the loss can be recognized and the task of grieving defined.

Progressive multiple loss involves not only the factor of many losses, but also that the losses continue and accumulate over time. Wars, plagues, and conditions of continued poverty and violence are examples of progressive multiple loss. In progressive multiple loss, along with the fact that the losses are traumatic, there is also the factor that the losses continue, that the task of grieving the deceased is constantly being interrupted and altered by yet another loss.

TRAUMA IN LOSS

As a diagnostic definition for trauma, DSM-III-R (1987) described "experiencing an event that is outside the range of usual human experience and that would be markedly distressing to almost anyone." The revision in DSM-IV (1994) provides a more specific and accurate definition of trauma as an experience that evokes "intense fear, helplessness or horror." Post-traumatic stress disorder (PTSD) is the diagnosis that defines the psychological impact of and symptoms of trauma. This includes recurrent and intrusive recollections or a reexperiencing of the traumatic event, avoidance of stimuli associated with the event, numbing of general responsiveness, and increased arousal (hypervigilance).

Simply stated, the enormity and impact of multiple loss is traumatizing to survivors. The tasks of grieving, of multiple grieving, are altered and extended by the experience of trauma. How trauma alters and extends the experience of grief can best be understood by examining the two primary components of post-traumatic stress: the emotional response and the cognitive response.

The emotional experience of trauma can best be described as a pendulum swinging between two extremes. On one end of the pendulum is an acute experience of the pain or horror of the trauma called *flooding*. Flooding is an uninvited sensation of the emotions associated with the traumatic event. It may have the intensity and vividness as if actually reexperiencing the trauma. In response to this overwhelming emotion, the pendulum swings to the other extreme, *to numbing*. Numbing is a decrease in general responsiveness, a way to dampen or interrupt the overwhelming emotion associated with the trauma. Numbing is characterized by restriction in the range of affect and often includes a sense of detachment or estrangement from others. The back-and-forth swing from numbing to flooding is involuntary, especially in the acute stages of trauma. It is a survival-oriented mechanism that the person relies on to modulate exposure to the pain of overwhelming life events. Like an internal circuit breaker it prevents psychological decompensation and allows for a manageable pace in the recognition of intense fear, helplessness, or horror.

The cognitive process associated with trauma can best be summarized as a loss of cherished assumptions about the self and the world. Janoff-Bulman (1992), in her book, *Shattered Assumptions,* explores in depth this loss of assumptions, which is defined in some posttraumatic stress disorder diagnoses as "loss of sustaining beliefs and values." According to Janoff-Bulman, the primary assumptions that are violated by traumatic events are as follows:

1. The self is worthy.
2. The world is benevolent.
3. Life has meaning.

Out of these primary assumptions, a number of other secondary assumptions are also questioned and often shattered by such trauma as the following:

1. There is a relationship between a person and what happens to him or her; that is, good things happen to good people.
2. We can control what happens to us through our behavior; that is, drive carefully and there will be no accident.
3. Events are orderly and understandable.
4. People are basically good and kind.

Trauma can turn some or all of these assumptions upside down. This is expressed in questions often heard from survivors such as, "Why me?," "Why this?," and "Why now?" The cognitive experience of trauma involves an upheaval of cherished beliefs about self and one's world. These beliefs, whether objectively valid or not, are the foundation of the capacity to feel good about who we are (i.e., the self is worthy), feel positive about going out and functioning in the world (i.e., the world is benevolent), and provide a sense of purpose (i.e., life has meaning).

For multiple-loss survivors, especially in progressive multiple loss, the emotional and cognitive impact of trauma is experienced and is part of their bereavement. Unlike in single-event trauma, loss is recurring, trauma is ongoing, and, as a result, the person is retraumatized. Sometimes this happens again and again to the person. In progressive multiple loss, the ongoing reparative recovery processes from trauma, along with grieving, are thwarted by new assaults. One of the results of this is that the emotional trauma response (the internal mechanism regulating the process of numbing to flooding) works constant overtime as new trauma requires more numbing to prevent psychological overload. Another result is that the rethinking of assumptions, which is the central cognitive task of trauma recovery, is interrupted and assailed by more loss and trauma. Like a tiny boat in a pounding surf struggling to find its moorings, more trauma and loss keeps pounding away at the sense of self-worth, sense of safety in the world, and sense of meaning.

GLOBAL LOSS

Along the lines of differentiating multiple loss from normal loss, and in examining the concept of trauma that defines the multiple-loss experience, the concept of global loss must also be understood to begin to comprehend the experience of gay men in the last decade of AIDS. An exponential increase in severity and complexity, global loss is different from multiple loss in at least three ways:

1. With global loss, no aspect of life or identity is unaffected. In other words, self-perception and internal experience become

consumed with loss and survival. Also, the roles, functions, and relationships that define the external world are lost or severely altered. Loss, therefore, touches all facets of the person's world.

2. There is a loss of community. To illustrate this, the author suggests that one should imagine community being represented as concentric circles around the self. The inner circles represent intimate friends, family, and lovers. The middle circles are acquaintances and colleagues. The outer circles represent the greater community such as culture and the collective future. For the self in the center, these circles, to greater or lesser degrees, provide the foundation for identity, relationships, and meaning. When global loss occurs, all the circles are gone or fragmented and broken. As a result, the following is true.

3. There is no safe haven. In multiple loss, some aspects of life remain stable. Typically, for example, the individual's support system or community is intact. In global loss, however, there is no place to get away from the impact of the loss and no place of psychological refuge. The Holocaust, Hiroshima, the enslavement of the African people, the genocide of Native Americans, and AIDS in the gay community are all examples of global loss.

It is important to note that, while global loss in the gay community occurs within the larger heterosexual society (which is comparatively untouched by AIDS), the ignorance or denial of this larger society makes community support largely unavailable for gay men. Small or large gay networks represent the only community where a gay man can be himself, where his erotic and emotional needs are valued rather than blithely ignored or viewed with repugnance. This fact may represent a fourth characteristic of global loss: dehumanization, disownership, or victimization by the greater society.

Dave is a gay man who has lived in San Francisco for ten years and has lost over 60 friends and acquaintances to AIDS. He describes community not as concentric circles but as a tree where the trunk, limbs, and leaves represent various people, from intimate to casual. Speaking of this network, Dave said matter of factly, "This tree has been cut to the ground." Then he paused and said, "I'm 45 years old. These were my friends for life and now they're gone. I don't know if another tree can grow in its place. I just don't know."

GLOBAL LOSS
IN THE GAY COMMUNITY

> "The more than 100 people I've lost. I try not to think about it. Altogether it's just this kind of mass. It's there but I'm kind of detached from it. But if I start thinking about individual people, names and faces, well then I'm afraid I would fall apart." (Anonymous. Expressed by a gay man living in the epidemic.)

Loss of this magnitude creates some seemingly unresolvable dilemmas for those living in it. Perhaps the most significant dilemma is the fact that while, on the one hand, no aspect of life or identity is untouched by loss, on the other, the enormity of the loss is too big to grieve and too pervasive to fully comprehend. So while grief, recognized or denied, is ever present, it is impossible to grieve the entirety of the loss. The metaphor often quoted is one of the "huge cloud of unprocessed grief" hanging over San Francisco and other communities hit hard by loss to AIDS. Grief and trauma are all around. Although survivors can become accustomed as to seem almost unfazed, that is not the same as being immune to its effects.

One long-time resident of a Castro Street neighborhood described it as a war that was taking place in incredibly slow motion. At "normal" speed, everything looked normal. But if the "camera" were speeded up, then it would show the battle raging in his neighborhood: the small victories, major defeats, survivors caring for the suffering and burying the dead, and still fighting on.

The psychological toll of living in the years of global loss is high. The struggle to remain functional and retain a quality of life is as real a struggle as is the struggle against AIDS itself.

LOSS TOO BIG TO GRIEVE

What follows is a look at the effects of this struggle and the symptoms that result. It is important to note that these symptoms are adaptive survival mechanisms. It is important to preface the symp-tomology of global loss in the gay community by reaffirming that these "symptoms" are adaptive, survival mechanisms to an unten-able situation. The pathology lies in the horror of the global loss from AIDS itself. This is particularly important given the larger society's history of pathologizing homosexuality and hence the gay community. In fact, it is a miracle of the tenacity, strength, and humanity of the gay community that functioning and quality of life remain at the levels that they do. But it is precisely because of this humanity that global loss has and will continue to cause great suffer-ing, and the symptoms of this suffering must be addressed. The enormity of loss represents perhaps the central dilemma of anyone living in the midst of global loss. In terms of global loss in the gay community, four symptoms of coping with pervasive loss are partic-ularly pronounced: psychological fatigue, depression, survivor guilt, and shame.

Psychological Fatigue

While not a clinical diagnosis, psychological fatigue deserves recognition because it is one of the inevitable and ongoing effects of global loss. It is an understatement to say that coping with traumatic loss is a stressful and demanding process and when repeated over and over, the capacity to meet the tasks of grief become more lim-ited. In turn, the energy to face those tasks becomes depleted. Psy-chological fatigue is a loss of energy, of resilience, and while it can eventually lead to depression, it does not have the clinical features of melancholia or hopelessness. It is simply profound weariness.

Depression

The accumulation and relentlessness of losses and their impact can make avoiding or controlling depression an uphill battle. Depression, which is a stage of grieving, becomes an ongoing expe-rience when loss continues without relief. Further, growing up gay in a heterosexual society means many gay men were not strangers to depression even before their first AIDS-loss experiences.

Because of the unique combination of homophobia and AIDS

global loss, specific depressive and dysthymic symptoms are empha-sized: fatigue, low self-esteem, and thoughts of death with or without suicidality. Along with this, several clinicians in the gay community have recognized the prevalence of mania as a defense against experi-encing overwhelming depression. Hyperactive, driven, overcommitted behaviors, whether productive or merely compulsive, are seen as manic mobilizations against underlying depression. Mania represents an exhausting and ultimately fruitless attempt to stay "one step ahead" of the emotional pain of global loss.

Survival Guilt

Survival guilt, a major component of traumatic loss (and seen vividly in such examples as the Holocaust, Hiroshima, and Naga-saki) brings in the element of grief, not only about the loss of loved ones, but more important, *grief about surviving.* Odets (1995) describes survival guilt in terms of an identification with the deceased that includes the survivor wishing to trade places with the lost loved one, confusion about why he is alive while his loved one has died, irrational feelings of being responsible for the death of the deceased, or that the survivor does not deserve to live. Odets eluci-dates that survivor guilt not only keeps survivors from being able to separate (decathect) from the deceased, but more important, he states, "much of the remorse is not about the loss of the dead person, but about the survivor's survival, an event which is ongoing, and cannot be grieved, because it is not over."

As with depression, most gay men are not strangers to guilt even before having had to cope with AIDS losses. Admitting homosexu-ality and coming out to loved ones who can be profoundly disap-pointed or respond as if it is a personal affront will leave an unre-solved sense of guilt that global losses and resulting survivor guilt can intensify.

Shame

Unlike guilt, which refers to remorse about one's thoughts, actions, or behaviors (real or imagined), shame refers to a sense of being inherently flawed or inadequate. Thus, it is not just feeling bad about what one did, but *who one is*. Simply being gay in a society that reviles homosexuality means having experience coping with shame. Negative judgments and values about homosexuality are internalized as shame. There are at least three characteristics of AIDS global loss that can exacerbate or trigger long-buried shame in gay men.

First, along with guilt about survival, there is also the powerlessness that is experienced in global loss, the perceived inadequacy felt in being unable to stop tremendous suffering in loved ones, community, or self. As described above, the occurrence of traumatizing events flies in the face of our sense of worthiness, safety, and meaning. In turn, vulnerability, fragility, and powerlessness are exposed, and shame is experienced.

Second, one of the most cherished assumptions in society is the idea of some kind of ultimate justice, where good people are rewarded and bad people punished. While it may allow for a sense of safety and benevolence for many people, if interpreted simplistically, it has a destructive effect in traumatic loss, especially in terms of shame. Not only does it become a justification for blaming the victim, but also in "victims" blaming themselves, resulting in feelings such as, "If bad things happen to bad people, then I must be a bad person or have done bad things."

Third, shame about being gay or the powerlessness of global loss is consistently reinforced by the larger society. Gay men are barraged with ideas, opinions, and images from many segments of the larger society, where they are portrayed, not as equal yet different members of the human family, but as morally reprehensible, mentally ill, or doomed victims of a deadly virus brought on by themselves. Along with the ongoing assault of AIDS itself, this societal shaming is nearly impossible to completely deflect.

CHRONIC TRAUMA

While post-traumatic stress disorder (PTSD) accurately reflects much of the symptomotology of global loss for gay men, there are at least two significant differences. The term itself, *post-traumatic stress,* implies a trauma that is about a traumatic event that is in the past. With AIDS losses, the trauma is ongoing. There is no post to the trauma. Second, PTSD does not address the difference between surviving a single traumatic event versus chronic trauma. Chronic trauma affects the individual differently, with certain PTSD symptoms becoming more pronounced as the trauma continues. Some of these symptoms get integrated into the survivor's way of functioning while others become less pronounced or even disappear.

Arnold, a 36-year-old gay, HIV-positive man, made the following comment in the context of his ambivalence about continuing to see a guy he had been dating:

> I don't want a relationship. A lot of the guys I see all the time when I go out, we have fun, we dance, we get our rocks off, but no one gets too close to anybody. There's just too much to lose.

Arnold's comment speaks to the effects of chronic trauma in global loss, and the symptoms that emerge as a defense against further traumatic loss. When discussing the effects of global loss for gay men, it must be recognized that chronic trauma refers to more than *ten years* of traumatic losses. The symptoms and adaptive mechanisms reflect the duration of exposure to trauma. As a result of this duration, four groups of trauma symptoms deserve special attention: anxiety, numbing and restriction of affect, avoidance of intimacy (detachment and estrangement), and the sense of a foreshortened future.

Anxiety

Watching friends, lovers, and community die, the ongoing vulnerability to HIV infection or disease progression, and the certainty of losing more friends, lovers and community produce, along with chronic trauma, persistent anxiety. Different from the hypervigilence of PTSD (which may even decrease with the repetitive inevitability of chronic trauma), anxiety expresses a rational present time or future anticipated fear. The disturbing or painful recollections associated with trauma fuel anxiety, but whereas the repetition of traumatic losses blunts the impact of trauma, anxiety about living in ongoing global loss and the heightened sense of mortality can increase over time. This expresses itself in any of the ranges of anxiety disorders: panic, phobias, and/or obsessive-compulsive disorders. Hypochondria, although defined as a *Somatoform Disorder,* is an expression of this same anxiety.

Numbing

Numbing is a natural defensive response as a way to blunt the overwhelming effect of traumatic loss. In normal loss or trauma, it is a temporary state, often manifested as shock or denial. In global loss, this instinctive coping response is often no longer temporary. The more traumatic loss accumulates, the more our capacity to absorb, experience, and work through it all becomes saturated and fatigued, and the more all the emotions associated with grief and trauma become too great to contain. As a result, the internal mechanism for regulating the powerful emotions associated with trauma, the pendulum between avoidance (numbing) and flooding, goes on overload. A more permanent state of numbness becomes the only way to contain overwhelming amounts of grief and horror. While this allows global-loss survivors to function, it decreases the quality of life since all emotions, not only grief or trauma, are numbed.

David, a gay man in his forties, describes his impatience about "feeling nothing," and a growing sense of boredom and restlessness in spite of a number of recent significant emotional events and positive accomplishments. "I know there's something underneath all this. I know there is, but I can't get to it. I don't feel like I'm depressed, but whereas I used to get really charged up, I feel nothing."

Intimacy Avoidance

Intimacy avoidance is a trauma symptom characterized by a sense of detachment and/or estrangement from others. It is another survival mechanism that has a temporary function in normal trauma and loss that becomes more permanent in the extreme circumstances of global loss. When multiple progressive losses are ongoing, when partners, friends, acquaintances, and community members become sick and die, the survivor's capacity to attach, open up, and reinvest in new relationships becomes affected. In global loss, its effects are subtle, oftentimes expressed as ambivalence about, or avoidance of, investing any meaning in relationships or allowing the development of emotional attachment. As with survival guilt, the preexisting conditions of intimacy problems for gay men, such as growing up stigmatized and programmed for heterosexual pairing, are exacerbated by global loss.

Steve, a 29-year-old gay man, described a conversation with Brad, a man he was dating. Wanting to get to know Brad better, Steve asked him about his career plans and about his hopes for the future. Brad, also in his twenties, offered, "I don't think too much about the future. You know, with AIDS and everything." Steve softly asked, "Are you HIV positive?" Brad said, "No. I told you before I'm negative. Why do you ask?"

Sense of Foreshortened Future

Living in global loss means that a war zone mentality can develop. Who lives and who dies, who stays well and who gets sick is random and arbitrary. The fragility of life is constantly reinforced. The idea of a future seems like a luxury, and planning for it can feel like compounding one's sense of loss. With feelings of survival guilt added, as well as the blurring of any difference between being gay and having AIDS, the development of a sense of foreshortened future for HIV-negative and -positive men is accentuated.

It should be noted that recognizing the ephemeral nature of every life, that is, recognizing one's own mortality, can have positive effects. An examination of what is and is not important, coupled with a renewed capacity to live in the moment, can add a richness and intensity to heretofore ordinary events. However, feelings of a foreshortened future can create panic, urgency, or sense of resignation that instead of enhancing life's quality, depletes it. Perhaps the most destructive element of the feeling of a foreshortened future is that it robs those living in global loss of considering the possibility of their own survival.

SEXUALITY

Growing up gay in a heterosexual family and community means that budding homosexual desire is defined by a sense of difference, shame, and a struggle to suppress these feelings. The impossible choice between acceptance and belonging, while admitting to being different, creates not only confusion but isolation. Thus, early sexual fantasies are often experienced by gay men as pleasurable, yet feared. At whatever point a gay man eventually acknowledges to himself his homosexuality, sexual desire motivates him, and the expression of his sexuality with other men becomes a critical dimension in discovering himself and viewing himself as worthy.

In sexual experiences a gay man does not have to hide his desires and he can affirm these desires as good. In sharing sex with another man, the sense of being different and alone is dissolved. Thus, for gay men, sex means affirmation and integration, as well as the universal meaning of pleasure and intimacy. Even for those gay men who are still in the closet, sex with another man provides a moment of relief from oppression, and oftentimes affords a feeling of wholeness.

AIDS, transmitted through the most intimate of gay sexual experiences, links sex and death in the minds of most gay men. Thus, shame is superimposed on sexual desires and activities, and the affirming power of gay sex is diminished in the minds of gay men.

In the context of global loss, avoiding HIV infection is far more complex than simply having accurate information about transmission. Some authors (Moon, 1995; Odets, 1995) have addressed the role of grief and survivor guilt in risky sexual behavior, especially in mixed HIV status couples. While HIV transmission must be prevented, it must also be acknowledged that the meaning and affirming power of sexuality is as important to many gay men as is the drive for survival.

DRUG ABUSE AND OTHER ADDICTIVE BEHAVIORS

Mood-altering substances or behaviors are attractive in their ability to change the way a person feels. In an environment of recurring trauma and loss, the desire to change or escape from one's feelings is understandable. Problems with substance abuse and addiction in the gay community did not start with the AIDS epidemic. The challenges and conflicts associated with being gay create a vulnerability to chemical dependency, compulsive sex, and codependency in many gay men.

The patterns of use and substances of choice have changed as a result of AIDS, however. The traumatic losses and their assault on self-worth, safety in the world, and meaning hinder the already difficult steps of recovery. Grief, depression, and trauma constitute an added dimension in the recovery process for those affected by loss to AIDS. A sense of hopelessness, coupled with survivor guilt, can create greater ambivalence in acknowledging abuse and seeking out help. This ambivalence is reflected in relapse for men who may have years of sobriety.

The dramatic increase in the popularity of methamphetamines in the gay community reflects the ongoing stresses of living in global loss. The effects of the drug (increase in energy, increased sense of confidence, and sexual arousal) artificially bolster the very areas that global loss hurts most: energy, self-worth, and sexuality. Even the intense depression associated with coming off the high can be seen as self-punishment as an expression of survival guilt. Matthew Denchla (Personal communication, 1995), a Marin AIDS Project counselor, describes methamphetamine use in the gay community: "They could be like, fuck it, I don't have much time left, or my body image is leaving me, or I'm depressed in general. If I do some crystal, then life is a cabaret!"

SURVIVAL IN THE CONTEXT
OF GLOBAL LOSS

The desire to self-medicate, to numb, or escape from all the symptoms of global loss is understandable. The motivation for recovery, with little sense of long-term future and a decreasing value in survival, is hard to sustain. The need to find other ways to cope with global loss is a major challenge for a significant number of gay men. In searching for these options they often turn to mental health providers for guidance.

With more than a decade of fighting for survival already past, the question of living–not merely existing–is more compelling than ever. Meeting the responsibilities of caregiving while bearing the burden of ongoing trauma and grief has taken most of the physical and psychological energy from individual gay men, as well as much of the gay community. There is currently no end in sight, and thus we are still evaluating what it means to have survived thus far, and what it means to continue to survive. Some even ask, "Does one even have the right to consider the possibility of some degree of happiness in the midst of global loss?"

There is limited data on the psychology of individual and community survival in global loss, and even less data on *continuing* global loss. Like an expedition of reluctant explorers trying to map a pathway through some uncharted and dangerous territory, there are many uncertainties. The territory of global loss seems uninhabitable, barren, and harsh. Yet, there is no going back. This is the current reality. As individuals and as a community, charting a map for living in global loss is a task that nobody chose, but one that challenges us daily. It is not so much a challenge about death and dying, however. Rather, it is about finding ways to live fully.

Increasingly, gay men are finding ways to live in global loss. Doing so has required major restructuring of how gay men define themselves and their world, while simultaneously redefining their expectations about life and ways of living. This same process needs to happen with existing conceptions of grief and trauma, which are based on assumptions that are not valid in global loss. Thus, to discover what is true and valid about grief and trauma of global loss levels requires a restructuring of existing concepts and the development of new models.

DEVELOPING A LANGUAGE
TO DESCRIBE GLOBAL LOSS

From 1988 to 1992 I worked as the HIV/AIDS Services staff counselor for The Pacific Center for Human Growth in Berkeley, California. The Pacific Center is a community counseling center for sexual minorities. My work involved providing short-term crisis counseling, supervising HIV-related support groups, and coordinating a local HIV antibody test site. The counseling and support group services were utilized by the worried well people who had recently tested HIV positive, people living with HIV, caregivers, and survivors. Early on, it became clear that the most important component of counseling was to help clients with whom I worked find ways to describe their experience. Additionally, I found that the support groups were most effective when participants were able to communicate what they were going through to one another, especially their emotional experience. In both individual and group counseling, *describing* and *communicating* the trauma and grief allowed for relief and a lifting of the burden that many felt.

Having worked in bereavement services, I knew that the experience of the men with whom I worked was not unique. What was different, however, was the particular challenge, felt by both clients and therapist, in being able to describe or reflect back the extent of the grief and loss that was being experienced. The existing vocabulary, I found, was insufficient to encompass the reality of global loss. Individuals and group members saturated with traumatic losses would communicate with their faces and eyes what they could not verbalize. There was a struggle to articulate their emotions and thoughts in ways people dealing with less extensive loss did not experience. One client compared it to "trying to describe the nature of water after being hit by a tidal wave." Yet, the need to express what seems inexpressible remained, and to the degree this was possible, the benefits were obvious. Consistently, I saw a palpable sense of relief and in many, a greater capacity to cope.

As the work progressed, and as the community experience of coping with AIDS grew, the answer to this dilemma began to emerge in the form of building a vocabulary to express global levels of grief and trauma. In counseling and support groups an evolution was happening. Concepts and metaphors for describing the experience of global loss were being created. The logic behind this concept was simple: While each person's experience is unique, the *process* of living in global loss, like any other grief or trauma, is universal. Working with and learning from these men underscored the importance of developing a vocabulary as a kind of language or road map for living in global loss.

A people without a language that accurately communicates their experience are isolated from one another. In global loss, the struggle to articulate the trauma and grief, to express what it means to experience such an enormity of loss, and what it means to survive, are all part of building an individual and common vocabulary. To be able to express the experience, and in so doing, end the sense of separation, is particularly crucial in the AIDS global loss of the gay community because of the nature of any global loss. AIDS touches on many of the taboos in society: sexuality, homosexuality, illness and suffering, disfigurement, death and dying, and substance abuse. As with any taboo subject, there is a societal prohibition against acknowledging, much less talking about, these issues. Along with this, the nature of any global loss is typified by traumatic loss of such an extent as to leave no aspect of identity or world untouched. This is characterized by what DSM-IV refers to as "intense fear, helplessness or horror." Again, the experience of global loss feels to be beyond words.

Historical examples of global loss speak to both the difficulty and importance of finding a language to capture the feelings and reactions of the loss. Primo Levi, the Italian concentration camp survivor who wrote the book, *The Drowned and the Saved,* emphasized the importance of "bearing witness," which he describes as a continuing affirmation and expression of the reality of the Holocaust. Only through bearing witness, he observes, could the horror of the Holocaust have any meaning, and only through having meaning could it be bearable. Drawing on this concept it becomes clear that to bear witness as a survivor is not just to know, but to be able to communicate the experience; that is, to tell the story. An article in *National Geographic* (1995) describes the inhabitants of the city of Hiroshima as "divided between those who can never forget and those who can never know." Here, global loss has divided a people, illustrating both the challenge and the compelling need to find a language to bridge the separate worlds.

Defining and communicating personal experience not only allows for releasing one's burden, but ends isolation and starts the move toward finding meaning in the experience. In the numbing enormity of global loss, it allows a bearable recognition and expression of grief. Concepts, models, and metaphors that accurately capture any aspect of global loss offer a kind of psychological *container* for recognition and expression of trauma that becomes bearable in the witnessing and in the transmission of the story.

FIGURE 4.1. The Global Loss Model

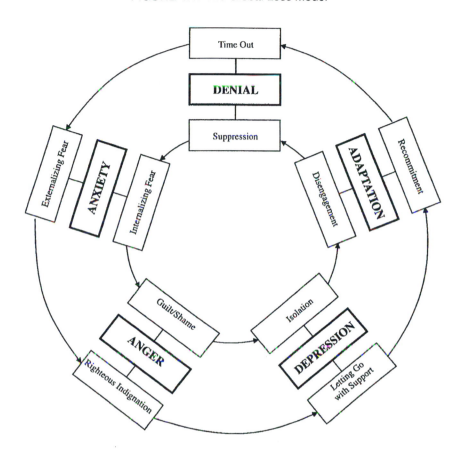

THE GLOBAL LOSS MODEL

The Global Loss Model (Figure 4.1) represents an effort to better define and reflect the experience of global loss than existing grief and trauma models currently do. It is one approach toward defining global loss. The Global Loss Model approaches the gas, y experience of loss from a clinical, therapeutic perspective. While this is a piece in the picture of the developing language of global loss, it is only one of many complementary approaches. Other approaches such as metaphor and ritual are equally as important, although they will not be explored in this chapter. An example of ritual in the gay community is the Names Project AIDS Quilt and the Candlelight Memorial March. Anyone who has participated in either of these has experienced how they allow for bearing witness while providing a place where the enormity of loss can be acknowledged, shared, and expressed.

The Global Loss Model is a grief model. Specifically, it is a model of grief and trauma that is about *living*. Whether HIV-negative or -positive, the experiences of living in global loss are challenges of living. Developed out of the perspective of gay men living in the AIDS pandemic, it addresses the question of how to live fully and productively in the context of ongoing loss and trauma. Unlike most existing grief or trauma models, however, the Global Loss Model is circular. There is no defined beginning or end. This more accurately reflects the experience of living in global loss than do linear models that are oriented toward a resolution of grief or recovery from trauma. Rather than seeking resolution at some end point when the grieving or trauma symptoms cease, the model is instead focused on how to live with the ongoing experience of grief and trauma in such a way that allows for better functioning and quality of life.

The circular Global Loss Model addresses the question of how one can live in a way that does not deny the ongoing losses and trauma without simultaneously feeling consumed. Reflecting this, the model is divided into the familiar stages of normal grief or trauma (denial, shock, anxiety, anger, depression). But rather than looking at these "stages" as temporary symptoms of a finite process, they are examined as part of the ongoing emotional world of living in global loss. Again, the goal is not to "get through and get over" these emotional states, but to recognize ways of being in an environment where grief and trauma are ongoing in a way that not only makes living more bearable, but also allows for more quality of life. In fact, gay men surviving and thriving in the global loss of AIDS are doing just that: living in a community where traumatic loss is ongoing and creating ways to live passionate and meaningful lives in the midst of it.

Each point of the model represents a continuum (Figure 4.2) from "more stressful" to "less stressful" ways of experiencing loss-

FIGURE 4.2. The Stages of the Global Loss Model

INCREASES STRESS	**DECREASES STRESS**
DENIAL	
Suppression	Time Out
This isn't happening. I'm going to block it out and not deal with it. If I don't think about it, it isn't real.	I acknowledge loss, but am not preoccupied with it. Loss/trauma is a piece in the picture of my life but not the whole gestalt. It's OK to take a break.

↓   ↓

ANXIETY	
Internalizing Fear	Externalizing Fear
Tension in body or breathing, feeling "keyed up," unable to relax, heightened sense of vulnerability, waves of fear about the future or distressing, vivid memories of loss, preoccupation with health status (hypochondria).	Giving myself permission to be afraid; it's OK. Getting support to examine fears: 1) of separation from loved ones 2) of not being in control (faced with uncertainty or feeling powerless) 3) of pain (emotional and physical) 4) of loss

↓   ↓

ANGER	
Guilt/Shame	Righteous Indignation
Survivor guilt: guilt about being alive, being healthy, or being happy—feeling undeserving. Anger turned inward toward self or shame: "bad times happen to bad people."	Addressing survivor guilt allows recognition of innocence. In this recognition, there is anger. Expressing anger—giving it a voice—focusing it outward in appropriate ways.

↓   ↓

DEPRESSION	
Isolation	Letting Go with Support
Immobilizing grief; despair—inability to see any hope or future, loss of drive, interest, or pleasure in living. Withdrawal from relationships. Psychological fatigue—coping mechanisms exhausted. Cherished life assumptions crumble under the onslaught of global loss, leaving a sense of insignificance, helplessness, and futility.	Reaching out and commiserating. Finding a safe place or person to be this vulnerable—to approach this intensity of pain and be understood and accepted. Grieving—not only the deaths of loved ones, but also recognizing and mourning the loss of our assumptions about self, world, and life; grieving the loss of our lives as we expected them to be.

↓   ↓

ADAPTATION	
Disengagement	Recommitment
1. Closing off of feelings (numbing) in attempt to "seal off" pain of losses. 2. Rallying of energy to avoid/ escape from sense of resignation or fatality; excessive activity/ involvement to avoid a nagging sense of emptiness. 3. Inability to open up, trust, be intimate —may also be use of/increase in mood-altering substances or behaviors —may also include self-destructive behaviors.	1. Rethinking of life assumptions that accepts the reality of ongoing loss and still allows for self-worth and meaning. 2. A cognitive/emotional shift: —from trying not to die—to living life fully. —from hiding, escaping, or "waiting for it to be over"—to recommitting to and participating in living. 3. Grieving, letting go of our lives "as we expected them to be" frees up energy to participate in the present. Renewal of vitality and the capacity for enjoyment.

↓   ↓

DENIAL	
Suppression	Time Out

↓   ↓

related denial, anger, or depression. Differentiating more from less stressful ways of experiencing a stage of traumatic loss provides not only a vocabulary or language for understanding the traumatic loss experience, but also represents a guide to make the experience of traumatic loss less stressful and therefore more livable.

The model is offered as a guide for clinicians working with gay men who have experienced repeated loss to AIDS and who are presenting with symptoms of grief, trauma, and/or post-traumatic stress. The model affords clinicians the opportunity to assess where the reactions of their clients fall with regard to a multitude of feelings and reactions of global loss. Some providers may find it useful to share the model with the client as a way of facilitating a better mutual understanding of these reactions to living with multiple loss.

Guidelines for Use

Most important in the guidelines are three points. First, the model is not written in stone. Rather, it is intended as an outline to support men living in AIDS global loss to individually and collectively continue to define their own vocabulary, language, and road map for living fully. In fact, the model should not be approached as conclusive since, just as ways of coping have changed over the past ten years of AIDS, so will they continue to change and evolve. Any model reflecting this will have to evolve also.

Second, people are at different points of coping with loss at different times. For example, George, a gay man in his early forties, was describing his battle with depression as "running around a lot but not really getting anything done." For George, loneliness and emptiness set in whenever he stopped long enough to catch his breath. Whereas the depression focused on the loss of so many close friends and lovers, he was very angry toward his family's seeming indifference to his situation. He also avoided his current (HIV-positive) lover's efforts to discuss the uncertainty of their future together. Instead, he would smooth things over with statements such as, "I know things will be OK," indicating his denial about this separate anticipated future loss. George's experience illustrates the complexity of global loss and is offered as a caution against oversimplification.

Lastly, there is no good-, better-, bad-, or worst-case scenario in the model. The "more stressful" responses are largely involuntary, unconscious survival mechanisms that will happen, whether we want them to or not. The key is understanding, that is, making the unconscious conscious. For in so doing, we can recognize the origin of these "more stressful" responses to the global loss and begin to change them. The removal of value judgments from the model interpretation is especially important because any loss amplifies the "inner critic." The internalized cultural or familial rules about acceptable versus unacceptable ways of responding to loss, or conceptions of "better" or "worse" only play into feelings of guilt and shame. The intent of the model is to encourage acceptance of what can feel like extreme emotional responses that in reality are an unavoidable consequence of the extreme circumstances of global loss.

Denial

Denial is the first line of defense against trauma or loss. In response to events that are painful to assimilate, this natural response is reflected in assertions such as "I just can't believe it," or "It's not real." Looking at the function of denial in ongoing global loss, it is viewed along a continuum, with denial that increases stress on one end (i.e., suppression), and denial that decreases stress on the other (i.e., "time out"). As with other components of bereavement or trauma, what in normal grief is a temporary point in a linear process becomes more of an ongoing adaptive mechanism.

For many men living in AIDS global loss, suppression can become a basis of functioning in the world. Suppression is a well-developed human capacity, and when compared to the magnitude of loss associated with AIDS, it can seem like the only alternative to total despair. The numbing effect of ongoing trauma reinforces suppression. As emotions are numbed, however, it also becomes easier to deny reality. Yet, although suppression is a natural response, it does not occur without psychological consequence.

To suppress one's experience takes energy. To suppress the reality of loss that leaves no aspect of identity untouched takes even more energy. Further, being in denial does not allow for any psychological growth, and actually hinders the bereavement process. Thus, even though it insulates the person from pain, it removes him from participating in life. The long-term effect of denial is disengagement, a chronic state of numbness.

Alternately, the "decreases stress" end of the denial also refers to a period of time out. This has also been described as "healthy denial" or "conscious denial," in that it is not based on a refusal to acknowledge loss, but instead is a form of stepping back from the pervasiveness of suffering, trauma, and loss. This form of denial entails taking time to rest, to be in an environment, relationship, or project that is not overwhelmed by AIDS loss. This provides an opportunity to recharge batteries and replenish emotional reserves. It is a temporary, but necessary, "weigh station" on the journey of living with global loss. The "time out" end of the denial continuum is actually only realized as a result of grappling with ongoing loss over time, for it takes some understanding of loss to be able to recognize the difference between supressing grief/trauma and taking a "time out." To be able to not get trapped in supression, and to instead develop the capacity to take a "time out" requires understanding the other points on the Global Loss Cycle, beginning with Anxiety.

Anxiety

The physical sensations of anxiety and the thoughts that produce them are not far below the surface for the men living in global loss. The psychological distress of multiple losses, as well as their traumatic nature, breaks through the barriers of suppression and brings with it waves of painful images and sensations, even panic.

On the "increases stress" side of the continuum, anxiety is defined as internalizing fear. Themes that increase stress involve a redoubling of efforts to suppress, avoid, or escape from these emotions. The body bears the suppressed anxiety in the form of stress-induced symptoms such as gastrointenstinal difficulties, skin problems, headaches, and confusion. In a cruel irony, these effects mimic many symptoms associated with HIV disease. Thus, like the person with AIDS, the individual finds himself preoccupied with his health, often to the point of hypochondriasis. Hypochondriasis, therefore, often expresses not only the fear of AIDS, but also the identification with loved ones who are living with AIDS.

The "decreases stress" side of the continuum of anxiety is externalizing fear. Here, the sensations and images associated with anxiety are still disturbing, but instead of internalizing or suppressing them, the fears are externalized or expressed. When fears are expressed, especially to another person, the power of the fear to consume us diminishes. In ongoing global loss of the gay community, past trauma with current and future-related fears blend together into a collage of emotions, sensations, and images that gnaw away at survivors, often overwhelming them tremendously.

To externalize the fear represents for the person a critical incident stress debriefing for AIDS global loss. Telling the stories again and again, especially with other survivors, provides a way to verbalize the anxiety that oftentimes feels paralyzing. This is not an easy process, as externalizing fear runs counter to our instinct, where suppression is the knee-jerk reaction, often rationalized with magical thinking: "If you talk about the fear out loud, you make the fear stronger"; "If I don't think about it, it will go away." In fact, however, talking about fears increases the feelings momentarily, but it is typically followed with a sense of relief. However, to externalize fear brings up other feelings including guilt, shame, and anger,

Anger

From the "increases stress" end of the continuum, defined as guilt and shame, to the "decreases stress" end of the continuum, defined as righteous indignation, anger represents one of the pivotal points in global loss. Unlike in normal grief, cumulative, progressive loss can undermine the capacity to recognize and express anger. This is best illustrated in examining the responses of the gay community during the past decade when the late 1980s brought witness to very focused anger, exemplified by groups such as ACT UP and Queer Nation. Individual and collective anger were focused as a way of mobilizing strength toward addressing such issues as treatment access; however, the corrosive nature of global loss diminished not only the ranks of these groups, but the energy and focus of the survivors as well.

As multiple losses accumulate for individuals and for the entire gay community, it becomes more difficult accessing and directing anger. Psychological fatigue, the sense of powerlessness to stop the dying, and ambivalence about survival diminish the vitality of anger. This is expressed on the continuum as guilt and shame, and thus naturally falls on the side of increasing stress. (See Figure 4.2.) As mentioned above, guilt and shame are separate experiences, yet both have in common their origin in the repression or displacement of healthy anger. As with guilt, shame represents an unconscious effort to maintain some sense of control.

Survivor guilt is highly pronounced in the more stressful expression of anger. There is a profound feeling of bewilderment or unworthiness to surviving. Here, the survivor takes on the burden of this perceived injustice as his own responsibility, and he unconsciously tries to atone for it by denying himself a future or sense of hope. He may punish himself for his undeserved lease on life, feeling that he does not really have the right to live. This self-denial or self-punishment may be acted out in overt or covert ways that are destructive to the person. For example, the person may defer on his capacity to fulfill his potential. The abandonment of being left behind challenges any meaning to living, and the anger that arises is directed to the self with comments such as, "I didn't do enough," or "I don't deserve to be alive."

Clearly, the power of survival guilt cannot be underestimated. The sense of bewilderment and unworthiness toward survival is an almost inevitable consequence of such extensive personal loss. For survivors, much of the guilt is unconscious. The person is simply unaware of the degree to which guilt impacts his life, and the manifestation becomes anxiety, hypochondriasis, difficulties around intimacy, and so on. San Francisco psychotherapist, Tom Moon, describes the depression associated with survivor guilt. He speaks to the "deadening" symptoms (i.e., loss of pleasure and energy, withdrawal) that are the unconscious expression of survival guilt, often expressed as "I don't have the right to be alive and happy when lovers and friends have suffered and died." Shame, part of the baggage of a homophobic world, gets triggered by the same powerlessness, the same sense of being "damaged goods." Both shame and guilt represent an unconscious effort to try to maintain some sense of control, when the onslaught of global loss threatens to expose it all as meaningless, indifferently cruel, or insane.

The "decreases stress" side of the continuum is defined as righteous indignation. Although the title, *Righteous Indignation,* is somewhat tongue-in-cheek, it captures the essence of anger that is not suppressed or turned against the self as guilt or shame. Anger is a natural and healthy part of coping with loss or trauma. When anger is acknowledged, accepted, and focused, it can reawaken vitality and creativity that global loss chips away. Of course, the expression of anger can be either creative or destructive. But it is in either the suppression of anger or its displacement as guilt or shame that it becomes damaging.

In order to reconnect with healthy anger in global loss, survivor guilt must be recognized and discharged. The right side of the continuum reflects this and is described in terms of "recognition of innocence." Admitting one's innocence means recognizing that nobody asked for this, nobody *deserves* it, and it is beyond our ability to change or control it. This involves challenging the imperatives of survivor guilt: "I am not worthy of survival," or "I am somehow responsible for his death. I didn't do enough." It means defusing the sense of irrational responsibility that survivor guilt carries, and acknowledging the sense of powerlessness that fuels it.

Though not an easy process, it is an essential task of finding a way of recovering the capacity to be fully alive. To the extent that one is able to work through survival guilt, the result is a recognition of innocence, a renewed sense of self-worth, and a return to the capacity for healthy anger. Healthy anger is conscious, focused, and appropriately directed. It is not only therapeutic, but also a source of energy and a catalyst for positive change. The understanding of survivor guilt and the recognition of innocence and anger is liberating, though it certainly does not resolve all the challenges of global loss.

As mentioned, Odets (1995) recognizes survival guilt as grief about survival. This grief eclipses and denies bereavement for the death of the lost loved one. As the burden of survivor guilt diminishes, what is uncovered is the raw pain of loss and abandonment, as well as the powerlessness to stop or end it. Further, working through the issue of survivor guilt and shame brings us face to face with the dilemma of the global loss versus our assumptive world. That is, if we are really innocent, then how and why could this happen? How does one make sense out of a life permeated by such suffering and loss?

Depression

The continuum of depression ranges from isolation, which increases stress, to letting go with support, which decreases stress. If the capacity for being fully alive is to be recovered, then grief must be addressed. When talking about grief with other gay men, there is an understandable weariness with the concept of grief. "I need to deal with my grief?" one man asked. "I've been dealing with grief for ten years. I'm sick of it. I don't need to grieve more; I need to find a way to be able to do something *other* than grieve. I want my life back." This sentiment could be echoed by many veterans of AIDS loss. Yet, depression is grief's calling card, and the same man who made the above comment described his day-to-day life in terms of "chronic depression."

Although it may seem like a contradiction to talk about depression that decreases stress, it must be acknowledged that depression is not only an unavoidable part of living in global loss, but also that grief-related depression can be experienced in ways that are less debilitating, and paradoxically, depression can even help a person recover the capacity to be more fully alive.

As with anxiety, there is a tendency toward magical thinking with depression. It is not uncommon for some to express the fear that admitting to feelings of despair will mean they will succumb to it. It is present whether we admit it or not. Unlike what our fears tell us, despair is not a final destination, but rather a step on the journey that leads away from despair. To take this step, however, we need a language for loss, a path to follow through the perilous "valley of the shadow" where there seems to be no hope or future.

The Isolation end of the depression continuum is summarized as "cherished life assumptions crumble under the onslaught of global loss," leaving a sense of insignificance, helplessness, and futility. This is global loss-related depression. Here, we grieve not only for the loss of loved ones, but the world as we knew it, life as we expected it to be, and the loss of life assumptions that we cherished and believed in as reality. It is a slow-motion nightmare, like the epidemic itself, rather than a big bang. Because of the pervasiveness and duration of loss there often is not a recognition that one is depressed. Rather, there is only an awareness of a decrease in the pleasure of living. Since it seems like a dead end, the only option seems to be denial and supression, or risk succumbing to despair. Without a language for communicating this dilemma, it is very difficult to unburden it and share it with others who may be going through the same experience.

"Letting go with support" offers hope. In order for despair not to be a final destination, two processes must happen. First, the isolation must be broken. Second, the loss of the assumptive reality must be acknowledged and the grieving started.

Adaptation

> Hate AIDS, not life. Look at AIDS as the guest at the party that won't leave. Yes, everyone hates him, but it's still your party.
>
> from the play, *Jeffrey,* by Paul Rudnick

In ongoing loss, there is no final stage to grieving. As described earlier, getting over and moving on is, at best, temporary because there is no way to be immune from future loss or trauma. But the human capacity to endure and adapt is extraordinary, and it is this potential that we as clinicians strive to develop in our clients.

Some men bristle at the concept of adaptation. One man said, "Adapt to AIDS? Never," as if adaptation means to diminish or belittle the enormity and tragedy of the loss. But whether admitted or not, to get up each morning and face the day means some kind of adaptation is taking place. The choice, therefore, is not whether or not to adapt, but how to adapt. The resistance to the concept of adaptation is often an expression of the survivor guilt variation of, "I don't have the right to have a life when so many have died."

The continuum of adaptation runs from more the stressful, disengagement, to the less stressful, recommitment. (See Figure 4.2.) Disengagement represents the cumulative effect of the resisting or denying coping mechanisms expressed in each of the previous points on the global loss cycle. The two primary components of disengagement are chronic numbing of emotions and an increase in activity as a way to escape the isolation of depression. In disengagement, the depression-stage tasks of reaching out and recognizing the loss of assumptive reality have not been addressed. In fact, the ability to address these tasks depends upon self-awareness, the availability of support, and the pacing of losses. Thus, most survivors go around the cycle of global loss many times before these critical tasks are achieved.

Disengagement highlights the traumatic effects of loss and increases stress in several ways. It is very hard to seal off whole sections of one's emotional life, and it is exhausting trying to stay preoccupied or active enough to avoid the emptiness that being emotionally shut down brings. Finally, the self-destructive behaviors that bolster avoidance and manifest in acting out unresolved guilt exact a high physical and psychological price.

Recommitment, on the other hand, is the end result of the hard and painfully realized self-exploration. There is an expression, "You have to fall apart in order to come together in a new way," and recommitment is this "coming together." Through fear, facing survivor guilt, anger, and addressing feelings of depression, it becomes possible to rethink one's life. This rethinking means no longer denying the reality that the worst does happen and there's no way of avoiding it. Living through global loss changes people. Many of the assumptions that once provided security, trust, and a sense of purpose have fallen away, questioning the worth of what remains. What remains is discovering how to live without these assumptions; that is, building security, trust, and a sense of purpose that survives even in global loss. As we do this we recover the capacity to participate more fully in life again, based on reality rather than on false assumptions. This is what recommitment means—examining which perspectives can endure through the corrosive effects of global loss. The past is full of ghosts and the future is full of uncertainty. What remains is an orientation toward the present, a decision to invent trust and purpose in quality of life in the moment. Psychotherapist Jeremy Hollinger, for example, says "For us, the future is today."

Renewal of vitality and the capacity for enjoyment is a result of recommitment. In fact, successfully addressing the tasks of depression and adaptation allow for and segue back into, "Time Out," which was defined previously as an opportunity to recharge our batteries and replenish emotional reserves. While recommitment does not represent a resolution of global loss, it does make it easier to experience less stress as the cycle continues.

It must be recognized that the loss and rethinking of life assumptions is not a single rite of passage, but is revisited again and again. The present-time perspective that is part of recommitment is difficult to sustain in the past and future orientation of the larger society. The orientation toward continuity, predictability, and security will inevitably reassert itself. Even with the acknowledgment that global loss breaks all the rules, we still hope to be exempted somehow.

It is human nature to attach meaning and self-worth to expectations of the past or projections into the future. This occurs even though it is the nature of global loss to undermine or destroy these attachments. It is unfair to ask ourselves to continue to love each other without our assumptive reality becoming invested in the experience. We can, however, remain cognizant of the cycle of global loss while living through it and remembering the truth that global loss exposes: that satisfaction is not behind or ahead of us, but must ultimately be found in the present, lest it elude us forever.

CONCLUSION

Throughout this chapter there has been emphasis placed on helping gay men to live a fulfilling life in the midst of the AIDS epidemic. The methods of coping and adapting, of finding ways of living full and passionate lives, demand that we live life as it is now; that is, a life less predicated on what we once expected and more on accepting the reality of AIDS global loss. Our challenge is to not be defeated by what is happening. AIDS is not going away, but neither is the tenacity, resilience, and vitality of the gay community.

In 1988 at the National AIDS Conference in San Francisco, an earlier version of the AIDS Loss Model was presented. As the ways of coping and adapting to AIDS global loss have changed, so has the model evolved, reflecting these changes. Naturally, questions arise about what the model will look like in another ten years. These questions bring both cautious hopefulness and trepidation. Certainly, the individual and community ways of coping and living will continue to change. As this occurs, the vocabulary and language of global loss will also grow and evolve. Although no one knows the future, what is known is that the quality of our future will depend upon our ability to communicate and learn from one another now, as we forge a pathway of living fully in global loss.

> Hope can be neither affirmed or denied
> Hope is like a path in the countryside;
> Originally there was no path. Yet, as
> people walk all the time in the
> same spot, a way appears.

Lu Xon
Chinese Poet, 1881-1936

REFERENCES

American Psychiatric Association. (1987). *Diagnostic and Statistical Manual of Mental Disorders,* 3rd ed. Washington, DC: American Psychiatric Press.

American Psychiatric Association. (1995). *Diagnostic and Statistical Manual of Mental Disorders,* 4th ed. Washington, DC: American Psychiatric Press.

Freud, S. (1953). Mourning and Melancholia. In *The Standard Edition of the Complete Psychological Works of Sigmund Freud.* London: Hagarth Press.

Hollinger, Jeremy. (1995). *Against All Odds: Surviving Catastrophic Multiple Loss.* Talk given May 5, 1995 at California Association of Marriage and Family Therapists, 31st Annual Conference.

Janoff-Bulman, R. (1992). *Shattered Assumptions: Toward a New Psychology of Trauma.* New York: Macmillan Inc.

Kübler-Ross, E. (1970). *On Death and Dying. New York:Macmillan*

Levi, P. (1989). *The Drowned and the Saved.* New York: Vintage Books.

Moon, T. (1994). Inventing Ourselves: A Survival Guide for HIV Negative Gay Men. Unpublished manuscript.

National Geographic. June 1995. Vol. 187, No. 6.

Odets, W. (1995). Survivor guilt in HIV negative men. In *The Second Decade of AIDS.* New York: Hatherleight Press.

Rudnick, P. (1994). *Jeffrey.* New York: Plume/NAL-Dutton.

Chapter 5

Balancing Autonomy and Intimacy in Lesbian and Gay Relationships

Diana Gray
Rik Isensee

After years of providing psychotherapy to same-sex couples, we have noticed a common theme: lesbians tend to bond emotionally with other women to a much greater extent than gay men bond to each other. The relative ability of lesbian and male couples to merge or remain autonomous creates strengths and weaknesses in most same-sex relationships. We view merging and autonomy as normal tendencies in lesbian and gay male relationships that result from sex-role socialization and from the dynamics of having two women or two men in a relationship. The lack of societal support for lesbian and gay couples also influences how these tendencies are manifested in same-sex relationships. An overall goal for therapists working with a same-sex couple is to help them create a conscious, satisfying relationship with a dynamic balance between intimacy and autonomy.

In the first section of this chapter, we will discuss merging in lesbian relationships and provide some clinical interventions. We will then discuss the tendency toward autonomy in gay male couples, showing how fear of intimacy can be exacerbated by mutual influence. Strategies for change will be suggested to help create healthier, more satisfying and longer-lasting relationships. As cultural diversity creates opportunities for all therapists to adjust and make theory meaningful to our clients, especially for same-sex couples, we strongly encourage therapists to use the following concepts, but to be sensitive to cultural differences in couples and modify the interventions appropriately.

MERGING IN LESBIAN RELATIONSHIPS

Question: What does a lesbian bring on her second date?
Answer: The U-Haul.

As lesbians we laugh nervously about the U-Haul joke, yet we acknowledge that women's tendency to join, to couple, to become one, is part of a cultural legacy. Humorous variations on this theme include the comments that lesbians "meet, mate, marry," or "meet, mate, merge." These jokes symbolize the ability of women to form intense emotional connections and couple quickly. Of all the psychological issues that women encounter in same-sex relationships, the issue of merging (or *fusion)* is the most talked about, written about, and even joked about in the lesbian community (Burch, 1985 and 1986; Falco, 1991; Kaufman, Harrison, and Hyde, 1984; and Krestan and Bepko, 1980).

Although the jokes typically refer to lesbian relationships, merging does occur between men or opposite sex partners, but frequently not as strongly or pervasively as with women. Clinically, we have found that women, regardless of their sexual orientation, have the capacity to merge in relationships with other women. The capacity to merge is not a function of their sexual orientation, but of the psychological dynamics of women and between women-loving women.

Merging

What is merging? Nonverbally, we can represent it as intertwined fingers. From a Gestalt perspective, the couple's energy is greater than the sum of its parts. Merging is frequently described as a psychological state between two women who have such a strong emotional connection that their ego boundaries collapse or merge into one. As a result of this merging, the women make decisions and function more as a couple or unit than as individuals. Falco (1991) describes merging as " . . . the tendency for two people to be as close together as physically and psychically possible" (p. 109). As an example, one might see couples sharing clothes, physical space, thoughts, or even dreams. Some couples may have the same friends and spend all of their recreational time together. Finances are often merged with unclear expectations about saving and spending priorities.

Origins of Merging

Psychological, social, and political analyses all provide explanations for why women develop the ability to merge. Psychological theories such as Mahler's (1954) originally described the need of infants and mother/caretakers to bond. Initially, this sense of "oneness" is needed for survival of the infant. With time and *good enough* mothering, the child separates from the mother and becomes more emotionally autonomous. While Mahler and others posit individuation and autonomy as an important developmental goal, it has become clear that men and women individuate differently.

Chodorow's (1978) and Dinnerstein's (1976) work suggests that women develop more permeable ego boundaries and are relationally focused because they are primarily raised by women. Early in our psychological development girls identify with and bond with their mother because she is the same gender. Because boys see themselves as different from their mother, they individuate earlier and with less difficulty.

Gilligan's (1982) research on women's ethical development shows that women even make ethical decisions differently. Gilligan found that women typically make decisions based on their desire to preserve and maintain personal relationships, whereas men generally make decisions using abstract standards about fairness.

The theoretical work of the Stone Center Scholars (Miller, 1986; Jordan et al., 1991) demonstrates that women's psychological development is best described by a relational model. Women are raised to view their interpersonal relationships with others as primary. Other psychological attributes, such as autonomy and independence, are less important.

In summary, there are numerous research studies and theoretical analyses that suggest women's socialization encourages women to make their relationships a priority. Women respond to these pressures by developing permeable ego boundaries and a tremendous ability to emotionally engage with others while having a concomitant difficulty disengaging from emotional relationships to act autonomously. The ability to merge is a normal part of women's psychological development. It has also been shaped by childrearing, nuclear family structures, division of labor, and sex-role socialization in the United States throughout the twentieth century.

Merging: Good or Bad?

If merging is a normal developmental attribute of women, why is it typically perceived as a negative condition of women and their relationships? Most psychological theories that evaluate mental health and normalcy are derived from patriocentric standards that highly value autonomy and independence (Mahler, 1954). Women's tendency to have permeable ego boundaries and their ability to engage profoundly with others is often labeled as psychological dependence and viewed as negative. Even within the lesbian community merging is often perceived as negative and the cause of "lesbian bed death," smothering, fusion, or even domestic violence. Merging is believed to be the primary cause of early breakups in lesbian relationships (Burch, 1985, 1986; Clunis and Green, 1988; Falco, 1991; Kaufman, Harrison, and Hyde, 1984; and Krestan and Bepko, 1980).

On a positive note, the ability of women to merge creates a very strong emotional bond and sense of connection to one another. This bonding is frequently cited by women as the primary reason for why women say they are lesbians (Gray, 1987). The tendency to merge, as described above, is a normal ability of women in either same-sex or opposite-sex relationships; however, merging is intensified when a woman is in a sexual and emotional relationship with another woman.

Merging versus Rescuing

The positive effects of merging need to be differentiated from its negative consequences. From my clinical perspective, it is not merging that causes negative consequences in same-sex relationships, but *rescuing;* however, when a woman merges, she almost invariably "rescues."

Rescuing is a concept that is described in the Transactional Analysis literature (Karpman, 1968; Steiner, 1974). The concept was later applied to lesbian relationships by Rabenold (1987). The psychological purpose of rescuing in relationships is to suppress conflicts that arise because of differences in individual needs. Without conflicts and individual differences, women can view themselves as similar, the same, connected, or as one. The rescue triangle describes major life positions, patterns, or scripts that all people enact to a greater or lesser extent. We tend to have feelings, make decisions, and behave in a way that is congruent with our primary script. The three primary scripts or positions are the *Rescuer, Persecutor,* and *Victim* (see Figure 5.1).

The rescuer is a helper who attempts to make everything smooth, nice, or okay. Rescuers frequently become consciously or unconsciously attracted to Victims and try to save them. Rescuing occurs when individuals consistently (1) do something that they do not want to do or (2) find themselves doing more than 50 percent of the work.

Victims are people whose life is frequently in crisis. They are often overwhelmed, and may state overtly or covertly "poor me," or "woe is me." Bad things do happen to good people, and we all have problems at times, but for people who have adopted a Victim script,

FIGURE 5.1. Rescue Triangle

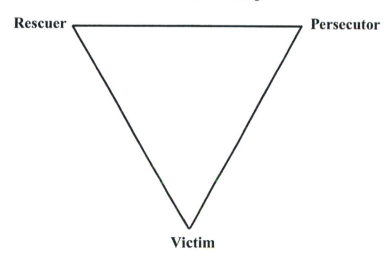

Rescuer   **Persecutor**

Victim

Note: Adapted from Karpaman, 1968

solving their own problems is difficult, and they tend to enlist Rescuers to save them.

The Rescuer tries to save (rescue) the Victim, but nearly always fails in the long run because Victims are never able to be rescued. They may get their immediate desire gratified, but the trouble stems from a core belief in an external locus of control. The worn-out Rescuer then typically shifts to the position of Persecutor. The Persecutor is resentful about giving up her own needs and often says with anger, "You never . . . " or "You always . . . ."

Alternately, the Rescuer may shift to a Victim role and feels victimized by the original Victim (who is now perceived as a Persecutor). In this role, the previous Rescuer may complain, "You made me . . . "; or, "I've tried and tried and you don't appreciate me"; "Because of you I've sacrificed . . . ."

From the earlier discussion of merging it is apparent that most women are raised to be Rescuers. Women value relationships as primary, even at the expense or exclusion of their own needs. In the process of caring for others, women often do greater than 50 percent of the work, and give up their own needs and wants in order to help others. Of course, we all need a little extra caring and attention at times. It is common, and by all means healthy, in any relationship for one partner to make some extra effort to help out during stressful times. The danger lies in taking care of others to the point where one's own needs are consistently neglected.

When our primary sense of self-worth is derived from helping others, we are likely to feel resentment when we are not appreciated, and guilt for asserting our own needs. Not recognizing where these resentments come from can lead to repetitive, unproductive transactions that cause chronic difficulty in lesbian relationships. Both partners often feel stuck and do not know how to move toward healthy choices.

The tendency of women to rescue is so encompassing, they may not even recognize that they are giving up their own wants and needs. They may confuse sacrificing their own needs with feelings of closeness. Frequently, their impulse to rescue is prompted by a desire to merge; that is, they believe they are trying to be nice, to help the other person, or even to help the relationship by being a good partner. As therapists, we can validate their impulse to be helpful. At the same time, we can help them differentiate between their desire for emotional closeness and the importance of taking care of themselves while caring for others.

The following scenario represents a common rescuing cycle.

> Maria and Jean are lovers. They met a couple of years ago and have been living together for about a year. Maria realizes that she has not seen most of her friends for a long time because she has been busy with night school, work, and forming a relationship with Jean. Most of her socializing is with Jean, and occasionally the two of them get together with another couple. Maria misses her friends. Carla, who is Maria's ex-lover and long-time friend, asked her to dinner and a movie this Friday so they can "catch up." Maria wants to go, but she usually spends Friday night watching TV with Jean. Feeling torn between the two options, she talks to Jean. Jean has had a particularly hard week and is depressed and tired. She had really been looking forward to spending Friday evening together. She is very hurt and angry that Maria wants to cancel their standing Friday night plans, especially this week. How does Maria solve this dilemma?

As a relationally oriented woman, Maria wants to preserve both relationships and make both people happy. Because her primary relationship is with Jean, she will probably be tempted to "rescue" Jean and stay home on Friday. To avoid a total rescue and keep Carla happy, perhaps she could reschedule with Carla for another night. How would Jean feel about this solution? Would Jean be any more comfortable or have less feelings of loss if the outing with Carla were rescheduled for another night of the week? If this works for her, then it may be an acceptable compromise. But Maria has a history of giving up her friends to spend time with Jean, so her need for outside friends (i.e., autonomy) may be increasing. Maria could decide to give in again this Friday and stay home with Jean, but she may become angry and resentful. After rescuing Jean, she may shift to an angry Persecutor role, deciding to go out with Carla some other time without even telling Jean. Inevitably, however, Jean would find out, become hurt and angry, and shift from the Victim role to the role of Persecutor, accusing Maria of betrayal. Maria, in turn, could shift into the Victim mode and say, "You never let me go out with my friends." Other moves are possible, but this scenario illustrates some common shifts within the dynamics of the rescue triangle. The role of the therapist is to help lesbian couples develop healthier choices that sidestep this cycle.

Interventions

As is obvious at this point, one of the key dynamics for most ongoing conflicts in a lesbian relationship is rescuing in an effort to suppress individual differences and conflicts. In the absence of social approval, lesbians often stay together for the interpersonal satisfaction they receive in their relationships. It is then terrifying for women to feel their emotional connection to each other lessening due to conflict, individual differences, or movement toward autonomy.

Most lesbian couples come to therapy in crisis. The crisis is sometimes an acute event but more likely stems from an ongoing series of conflicts that never seem to get resolved. Both women are frequently sad, hurt, angry, and very scared that the relationship is over. The therapist's task is to be the holder of hope for the relationship. We can help the couple identify the source of their conflict, as well as offer strategies to help solve the problems that arise from neglecting their own needs.

To encourage the positive aspects of merging and discourage the negative aspects that accompany rescuing, the therapist can educate clients about the psychodynamics of merging and differentiate it from rescuing behavior. The therapist can assist couples by using their presenting problems to familiarize them with the rescue triangle and the three script positions. Communication skills, such as "I" statements, and active listening techniques, such as paraphrasing, can help them identify underlying feelings and desires. Role-playing and step-by-step problem solving can be used in session to practice clear communication and teach negotiation skills.

For example, in the scenario above, Maria and Jean would be encouraged to clarify their own wants and needs by stating 100 percent of what they want. This is frequently very hard for women to do because it counters our socialization to place others' needs and feelings first. We accommodate to the perceived feelings and wants of others without even realizing it. Coaching by the therapist is often needed to identify the clients' own feelings and desires.

With practice, the conflict can be negotiated into a win-win situation with neither woman rescuing, persecuting, or being a victim. Homework assignments, such as having each person ask the other for 100 percent of what they want, can be given for the couple to practice their negotiating at home while monitoring themselves for rescuing.

Returning to the Rescuing Scenario, Jean might say that she wants Maria to spend Friday night with her (100 percent of what she wants). Maria could say that she wants both Carla and Jean to be happy, and she wants to spend time with both women (100 percent statement). Maria may suggest that she could stay home with Jean on Friday and go out with Carla on Saturday (a compromise solution). Hopefully, Jean can accommodate Maria's independence if she gets some of what she wants and is supported by the therapist. The therapist can encourage Jean to use the time to go out with a friend of hers, or if it is not too anxiety-provoking, to spend some time by herself.

In addition to the above strategies, the therapist can emphasize the dynamic balance between autonomy and intimacy that is essential in any long-lasting relationship by encouraging couples to do the following:

1. Have individual friends and see them regularly;
2. Have time alone weekly in the house, while hiking, or even on vacation;
3. Schedule quality time with each other such as going on dates to have fun and romance;
4. Decrease the amount of life-maintenance time together such as doing laundry or grocery shopping;
5. Talk to one another about the issues of rescuing and monitor one's own rescuing behavior;
6. Read self-help books about rescuing or codependency and discuss them with each other; and
7. Schedule weekly time, typically for half an hour to an hour, for the two to meet together and talk about feelings, problems, and appreciations they have for one another.

By doing the above, couples can check in with how they are doing with their goals of decreasing rescuing, taking care of themselves, and achieving a balance between autonomy and intimacy.

Summary

Lesbian relationships can be vital and long-lasting if partners learn to develop a dynamic balance between intimacy and autonomy. To do this, women have to learn to decrease rescuing, negotiate differences, and tolerate the natural wave-like movement of intimacy in relationships. At times women are closer together and at times they are further apart. Conscious relationships and intimacy are dances, and these dance steps can be learned, but must be practiced often to develop a high degree of skill.

FEAR OF INTIMACY IN MALE COUPLES

What is unique about gay male relationships? How we relate to one another is influenced not only by our emotional and sexual attraction for other men, but also by how we have been socialized as males in a homophobic society. Homophobia isolates us, and male conditioning inhibits our awareness of feelings. The gay male subculture also tends to reinforce men's reluctance to self-disclose.

Successful gay male couples report a high level of emotional intimacy (Deenan and Van Naerssen, 1994). It seems that once men experience sustained intimacy, they like and value it. Yet male dating patterns are often oriented toward sexual contact, with studies showing that gay male "scripts" are more sexually oriented and less intimacy-focused, than those of lesbians (Klinkenberg and Rose, 1994). I have worked with many gay male couples who got together because of an initial sexual attraction, but who are having a hard time negotiating an emotional relationship.

This section examines how therapists can help gay male clients and couples deal with the discomfort and ambiguity that arise while dating and forming intimate relationships.

Male Socialization

Some research indicates that men tend to disclose less about themselves than women do, and that both sexes reveal more personal information to women than they do to men (Jourard and Richman, 1963). It is possible that each partner in a male couple may communicate less about how he feels than either partner would in a heterosexual relationship. The authors believe men's reluctance to disclose emotional vulnerability stems from real-life experiences. Often, men learn early on that it is dangerous to reveal much about our emotional lives to other men. Because men lack extensive experience dealing with emotions, it is often difficult and uncomfortable for them to talk about how they feel.

Socialized to be analytical and critical, both members of a male couple may be so focused on their own independence that neither is oriented toward the emotional needs of the relationship. Unaccustomed to disclosing their feelings or listening to others, they withdraw emotionally or end up in competitive arguments over who is "right," rather than saying how they feel.

Ambiguity in Gay Relationships

Many men feel an initial sexual attraction toward another man without having any idea as to whether they will find themselves compatible in other ways. Of course, some gay men enjoy recreational sex without expecting an ongoing relationship, but this is often left unspoken. They may end up sleeping together once or twice, and then feel awkward trying to define the relationship.

What may simply be a desire on the part of one man to reclaim himself, may be misinterpreted by the other as a lack of interest in building a relationship. Neither partner may be ready to make the commitment that continued sexual involvement might imply, but instead of dealing with that uncertainty by talking about their expectations, it may seem easier not to see each other.

The Split Between Sex and Intimacy

Both heterosexual and gay men often have a hard time integrating sex and intimacy. Whether this is due to some essential male trait (i.e., "to spread one's seed"), male socialization, or a combination of both, is an ongoing debate between essentialists and social constructionists that may never be resolved. For gay men, it is useful to look at how homophobia contributes to the split between sex and emotional intimacy.

For many boys, it is seen as acceptable to "fool around" as long as feelings of affection are not shown. Some men translate this into an acceptance of having sex with another man, maintaining that they are not homosexual, just "horny." Homophobia interferes with same-sex relationships by undermining the belief that intimacy with another man is even possible. It inhibits men's ability and willingness to be emotionally vulnerable, discounts men's feelings of love and attachment, and associates both sexual and emotional involvement with guilt and shame.

Depathologizing Fear of Intimacy

It makes sense, then, that men might feel cautious about being emotionally vulnerable, since they learned it was not safe to share their innermost thoughts and desires. But as adults, some of these strategies may interfere with developing intimacy with other men. Although a "fear of intimacy" may be a real issue in a relationship, I believe that there is more to be gained by understanding this fear as a learned reaction, rather than as a pathological trait. Fear is a feeling, not a character deficit. Avoidance of intimacy can be seen as a protective coping strategy in response to early homophobic experiences, rather than as a permanent part of one's personality.

Parents who are overly invested in their son's becoming heterosexual may lead some gay men to associate intimacy with emotional intrusiveness. A fear of abandonment for disclosing who we really are can lead to the development of a false self, which makes it difficult to say how we really feel. Empathizing with these sources of fear and discomfort can help clients deal with underlying feelings, rather than pathologizing them. Feeling supported and understood, they will be more open to learning healthier ways of negotiating ambiguity in their relationships.

Helping Couples Develop Emotional Intimacy

We can help our clients develop the skills of emotional involvement by teaching them how to listen, how to empathize, and how to say what they want in a way that elicits a more cooperative response from their partners. We can acknowledge the effects of homophobia and male socialization, and explain how feelings work. For example, it is helpful for clients to hear from us, "You don't have to justify feelings; feelings often shift once they're acknowledged; being aware of a feeling doesn't mean you have to act on it, etc."

Once couples have learned these basic communication skills, it becomes easier for them to hear one another's feelings and they can begin to problem solve. Rather than arguing about the first solution that comes to mind, they can negotiate solutions that take the concerns of both partners into consideration. Practicing these skills usually helps couples feel more hopeful about their situation. As they learn to empathize with each other, they are less likely to have their feelings escalate; however, some couples become entrenched in patterns of conflict that are hard to deal with. When this occurs, we try to elicit their help in discovering patterns of mutual influence.

Mutual Influence

Systems theory commonly describes relationships in terms of mutual influence, a term that acknowledges that each person's behavior influences (and is influenced by) his partner. Understanding this influence, members of the couple are less likely to assume either partner is "bad" or "crazy" for reacting in a certain way. In addition, feelings and behavior of each person begin to make sense within the context of the relationship. While each partner brings his own issues to a relationship, a move toward closeness or distance can be often understood as a function of mutual influence between partners.

For example, a fear of intimacy is often a sense of inadequacy in handling conflict. The one who withdraws does so partly because he does not know how to talk about his feelings or needs without feeling guilty or becoming defensive. He may experience his partner's desire for contact as intrusive, not recognizing that he elicits "clinging" behavior by withdrawing. By developing new strategies for handling conflict, he is less likely to withdraw, and his partner will feel less deprived.

Likewise, what we call *dependency* is usually an ineffectual response to deprivation. The one who desires more closeness often experiences his partner's withdrawal as emotional abandonment. He may then be tempted to make emotional demands that elicit further withdrawal by his partner. But if he can learn to communicate his desire for contact instead of blaming, he may be able to interrupt this cycle. Then they are more likely to negotiate a level of contact that suits them both.

A Mutual-Influence Scenario

> Mike has made dinner, looking forward to spending time together when Al comes home from work. But when Al gets home, he turns on the TV as soon as they sit down to eat. Mike tries to engage Al in conversation, but he keeps getting one-word answers. Finally, to express his frustration, he takes his dinner to the living room to eat by himself. Al follows him and asks him what is wrong. Mike says, "If you can't figure it out, I'm not going to bother telling you," at which point Al stomps out of the room.

Discussion

In the next few sections we will outline a way to work with male couples dealing with issues of intimacy and autonomy by looking at the above scenario. This approach includes four parts: (1) Identifying unspoken accommodations; (2) Looking at projective identification; (3) Reclaiming projections; and (4) Increasing empathy by talking about the pattern, rather than acting it out.

Unspoken Accommodations

A major source of problems in relationships is the tendency for partners to accommodate one another without negotiating their desires (similar to what was referred to previously as rescuing). They may not realize how much they have given up until they feel resentful, stubborn, or unwilling to cooperate over a seemingly minor dispute. These concessions often contribute to the very patterns that manifest in therapy. Identifying the couple's accommodations can help each partner feel recognized for the effort he has made to make things work, while at the same time help each person understand the source of his resentment.

In the above scenario, Al may have wanted some time to himself to unwind from work, but instead of saying so he sat down to dinner and turned on the TV. Mike made a nice dinner in hopes of having a pleasant evening together. He was disappointed in what he saw as Al's withdrawal, but instead of talking about his expectations, he tried to compete with the TV for Al's attention.

Projective Identification

Projective identification (Klein, 1946) occurs when we not only see a trait in our partner that we do not recognize in ourselves, but we also pressure him—in unconscious ways—to experience and act on our projection.

In a couple dealing with approach/avoidance, the Approacher (in the above scenario, Mike) may feel insecure about his own desires for separate activities. Doing things on his own may feel too risky or it may seem contrary to his notions of intimacy. So he projects his desire for independence onto the Distancer (he sees Al as being the one who wants distance in the relationship). In fact, he elicits distancing behavior in Al by making emotional demands when Al is not likely to respond favorably. By doing so, he is able to experience some degree of independence, but he sees this desire as coming from Al. Meanwhile, Mike feels miserable because Al is "so aloof," and he remains oblivious to his own part in eliciting Al's rejecting behavior.

If Al did not have any unresolved ambivalence about intimacy, then he might be able to identify Mike's double message: Mike says he wants to be intimate, yet he pushes Al away. Commenting on this dynamic, Al would be less likely to play his part in the pattern that has developed between them, and Mike could get in touch with his own ambivalence about closeness and independence.

However, we often find partners who complement our own unconscious needs for projective identification, and they will play right along with us. For example, Al may be anxious about being too close, so he projects his desires for closeness onto Mike. He sees Mike as the one who is needy, but then Al elicits clinging behavior from Mike by not being emotionally available when Mike is obviously in pain. In this way, Al is able to experience feelings of closeness, but he sees this need as coming from Mike. He is tired of Mike's clinging, but he does not see what he contributes to the cycle. Mike could also comment on Al's double message: Al wants some time to himself, yet instead of saying so he draws Mike into competition for attention.

A move toward intimacy by one partner may elicit a corresponding move toward autonomy by the other. Likewise, a move toward distance may elicit a desire to affirm closeness. Male couples often experience this dynamic shift back and forth between them as the pursuer gives up and withdraws and his partner then pursues him.

If they could both reclaim their desires for intimacy *and* autonomy they would not have to project these needs onto each other. The goal is for each man to experience his own ambivalence about closeness and independence without having to project one part of his ambivalence onto his partner. This will enable them to find more of a balance between intimacy and autonomy in their relationship. They would then be far less likely to elicit the very behavior in their partner that they fear experiencing in themselves (Isensee, 1990).

Interventions

How can therapists best help clients break out of a projective identification cycle? Part of the problem is that this process takes place outside of their conscious awareness. I have found the following steps helpful in assisting clients to identify and reclaim their projections.

Reclaiming Projections

1. Ask each partner to consider the possibility that he may be projecting. For example, questions such as, "What does your lover do that bothers you?" or "Could this behavior be a tendency you dislike about yourself?" help clients to think in this style.
2. Ask clients how emotional roles are divided in the relationship. For example, "Is one of you *reasonable,* while the other is *emotional?*" "Is one of you affectionate, while the other keeps

to himself?" "Do one of you express feelings, while the other is more reserved?" "Does one of you want closeness, while the other wants distance?"

3. Ask each member of the couple, "How might you be contributing to this division of labor?" "Is there anything you do that tends to elicit a complementary response from your partner?"
4. Assist the client in identifying mixed messages he sends to his partner. For example, does one person say he wants to be close, while simultaneously pushing his partner away?
5. Assist clients with the active process of listening and reflecting each other's fears and desires.
6. Encourage clients to openly discuss their expectations around emotional intimacy and independent activity.

A Guide for Handling Patterns

The recognition that both partners contribute to patterns of mutual influence can reduce blame and defensiveness. We can help clients recognize their own ambivalence instead of projecting it onto a partner. When they find themselves caught in a negative pattern, they can use this insight to consider what it is they are doing to elicit the very behavior they object to in the partner. Here are some techniques I have used to help clients break their usual cycle and talk about their pattern.

To Identify the Underlying Source of the Conflict

1. Encourage each person to ask whether they are judging themselves for unacceptable or petty feelings;
2. Help clients identify that feelings of annoyance with their partner may be a signal that they have accommodated their partner without saying what it is that they, the individual, wants;
3. Encourage individual members of the couple to reclaim any feelings they may be projecting onto their partner.

To Keep from Escalating

1. Encourage clients to talk *about* their feelings and impulses rather than act on them. For example, instead of putting down

TV in a bid for Al's attention, Mike could say, "I find myself competing with the TV, and I realize I'd like some attention." Further, instead of withdrawing when he feels pressured, Al could say, "I notice I'm withdrawing so I realize I must be feeling pressured."

2. Help clients identify patterns of relating rather than just arguing. For example, instead of putting Al down for being "afraid of intimacy," Mike could say, "It seems like we're having that problem again where I'm wanting attention when you'd rather be by yourself." And instead of putting Mike down for being "too dependent," Al could say, "It seems like we're having that problem again where I'm wanting time by myself when you're wanting some attention."

3. Help clients learn to empathize with how hard it is to have this conflict instead of just automatically becoming defensive. For example, instead of blaming his partner for being "dependent" because he wants attention, Al could say, "Oh, you must be feeling neglected. Maybe you're wondering whether I even want to be with you." And instead of blaming Al for being "aloof" because he wants to withdraw, Mike could say, "It must be a drag to feel pressured again." Thus, by saying how they are feeling and by reassuring one another, Mike and Al avoid escalation into conflict.

Summary

It is inevitable in male couples that one partner will want some attention when the other wants time for and by himself. Sometimes this dynamic shifts simply by recognizing it. This recognition will enable the male couples you work with to negotiate whatever level of contact works for both of them.

Obviously, the ability to identify patterns and empathize with each other takes a lot of practice. As therapists, we can help male couples overcome negative patterns and develop intimacy by teaching communication skills, normalizing their emotional reactions, encouraging a spirit of experimentation, recognizing their efforts, and empathizing with their situation.

Practicing these skills enables couples to develop empathy for each other. Whatever fear they may have associated with intimacy is often soothed by empathic sharing. This instills a sense of hopeful-ness that they can resolve conflicts in a way that takes the needs of both partners into consideration.

CONCLUSION

Sex-role socialization has an impact on same-sex couples that often differs from heterosexual couples in the ways we have out-lined. We recognize that assigning the issues of merging to lesbian couples and fear of intimacy to male couples is a generalization. Obviously, some men have issues with merging and some women have a hard time expressing their feelings. Finding a balance between autonomy and intimacy is a task for any couple, regardless of sexual orientation.

As therapists, we can help lesbian couples validate their emo-tional bond, while also assisting them in reclaiming themselves as individuals. They can then negotiate their needs from a basis of strength and self-worth. And we can help male couples increase their ability and willingness to share their emotional lives and empa-thize with their partners. This will enable them to experience the depths of intimacy they long for in loving another man.

REFERENCES

Burch, B. (1985). Another perspective on merger in lesbian relationships. In L. B. Rosewater and L. E. A. Walker (eds.). *Handbook of Feminist Therapy.* (pp. 100-109). New York: Springer.

Burch, B. (1986). Psychotherapy and the dynamics of merger in lesbian couples. In T. S. Stein and C. J. Cohen (eds.). *Contemporary Perspectives on Psycho-therapy with Lesbians and Gay Men.* (pp. 57-71). New York: Plenum.

Chodorow, N. (1978). *The Reproduction of Mothering.* Berkeley: University of California Press.

Clunis, D. M. and Green, G. D. (1988). *The Lesbian Couple.* Seattle: Seal Press.

Deenan, A. A., Gijs, L., and Van Naerssen, A. (1994). Intimacy and sexuality in gay male couples. *Archives of Sexual Behavior.* 23(4):421-431.

Dinnerstein, D. (1976). *The Mermaid and the Minotaur.* New York: Harper Colo-phon.

Falco, K. (1991). *Psychotherapy with Lesbian Clients.* New York: Brunner/Mazel.

Gilligan, C. (1982). *In a Different Voice.* Cambridge, MA: Harvard University.

Gray, D. (1987). *Women's Sexuality: From the Margin to the Center.* Ann Arbor, MI: University Microfilms.

Gordon, J., Kaplan, A., Miller, J. B., Stiver, I., and Surrey, J. (1991). *Women's Growth in Connection.* New York: Guilford.

Isensee, R. (1990). *Love Between Men.* New York: Fireside/Simon and Schuster.

Jordan, J., Kaplan, A., Miller, J. B., Stiver, I., and Surrey, J. (1991). *Women's Growth in Connection.* New York: Guilford Press.

Jourard, S. M. and Richman, P. (1963). Disclosure output and input in college students. *Merrill-Palmer Quarterly of Behavior Development,* 9:141-148.

Karpman, S. (1968). Script drama analysis. *Transactional Analysis Bulletin,* 7:39-43.

Kaufman, P. A., Harrison, E., and Hyde, M. L. (1984). Distancing for intimacy in lesbian relationships. *American Journal of Psychiatry,* 141(4):39-43.

Klein, M. (1946). Notes on some schizoid mechanisms. *International Journal of Psychoanalysis,* 27:III.

Klinkenberg, D. and Rose, S. (1994). Dating scripts of gay men and lesbians. *Journal of Homosexuality,* 26(4):23-25.

Krestan, J. and Bepko, C. S. (1980). The problem of fusion in the lesbian relationship. *Family Process,* 19:277-289.

Mahler, M. (1954). *The Psychological Birth of the Human Infant.* New York: Basic Books.

Miller, J. B. (1986). *Toward a New Psychology of Women,* second edition. Boston: Beacon.

Rabenold, D. (1987). *Love, Politics, and Rescue in Lesbian Relationships.* Santa Cruz: Herbooks.

Steiner, C. (1974). *Scripts People Live.* New York: Grove.

Chapter 6

Gays and Lesbians
Choosing to be Parents

Marcia Iris Baum

In the gay and lesbian community of the 1980s and 1990s, there appears to be a pendulum swing between birth and death. While the AIDS epidemic has taken a horrific toll on gay men, many lesbians are choosing to bear children and raise families. Alternately, many gay men are also considering parenthood through adoption, foster parenting, or coparenting with lesbians *(coparenting* is a term used to describe two or more persons who assume responsibility to parent a child together). Clearly, the *family* is being redefined. Baby boomers have grown up in single-parent households, been reared by grandparents, blended into stepfamilies, or been raised in communal or extended family settings, but only during the last two decades has the gay and lesbian family system emerged. What distinguishes nontraditional alternative families, which I will discuss, from the traditional "mom and pop" family is that one or both of the primary caregivers identify as gay or lesbian.

Gay men and lesbians who choose parenthood are typically in their thirties or early forties, although the planning process begins, for many, as early as their twenties. This parallels the experience of many heterosexual parents-to-be, and thus the baby boom within the gay and lesbian subculture is a microcosm of the baby boom within the larger culture. What is so radically different for gay and lesbian families, however, is the purposeful planning, analytical decision making, and time spent in considering whether to parent. Considerations are given to moral and ethical concerns, legal ramifications, family-of-origin impact, societal homophobia, discrimination, and so on. Because lesbian and gay families are built on choice, the children are wanted, unlike so many children who are conceived by accident.

Within the gay and lesbian community there is a commitment to build healthy and functional families through education and self-awareness. Groups for lesbians and gay men considering or choosing parenting are available through specialized facilities throughout the country, such as Lyon-Martin Health Services in San Francisco. There are books and literature available that provide information on this topic, such as *Considering Parenthood: A Workbook for Lesbians* (Pies, 1985), *The Lesbian and Gay Parenting Handbook: Creating and Raising Our Families* (Martin, 1993), and the novel, *Family Values: Two Moms and Their Son* (Burke, 1993).

In my psychotherapy and counseling practice with gays and lesbians, the decision to become a parent was never considered an option ten to fifteen years ago. At that time, gays remained closeted and only had children within heterosexual marriages. Today, it is not uncommon for a couple to come to therapy to evaluate their feelings about becoming parents and explore the self-sacrifice involved in putting a child's needs first. Often, a single gay male or lesbian will enter therapy to explore the possibility of parenting alone in spite of the pressures, both within and outside of the gay and lesbian subculture or to be in a couple and not be a single parent.

CASE EXAMPLE

The following is based on the experience of one lesbian couple who used an anonymous donor. The time and soul-searching that went into their decision to coparent, as well as the legal ramifications involved, are highlighted as a way of demonstrating some common themes therapists will either see or may need to anticipate for their clients. Although this couple was viewed as pioneers by some, they did not set out to be trailblazers.

Sarah and Judith met in graduate school. Both "came out" together and set up a household two years later. Both Sarah and Judith are only children of Jewish, working-class background, and both live a fairly middle-class life, complete with economic and relationship stability. It was during her late twenties that Sarah introduced the possibility of raising children, thereby establishing a nontraditional two-mom family. Sarah kept telling Judith how happy she was with her, and how she felt that Judith would make a great parent. Sarah's proverbial biological clock was ticking away, and with it came a maternal pull to give birth to a child.

MAKING A DECISION TO RAISE A CHILD

Judith's immediate reaction to Sarah's request was a combination of interest, ambivalence, curiosity, and fear. Her internalized societal homophobia pulled on her to conform and "do right." She knew that she and Sarah could provide a nurturing and warm environment for a child, including a home filled with love, mutual trust, and honesty, which was very similar to her own childhood experience. She was reticent, however, and frequently worried about what her mother and father would think. She also had concern over what the neighbors would say and how this might affect the well-being of their child.

Clearly, from a clinical standpoint, Judith was struggling with her own desires versus what she felt was right by society's standards. Many gays and lesbians view "fitting in" as being accepted by their heterosexual counterparts. This internalized homophobia fuels and drives the individual to conform to the established norm and to be liked by and to be *like* everyone else.

Sarah knew that it would take some time before Judith would agree to participate in what would be the biggest and most important decision in her life: giving birth and raising a child. Judith was afraid for the child because of the hateful attitudes often afforded gays and lesbians. She knew the child would have an uphill battle and would need a strong sense of self to endure any hostility.

Judith is a practical person, a thinker who does not make decisions impulsively. Rather, she weighs all the pros and cons involved in decisions of importance. In discussion with Sarah, the two agreed that the most important thing is to have a child who feels wanted, given their familiarity with children who were unwanted and, therefore, suffered rejection and feelings of abandonment all their lives. They were clear that their child would develop a positive sense of self, feel wanted and loved, feel secure and esteemed, and that this would hopefully carry over into other areas of the child's life. Both Judith and Sarah agreed that a family which modeled caring and loving between its members would impart a sense of well-being for the child, regardless of the gender of the parents.

After seven long years of discussion and processing (i.e., an intensive, introspective understanding of one's thoughts, feelings, attitudes, and behaviors in relationship to oneself and/or in relationship to significant others), Sarah and Judith agreed that a child would enrich the quality of their lives and that they would be able to provide a stimulating, nurturing, and loving life for a child. They both realized that parenting was the single most important thing either one of them would ever do. It was agreed that Sarah would be the *biological* parent, but that Judith would legally adopt the child as a second-parent (second-parent, same-sex adoptions are legal in San Francisco County).

THE DADDY DILEMMA

As is true with many lesbians choosing to have children, the *daddy question* (or "no-daddy dilemma," as it is sometimes called) did create an obstacle and delay Judith's decision to commit to parenthood. Sarah did not want to be a single parent and risk the loss of her relationship. At first, the dilemma loomed large and became a giant boulder blocking the path. Because of their commitment, and with much discussion, the boulder changed form and broke down into tiny pebbles (thus less formidable and metaphorically less difficult of a challenge to overcome). The couple wanted to have a significant male figure involved in their family system. They methodically approached the task and started by making a list of all their male friends, both gay and straight, whom they could ask about fathering a child (thereby challenging the myth of lesbians as separatists who hate men and only socialize with other women).

To address this and other areas of concern, Judith and Sarah agreed to do time-limited couples counseling. Professional counseling helped facilitate a discussion between them about the daddy dilemma, as well as issues of changing roles and responsibilities after their child was born, financial and emotional stressors, body image, and sexual frequency changes. Of particular emphasis was how a third parent would affect their primary relationship. They were concerned about the stress, pressures, and demands that a third parent might bring to their relationship.

Further, they openly discussed their expectations of a known father. They did not want the man to financially support the child or be legally responsible for the child in any way. They were also clear that they wanted to maintain their own separate residence. They wanted the father to have contact with the child and be a part of his or her life to the extent he wanted to, but they did not want him to be liable for any of the traditional responsibilities afforded fathers.

Sarah and Judith approached one gay male friend, Bryan, who had foster parented a son in his home. The three discussed the possibility of creating a family together, but Bryan had his own agenda and list of expectations (including a request that Sarah quit her job and move into his condominium). Sarah was completely dumbfounded by his demands, thought them to be self-serving, and very disregarding of her primary relationship. They then contacted Andrew, a heterosexual man who was married and had children of his own. Extensive discussion ensued between Judith, Sarah, Andrew, and his wife. Though Andrew's wife eventually agreed, albeit reluctantly, Sarah, Judith, and Andrew decided not to use Andrew as a sperm donor.

After one year of searching for a surrogate father, they decided not to have a known male involved. This was a difficult and painstaking decision because the future impact on child development without a male role model is unknown. Longitudinal and developmental research may be able to clarify these issues, but for now it is too early to determine how the children will be affected not having a known father. My experience is that some children raised by single, lesbian mothers, with minimal paternal contact appear to do fine. It has been suggested that a child's ego development and self-esteem may be impacted more by the negative judgmental beliefs and bias held by others toward the lifestyle of the parents than by not having a known father. This line of thinking stems from the notion that society fosters homophobia, and thus children are vulnerable to attitudes of the Religious Right and others who consider same-sex parenting immoral and selfish.

Judith certainly realized she could not fully protect her child from bigotry and prejudice, and the painful truths and realities of being gay or lesbian in our culture, but through counseling she explored her ambivalence and fears. She supplemented her individual therapy with writing in a journal, doing recommended homework exercises, and drafting an unmailed and uncensored "Dear Mom and Dad" letter to help her identify what she needed and wanted to share with her parents. Finally, she spoke extensively with friends, interviewing them, if you will, and eventually decided on using the sperm of an unknown donor.

LEGAL ISSUES

For lesbians choosing to have children, heterosexual intercourse is not a preferred or viable option. Judith and Sarah opted to utilize the services of a local sperm bank. This allowed them to select an unknown sperm donor who agreed in writing to be known to the child on her eighteenth birthday, if she so desired. This is a fairly common arrangement with many sperm banks. The use of a sperm bank may also provide legal protections for same-sex couples, such as ensuring that the male sperm donor has no legal rights or child-custody entitlement to the child in the future. Therapists should encourage their clients to fully investigate and understand how each sperm bank, as well as local laws, handles the rights of the male donor vis-à-vis the rights of the recipient. Laws vary widely on sperm donor child entitlement, and state laws may override legal protections for unmarried women. California Civil Code Section 7613, the Uniform Parentage Act, specifies that the donor has no parental rights if the insemination is performed by or under the supervision of a medical doctor (The National Center for Lesbian Rights).

Couples who use sperm from friends without using a medical site or sperm bank as an intermediary run the potential risk of custody challenges by the donor. Verbal promises or written and notarized contracts do not guarantee or protect the lesbian biological mother's rights to that child. Similarly, gay men using a birth mother may not have protected rights to that child by the presence of a written agreement.

For lesbians, the nonbiological parent has no custody rights unless she legally adopts her partner's child. Unlike the heterosexual couple, whose marriage is legally sanctioned and recognized, the nonbiological mother is not recognized and, therefore, is advised to consult a family law or lesbian/feminist attorney to proceed with a second-parent adoption.

Recent history has demonstrated an inherent bias and prejudice toward gay and lesbian parents on the part of the courts. Although court rulings may imply that lesbianism in itself does not make a mother unfit, homosexual conduct is a felony under some state laws, and judges have used this argument in removing a child from his or her maternal home. For example, in September 1993, the circuit court of Henrico County, Virginia, awarded custody of three-year-old Tyler to his maternal grandmother. Judge Buford Parsons Jr. ruled that a woman's lesbian relationship makes her an "unfit parent" and that "her conduct is immoral." The mother, Sharon Bottoms, appealed this decision to the Court of Appeals in Virginia. The Virginia Court of Appeals declared that the circuit court judge erred in this ruling. The grandmother appealed this decision to the Virginia Supreme Court. In April 1995, the Virginia Supreme Court refused to award Sharon Bottoms custody of her son because, "active lesbianism practiced in the home could stigmatize the child."

A CHILD IS BORN

Sarah, by way of alternative insemination by donor (AID), gave birth to a daughter. She and Judith agreed that when their daughter becomes inquisitive and asks about her conception, they will be honest and tell her what she can understand for her age. It will be no different from any other child asking, "Where did I come from?" Perhaps when that time comes, AID may not be that uncommon or unusual.

Sarah and Judith told the grandparents-to-be the news after Sarah completed her first trimester and knew she had a healthy baby. Fortunately, both sets of grandparents were delighted, after the initial shock wore off, of course. In fact, they acknowledged Sarah and Judith's partnership in a very different way than before. The tacit messages that their lesbianism was a phase and that they would break up were now gone. It had not been too long before this time that Sarah's mother asked her, "Who is the man and who is the woman?" in her relationship.

Children do not typically get confused or have difficulty discerning the difference between each same-sex parent. Rather, the child sees both as his or her parent, each with an individual personality. Rachel, Judith and Sarah's daughter, now in elementary school, knows she does not have a daddy and that her family is different. But she also knows that *difference* is not about good or bad, right or wrong. Like most children her age, she is inquisitive and wants to learn. Thus, once she asked, "What does gay mean?" Sarah answered, "It is when two women or two men love each other."

COMING OUT
AS A GAY OR LESBIAN PARENT

My clinical and personal opinion is that it is in the best interest of our children for the gay or lesbian parent to be out, that is, known as being gay or lesbian. While it is stressful to continually come out, it makes us visible and sends a message of pride to our children. We cannot afford to blend in, deny our true selves, and/or hide behind a veil of secrecy. It only perpetuates shame, and given that children are extremely intuitive, they easily pick up on these feelings. Of course, good judgment needs to be exercised about when and where to come out, as not everyone lives in communities and cities that are open and supportive of different families.

Therapists are encouraged to explore the realities of coming out with gay and lesbian parents, taking into account regional and other personal variables. Coming out as a gay parent takes time and energy and involves educating people we probably would not have talked to otherwise. One gay father, Norman, best illustrates his gay pride through visibility and education when he comes out to strangers in supermarkets and at toy stores in order to dispel myths that his child's mother must have French-braided her hair.

Being out and coming out in the schools is yet another sphere where gay and lesbian parents need to educate the educators, as well as the parents of other children's classmates. Thorough discussion and role play can help clients anticipate how to handle these situations, although disclosure often happens at unpredictable times. For example, Amanda, a classmate of a child with two mothers, was eager to tell her own mother about her friend's family. When her mother arrived at school, Amanda blurted out, "Emily has two mommies, wow!" Amanda's mother put a finger to Amanda's lips and said, "Don't say that." This clearly communicated a negative message to Amanda that it is not OK to talk about these differences. Upon hearing this, Emily's mother said, "Yes, it's true that Emily has two mommies and she is a lucky kid." Amanda's mother blushed.

It is important that we validate for our clients and others that there are all different kinds of families, and that there is nothing inherently wrong with difference. The earlier this message is conveyed to children–not just our own but all we come into contact with–the better they will be able to cope. Four-year-old Joseph lives with one mom and one dad, but he plays with a child from a two-mom family. When his classmate told him only a man and woman can marry and have a family, Joseph said, "That's not true. You can too have two mommies and a family."

Being "out" as a gay father in the gay male community presents an even greater challenge than being out in the heterosexual community. To some, gay men have a reputation for being narcissistic, self-involved, and "looking for a good time." Mike, a single gay father, said that he now feels invisible when he walks with his young daughter down Castro Street. He said all eyes were upon him when he walked down the street alone and now he is hardly noticed. Gay men and lesbians often report that their peer groups change after having a child and often include more heterosexual parents with children.

WORKING WITH GAY AND LESBIAN FAMILIES

Gays and lesbians are vulnerable to attack by conservative mainstream America, the Christian Right, and the Republican-sponsored "Contract with America," because we are perceived as incapable of forming committed relationships and stable homes for raising healthy children. There is an increase in antigay legal action around the country that seeks to deny and threaten the rights of the nontraditional family. In eleven states, legislation to prohibit lesbians and gay men from adopting children is being considered. State laws in Florida and New Hampshire ban adoption by lesbian or gay couples. In Oregon, legislation to deny unmarried women access to alternative insemination procedures has been introduced. In Nebraska, the Department of Social Services has announced an interim policy of no longer placing foster children in the homes of prospective foster parents who identify as gay or lesbian.

Gay and lesbian families will be open to scrutiny by clergy, health professionals, educators, the legal profession, and lay persons when our relationships fail, when couples separate, or when our children behave negatively (i.e., "act out"). Our lifestyles will be cited as the cause. The alternative family encounters many of the same challenges and pressures that the traditional family encounters, except that homophobia compounds and adds to the daily stress and pressure. We are already witnessing the first wave of "divorced" gay couples, gay stepparents, and gay blended families, and this presents new challenges and opportunities for the mental health profession.

In light of these pressures and realities, a professional therapist can be vital to the gay or lesbian family, both to the couple and the children. Children, in general, often have a hard time expressing what is bothering them. Child, group, and/or family therapy can help children recognize and talk about anger, sadness, and other feelings they experience. It can help them identify any fears or concerns they might have about growing up in a nontraditional family. Due to condemnation of their parents' lifestyle, overt or hidden, the children may encounter ostracism or social rejection by their peers. Normalizing and exploring a child's feelings associated with this can be very therapeutic.

With a young child, three to ten years of age, the mental health clinician can utilize play-therapy techniques such as board games, puppets and dolls, a feelings poster, fairy tales, and storybooks for therapeutic work. Younger children have experienced less social conditioning and exposure to homophobia and bigotry, and, as a result, often see nothing wrong or shameful with their family. Therapeutic work can help foster and strengthen this perception.

During the adolescent stage of development, "fitting in" and belonging to a group is vitally important to one's self-esteem and identity. Concurrently, sexual identity and dating issues come into play. It is not uncommon for most teenagers, and particularly those with gay or lesbian parents, to question their own sexual preferences, and often exclaim, "I'm not gay!" Individual counseling or groups facilitated by a therapist can provide a structured and safe milieu for adolescents to explore these issues and work toward acceptance by peers.

Family therapy is another vehicle for families to consider in order to facilitate expression among family members. Particularly with older children, 12 years and up, having a structured and neutral setting may help them feel safer communicating their questions, concerns, and feelings with their parents.

Parents often need the therapist to anticipate potentially problematic areas. To this end, I have found the following guidelines helpful.

1. Instruct parents on how to help their children cope with any tension, anxiety, or stress that develops around feelings of being in a gay or lesbian family. Particular emphasis should be placed on helping parents learn how not to minimize and/or deny such feelings.
2. Help parents prepare their children for the challenges in life that may trigger uncomfortable feelings or put the child in an awkward situation, such as entering kindergarten, being called "queer," or being confronted with a bully.
3. Some children will have periods of feeling different because they live in a gay or lesbian family. This will often include feelings of anger and sadness. Normalize this for parents, and encourage parents to seek out other gay and lesbian families. This helps the child feel that their family and experience is less unusual.
4. Finally, it is important to try to instill a sense of pride in the parents and children. Emphasize that love and caring are what makes a family. Involvement with social and educational groups can foster this sense of pride, while offering support. A recently formed group, COLAGE (Children of Lesbians and Gays Everywhere) is one example of a group that provides support for kids of all ages such as a pen-pal program, booklets, social groups, video projects, etc. Many communities have social and support groups for gays and lesbians with

children, and these can be tremendously beneficial and affirming for parents.

This chapter has reviewed many of the personal, couple, and family struggles that gays and lesbians encounter when they seek to develop a nontraditional family. A general theme through much of this is the feeling of not being seen as a family, and having one's goals of parenting children invalidated by others. Homophobia is a social disease, and we need to raise consciousness while we raise children.

REFERENCES

Burke, P. (1993). *Family Values: Two Moms and Their Son.* New York: Random House.

COLAGE: Children of Lesbians and Gays Everywhere. 2300 Market Street, Box 165, San Francisco, CA 94114.

Martin, A. (1993). *The Lesbian and Gay Parenting Handbook: Creating and Raising our Families.* New York: HarperCollins.

Pies, C. (1985). *Considering Parenthood: A Workbook for Lesbians.* San Francisco: Spinsters Ink.

Chapter 7

Clinical Issues in Identity Development in Gay Latino Men

Richard A. Rodriguez

Listen carefully, this is an important point. This system is something that we use against ourselves—our brothers and our sisters. It is called *internalized oppression.* I have heard it many times, "Well, he's not a real Chicano, he doesn't even speak the language;" "she's a sell-out; her old man is White." We even do it to ourselves, "Man, I don't know if they will accept me; I don't even know my history;" or my skin *es tan guero*, or too dark. Our men have used it against our women. And, our women have used it against each other. And homophobia continues to rage in our communities. Whether we recognize it or not, it infects our self-expression, and that of our niños y niñas. The list goes on and on . . . ."[1]

INTRODUCTION

During the last several decades, much has been written on the psychological, social, and political processes of ethnic identity development (Atkinson, Morten, and Sue, 1979; Parham, 1989).

---

1. From Chicana/Chicano Identity: A True Story. An unpublished manuscript by Rocha-Singh, PhD.

The author greatly appreciates the feedback on earlier drafts of this chapter by Anne Marshall, MS, and Indra Rocha-Singh, PhD.

These authors proposed stage-sequential processes in the identity development for people of color. The processes involve a conversion of attitudes, values, beliefs, and behavior from a dominant culture (Anglo) to those of a minority culture (ethnic). The result is identification with a primary cultural group and acknowledging, accepting, and valuing ethnicity as a positive aspect of self.

Likewise, several researchers have proposed stage-sequential theories for gay and lesbian identity development (Cass, 1979; Troiden, 1989). They posit a similar conversion of attitudes, values, beliefs, and behavior from a dominant culture (heterosexual) to those of the minority culture (gay/lesbian), in which gay/lesbian identity becomes an aspect of a person's internal definition and social presentation of self.

These models operate on the basis of two dichotomous variables (e.g., Latino and Anglo, gay and nongay). Ethnicity and sexual orientation are considered constructs on a continuum with two mutually exclusive endpoints and identity development becomes a process of rejecting one side and accepting the opposite. These models, however, are not sufficient to accommodate the process of identity development for individuals with multicultural backgrounds. Subsequent models have been developed which incorporate multiple racial, ethnic, cultural, and social identities and identify strategies for self-identification (Oetting and Beauvais, 1991; Root, 1990).

A review of the ethnic identity development models, however, reveals several inconsistencies. There is little agreement in definitions of ethnicity and culture, research paradigm (process/content), linear sequences of stages, and in the generalizability to various ethnic groups (Berry, 1993; Knight et al., 1993; Phinney, 1993). A degree of caution must be exercised when attempting to apply a model to a specific group.

More recently, research has focused on identity development that includes ethnicity and sexual orientation. Studies have focused on African-American gay men (Icard, 1986; Loiacano, 1989), Asian-American gay men and lesbians (Chan, 1989; Wooden, Kawasaki, and Mayeda, 1983); and Latina lesbians (Espín, 1987). A recurring theme in these studies is that gays and lesbians of color express a need to find validation in each community (ethnic and gay/lesbian) and a need to integrate both cultural identities. When presented with an "either-or" choice of preference and/or dominance of one culture over another, many gay and lesbian people of color reported feeling stressed and pressured.

A body of literature is now developing with respect to clinical issues with gay men of color, with increased focus on gay Latino men. Most of the research has focused on identity issues (Morales, 1990a; Rodriguez, 1991), sexual behavior and HIV prevalence and prevention (Carrier, 1985; Carrier and Magaña, 1991; Diaz, 1995; Diaz et al., in preparation; Morales, 1990b), general counseling issues (Morales, 1992), and considerations in counseling gay Latino men with HIV/AIDS (Carballo-Diéguez, 1989; Parés-Avila and Montano-López, 1994).

Gay Latino men face several challenges in today's society. Developing and maintaining an identity can be a struggle in a society that places heavy emphasis on conformity. Dealing with racism and homophobia in covert and/or overt situations can be quite taxing. Just wanting to be oneself in a public setting can be anxiety provoking; sometimes it is dangerous. Though, at other times, being one's true self can be beneficial for the individual, the family, and the culture. Interacting with these stressors, HIV infection rates for gay Latino men continue to rise (Diaz, in press). These issues warrant a critical look at the barriers and supports to developing identity as a gay Latino man, issues that may manifest clinically.

DEFINITIONS

The literature on ethnic and gay identity development is filled with concepts and terms that carry a variety of meanings. In some cases, terms are used interchangeably, with no conceptual or practical definitions. The following are definitions of common terms and concepts used in this chapter.

Based on a review of the literature on gay identity, Troiden (1984) offered the following definition of identity.

> Formally stated, identity refers to organized sets of characteristics an individual perceives as definitely representing the self in relation to a social situation (imagined or real). (p. 102)

Cognitive, affective, and behavioral components are included, both internal (perceptions) and external (social behavior and interpersonal interactions).

In defining the terms *homosexual* and *gay*, Warren (1974) and Rodriguez (1989) offered similar distinctions. They noted that "homosexual" describes sexual orientation and is primarily based on sexual behavior, whereas "gay" implies affiliation with a community, a culture, and describes people who have adopted a particular worldview. For purposes of this chapter, the term *gay identity* is used when referring to people with a homosexual identity who have adopted a psychosocial, political, and cultural affiliation with the gay community.

Keefe and Padilla (1987) defined *ethnic identification* as "self-identification among group members as well as their attitude toward and affiliation with one ethnic group and culture as opposed to another" (p. 8). The authors noted that *acculturation* refers to the social, economic, and political integration of an immigrant or ethnic minority group member into mainstream society." *Assimilation* assumes the disappearance of any continuing self-conscious ethnicity on the part of the former group members and their children (DeVos, 1993, p. 236). In order for someone to assimilate, he or she must have become acculturated to some extent, but that acculturation does not ensure assimilation.

Ethnic identification also implies taking on a label, which implies adoption of a certain set of ideologies, experiences, and worldviews. For the population of focus in this chapter, controversy exists with regard to choosing a single, identifiable label. There are similarities (language, common customs) as well as differences between cultural groups from various national origins (e.g., a second-generation Chicano and a first-generation immigrant from Cuba). Further, in their study of Mexican-American ethnic labeling with seventh-grade children from southern California, Buriel and Cardoza (1993) found a relationship between students' generation and their label selection. Given all of the above, the term *Latino* will be used as an umbrella term to describe the common social, political, and historical experiences of people of Latin-American descent. It is also acknowledged that individual differences exist in this heterogeneous group of peoples, and that caution must be taken with respect to overgeneralizing the following issues to all gay Latino clients.

IDENTITY DEVELOPMENT MODELS

Cass (1979) proposed a six-stage model of homosexual identity acquisition. The framework of the model is based on interpersonal congruency theory, that is, it takes into account the person's own perception of a characteristic of self, the resulting behavior related to the characteristic, and the individual's perception of another person's view of that characteristic. The time it takes to proceed through the stages varies by individual. Cass' six-stage model is presented in Table 7.1.

Atkinson, Morten, and Sue (1989) reviewed the literature on racial/ethnic identity development and proposed an inclusive Minority Identity Development model (MID). The five-stage MID

TABLE 7.1. Cass' Gay/Lesbian Identity Development Stage Theory

Stage	Developmental Task/Issue
1. Identity Confusion	Resolve the personal identity crisis of "Who am I?"
2. Identity Comparison	Deal with social alienation.
3. Identity Tolerance	Decrease social alienation by seeking out lesbian/gay others.
4. Identity Acceptance	Deal with inner tension of no longer subscribing to society's views; attempt to bring congruency between private and public views of self.
5. Identity Pride	Deal with incongruity of views of heterosexuals as unresponsive and unacceptable and actuality of heterosexuals responding positively to self-disclosure.
6. Identity Synthesis	Integrate lesbian/gay identity so that instead of being *the* identity, it is one aspect of self.

is presented in Table 7.2. The MID model is not proposed as a comprehensive theory of personality development, but rather as a schema to understand minority-client attitudes and behaviors within existing personality theories. The model also takes into account the differences that can exist between members of the same minority group with respect to cultural identity and the potential each person has for changing his/her sense of identity.

Morales (1990a) discussed implications of an identity development model for ethnic gays and lesbians. Rather than employ the term "stages," Morales proposed five "states" that are experienced

TABLE 7.2. Minority Identity Development Model

Stage	Attitude Toward Self	Attitude Toward Others of the Same Minority	Attitude Toward Dominant Group
1. Conformity	Self-depreciating	Group-depreciating	Group-appreciating
2. Dissonance	Conflict between self-depreciating and self-appreciating	Conflict between group-depreciating and group-appreciating	Conflict between group-appreciating and group-depreciating
3. Resistance and Immersion	Self-appreciating	Group-appreciating	Group-depreciating
4. Introspection	Concern with basis of self-appreciation	Concern with nature of unequivocal appreciation	Concern with the basis of group depreciation
5. Synergetic Articulation and Awareness	Self-appreciating	Group-appreciating	Selective appreciation

Note: Adapted from Atkinson, Morton, and Sue (1989). *Counseling American Minorities.* Dubuque: William C Brown Publishers.

by gays and lesbians of color. Each state describes processes for managing anxiety and tensions. As a person experiences cognitive and behavioral changes, there is a tendency toward greater understanding of self from the contexts of both one's sexual orientation and ethnic background. Morales' model is presented in Table 7.3.

Rodriguez (1991) interviewed fifteen adult gay Chicano men from three southern California counties (Los Angeles, Orange, and San Diego). Transcripts of the interviews were analyzed via qualitative methodology, yielding 38 discrete themes, grouped under three general headings: Chicano identity development, gay identity development, and integration of Chicano and gay aspects of identity. A grounded theory, derived from data from the research participants, was proposed, describing the process of identity development as well as the blocks, supports, and strategies utilized for identity maintenance. Results from this study are presented throughout this chapter.

The inconsistencies previously mentioned in the research on identity development models raise the question of "What is really being measured?" Phinney (1993) noted that most research has been based on cultural *content* (attitudes, values, behavior) and very little based on the *process* of ethnic identity formation and the management of differences. Knight et al. (1993) presented a social cognitive model and stated that it was highly probabalistic. In some cases a person's behavior may have more to do with temporal contextual factors than cultural value systems. Berry (1993) further raised the issue that less attention has been paid to the events that take place as a result of contact with other cultures and the effects this may have on developing individuals.

The perceived linear nature of stage-sequential identity development models is also under question. The multidimensionality of a person is easily lost and a hierarchical framework of viewing a person in a more/less than diagnostic category becomes the resulting paradigm. It is clear that a "one-size-fits-all" model does not exist. More research is needed in testing the theoretical models for applicability to particular groups. The models do, however, provide an invaluable set of knowledge-process variables in identity development. These variables have significant clinical utility in that they can be examined in a particular cultural context of the client. Thus,

TABLE 7.3. Morales' Identity Formation Model for Ethnic Minority Gays/Lesbians

State	Identity Management Issues
1. Denial of Conflicts	During this phase, people tend to minimize the validity and reality of discrimination they experience as ethnic persons and believe they are treated the same as others. Their sexual orientation may or may not be defined, but they feel their personal lifestyle and sexual preference have limited consequences in their life. The focus of therapy centers around developing a more accurate picture of how the environmental stresses affect their functioning and how their multiple identities can be assets in their personality and lifestyle.
2. Bisexual versus Gay/Lesbian	The preference for some ethnic minority gays and lesbians is to identify themselves as bisexual rather than gay or lesbian. Upon examining their sexual lifestyles there may be no difference between those who identify themselves as gay/lesbian as compared to those identified as bisexual. The focus of therapy may be to explore the sense of hopelessness and depression resulting from the continued feelings of conflict.
3. Conflicts in Allegiances	The simultaneous awareness of being the member of an ethnic minority as well as being gay or lesbian presents anxiety around the need for these lifestyles to remain separate. Anxiety about betraying either the ethnic minority or the gay/lesbian communities, when preference is given to one over the other, becomes a major concern. The need to prioritize allegiances in order to reduce the conflict becomes the focus in therapy.

State	Identity Management Issues
4. Establishing Priorities in Allegiances	A primary identification to the ethnic community prevails in this state, and feelings of resentment concerning the lack of integration among the communities becomes a central issue. There are feelings of anger and rage stemming from their experiences of rejection by the gay community because of their ethnicity. The need to re-examine the feelings of anger and rage as they relate to their experiences becomes a central focus in therapy.
5. Integrating the Various Communities	As gay or lesbian persons of color, the need to integrate their lifestyle and develop a multicultural perspective becomes a major concern. Adjusting to the reality of the limited options currently available for gay and lesbian people of color becomes a source of anxiety facilitating feelings of isolation and alienation. The focus of therapy centers around reassuring them that they are aware of the various dynamics they experience and can better predict outcomes and consequences.

Note: Adapted from Morales (1990). Ethnic minority families and minority gays and lesbians. In Frederick W. Bozett and Marvin B. Sussman (eds.), *Homosexuality and Family Relations*, pp. 217-239.

clients do not have to be pushed or prodded through a sequence of stages as dictated by a model. Rather, a therapist can help a client examine the effects of these process variables on self-concept, self-esteem, and behavior. This perspective forms the framework for this chapter.

CULTURAL CONTEXT

According to Comas-Díaz (1985), understanding the cultural context is a critical factor to providing effective mental health services to Latinos and all other ethnic groups. In this chapter, a social constructivist view of identity development for gay Latino men will be used, addressing significant events, social, psychological, and political issues. The basis lies in Rodriguez' (1991) qualitative study of men "telling their stories" and uses quotes from participants. Latino values, attitudes, and beliefs that influence how gay Latino men may think, feel, and act are discussed in terms of how the issues may manifest in psychotherapy.

DEVELOPMENTAL ISSUES

In this section, I will cover the following issues affecting the identity development process: Family as the basis for socialization, social class, religion/spirituality, machismo, gender role socialization, not being brown enough/acculturation, language, *familismo,* family dynamics, coming out, socialization in multiple worlds, dating partners, survivors of childhood sexual abuse, HIV/AIDS, and redefinition of *familia.*

Family as the Basis for Socialization

> I mean even my parents sometimes, you know, like, when I was younger, we used to celebrate some of the, I guess, Mexican holidays . . . . So like the Santos, Dia de los Reyes, you know . . . they would like celebrate Dia de las Madres on the 10th of May instead of where they do it here.

> My parents raised us very Anglicized, you know, very . . .
> mainstream culture. And so, I didn't feel like I grew up Latino
> at all . . . . It wasn't until much later that I started identifying
> more that way, you know. But my parents just preferred not to
> really talk to me about that part of my identity or their identity.
> I don't think that they thought it was as strong a part of their
> identity that they wanted . . . or that they felt that they needed
> to, you know . . . impart it to me.

In Rodriguez (1991), the family was viewed as the primary
source of learning about Latino culture, attitudes, and beliefs, and
normative behavior and was cited as the source of emotional, financial, and moral support within the Chicano community. For six
respondents, Spanish was the primary language spoken in the
home; six reported that English was the primary language; and three
respondents grew up in bilingual households. For those being raised
in identified Mexican barrios, respondents related speaking Spanish
with family and peers, eating Mexican food, and celebrating Mexican traditions. Several respondents reported being raised in "Anglicized" homes where only English was spoken, social contacts were
with Anglo friends, and only American traditions were celebrated.

Growing up without a solid sense of Latino identity is often a
significant issue raised in therapy. There is often a degree of embarrassment, anger, and blame (of self and/or parents) attached to the
absence or lack of proficiency in Spanish or the lack of knowledge
of Latino traditions. Another version of this may be heard as
"Being Latino isn't an issue for me." Exploration of how the client
sees himself with respect to his ethnicity, attributions of the reasons
underlying the cultural gap, and his current level of investment in
learning more about his culture would be an appropriate approach.

Social Class

> I'm the only one who went to college. And he [father] appreci-
> ates that because he wishes all his kids would go to college.
> But then again, he understands that not all of them want to.
> And he's very proud of the fact that I went to college and he
> says he wishes he could . . . . I think I get a lot from him . . . .
> My father is very dynamic in that he moved up here when he

was 15 or 16. He lived here and supported his family in Tijuana, while he worked. And, uhm, then after awhile, he went to the community college to take some courses that he wanted to learn. And he learned English by himself. He just picked it up. He still has trouble, uh, remembering how to write certain words and sounds and stuff like that. But he asks me about it and I clear it up. But he's always wanted to continue and get a college education. I think he will in the future.

As noted in Morales (1992) and Parés-Avila and Montano-López (1994), socioeconomic class plays a significant role in the development of cultural values and social networks. Latinos tend to be proportionally overrepresented in the lower socioeconomic classes in the United States. The norms, values, and beliefs associated with class influence a person's view of himself, his family, his culture, and the community at large. They also greatly affect behavior.

The interaction of socioeconomic class, Latino culture, and sexual orientation may play a significant role in identity development. For example, a client presents in therapy with coming-out issues. He is the primary contributor to the family income and chooses not to be out due to fears of being fired from his job. Risking the loss of resources to the family income may be the primary reason for not coming out and may be a very real consequence. In light of this, assessing the priorities for decision making will be important. Sometimes the issue is homophobia, sometimes internalized homophobia, sometimes it is a function of class values in terms of economic survival, and sometimes it is an interaction effect of all of the above.

Religion/Spirituality

But as far as church, I've always gone to church . . . well we used to go to mass at Delhi church, and that's about as Mexican as you can get, I guess, uh, in Spanish. And I was an altar boy, for about 4 years.

All participants in the Rodriguez (1991) study discussed or made reference to having been raised in a religious environment and having at least one parent raised in the Catholic faith. Many clients feel like the person who commented, "You can't separate Catholicism from being Chicano–they're one and the same thing." Those who identify with indigenous peoples have also discussed their faith in the healing powers of attending a ceremony in a sweat lodge as a spiritual cleansing.

Given the religious backgrounds of the mostly Catholic participants, several noted feeling guilt regarding their homosexual feelings and behavior. They reported praying to God on a nightly basis to be able to "change." Some felt that God had rejected them, while others coped by rejecting organized religion and/or God.

> So I hoped it [gay feelings] would go away. And I hoped and prayed that it would go away. I remember just praying for it to go away. I would cry myself to sleep sometimes. And it wouldn't. And I'd come to school the next day and the next morning I'd say, "today it's going to be totally different."

Interestingly enough, two participants stated that even with the antigay stance of organized religion and the pressures they felt to conform, they believed it was their faith in God that helped them cope.

> At the ripe old age of 21 [when I came out], I could look back at everything that had happened: my sisters all knew; my family knew; I had all kinds of friends. And I thought, Oh, this is great. And I could look back and say, "You know what–there is a God. Because if there wasn't a God, then I wouldn't be so happy." I prayed and I prayed and I prayed. He didn't change me. He helped me accept myself for who I am. So to this day I still believe in God. You know, He's a different God; He's not an angry God or mean–He's a beautiful God.

As Parés-Avila and Montano-López (1994) pointed out, although Catholicism is the predominant religion, it is important to consider the influence of other religious beliefs and folk practices. The following belief systems were described: (1) *Curanderismo* (common in countries with strong, indigenous influences) in which *curanderos* use prayers, massage, and herbs to cure physical, spiritual, and emotional ailments; (2) *Santería* (common in Cuba and Caribbean countries), which combines Yoruban deities introduced by African slaves with Catholic saints/rituals; and (3) *Espiritismo* (common in Puerto Rico) in which spirits of the dead manifest and intervene with the living.

Whether it be religion, folk beliefs, or other practices, it is important to include a client's sense of spirituality in the overall assessment of his level of identity development. A client may or may not currently practice these beliefs but may still hold them as significant influences on how he perceives himself in relation to family, culture, society, and the universe. For some clients, a therapist supporting consultation with a spiritual healer may make the difference between feeling misunderstood/judged/diagnosed, and improving overall functioning.

Machismo

> I learned what it means to be macho–if you're a man–to not cry; to be strong, you know, be the boss . . . oppressive (chuckles) . . . and very . . . authoritative. You know, stick up for anything. It doesn't have to be even if you're right. But . . . in other words, getting into a lot of good fights . . . mess around with a lot of women. And, you know, I got a lot of that from all my family. My dad would tell me stories–navy stories–that he and his buddies would go around, beating up the fags and, you know . . . and I was a pretty sensitive kid and I'd cry and I'd always hear from my uncles and my cousins, *joto, maricon,* you know, fag.

The concept of machismo has been viewed as a set of standards and norms for masculinity in Latino culture. Definitions for the term vary. In Rodriguez (1991), not only did respondents equate machismo with Chicano culture, but they tended to use the term as a way to talk about their father's negative behavior and treatment of them as children. It is interesting to note that the original definition of the term included protection of family and provision of love and sensitivity to family members, qualities that tend to be omitted from most contemporary definitions (M. L. Bañuelos, 1990, personal communication).

The negative effects of machismo on the self-esteem and behavior of gay Latino men often becomes a clinical issue. Internalized homophobia and racism are often the result of years of listening to and/or observing what happens to men who violate the norms of machismo. Homophobic comments and actions become indelibly etched into the minds of young boys struggling with conflicting feelings of sexual attraction. For those who decide to come out and break the image of a macho man, the negative consequences often lead to hurt, anger, anxiety, or depression. Unrecognized, these feelings can become internalized as a negative aspect of Latino culture, resulting in fears of interacting with or a sense of detachment from other Latino men.

Gender Role Socialization

> I don't remember the incident, but it was like drilled into my head so many times . . . My father wanted to buy me a Texaco truck, I guess it was like a gas truck or something. And he wanted to get it for me and I guess it was kinda for a kid; I guess when you're a kid, you sit on it and you push it around and something like that. And I wanted a doll. I wanted a Barbie doll or something like that. And he got so angry with me–he used to tell me this story, many times. He got so angry with me that he didn't get me anything (chuckles).

For study respondents, memories of learning what was culturally and socially appropriate behavior for boys during their growing up years are very clear. There is little doubt about what is appropriate behavior for Latino boys and punishment/ostracism is quickly expected if norms are violated. In a recent talk with Chicano/Latino college students, gender-role expectations and characteristics were discussed. Perceptions fell along the lines of men being intelligent, hard-working, and competitive and women being cooperative, caring, and nurturing. When the students were asked how they would privately describe themselves as individuals, however, most responded with both stereotypically masculine and feminine traits. A final question was asked about the consequences of publicly going outside the boundaries of these expectations. The response was unanimous: stepping outside the bounds of set gender-role criteria implied that men were gay and women were lesbian. Being gay or lesbian is, therefore, viewed as rejection to fulfilling set gender roles, a critical norm in Latino culture.

Given the heavy emphasis on demonstrating appropriate gender-role behavior, it is important to examine how the meaning of behavior influences the definition of sexual identity. Several authors have described possible differences in the definitions of "homosexual behavior" and "being homosexual." Carrier (1985) stated, "Heterosexuality is considered superior to homosexuality in Mexico. A Mexican male's gender identity, however, is not necessarily threatened by his homosexual behavior as long as he is masculine and plays the inserter role" (p. 84). Other researchers have noted this point and advise that one may get a different response from Chicano or Latino men when asking, "Have you ever engaged in sexual behavior with another man?" rather than "Are you gay/bisexual?" (Carballo-Diéguez, 1989; Carrier, 1985; Morales, 1990b). The label that a man uses may actually have little or nothing to do with his private sexual behavior. Parés-Avila and Montano-López (1994) responded as follows:

> This interpretation is questionable because there is no evidence that the active homosexual role is accepted among Latinos. Rather, the active partner's identification with a heterosexual life-style despite his bisexual behavior may reflect the active partner's mechanism for coping with homophobia in his community of origin. (p. 348)

A man's homosexual behavior may be known within the family, but there is a tendency within the culture to deny that homosexuality exists. At times, homosexuality may be met with silent tolerance as long as the man continues to play out his expected cultural role as provider, husband, and father. Carballo-Diéguez (1989) believes that having to hide or lie about aspects of true self in order to maintain the support of family can have a negative impact on a man's self-esteem. Helping a client understand the definition and meaning of sexual orientation and gender roles can help relieve anxiety and guilt often associated with not living up to cultural norms and expectations.

Not Being Brown Enough/Acculturation

> Basically in high school they used to call me a coconut [brown on the outside, white on the inside], you know, because I used to hang around with the white Americans. Because in our neighborhood there wasn't any . . . Mexicans around there . . . but they [*cholos* at school] would hassle me for me hanging around with the Anglos . . . .

Many Latinos (especially second generation and beyond) feel discredited by members of their own culture based on not being "brown enough" based on physical appearance, cultural knowledge, language preferences, or the ethnicity of the peer group with whom they socialize. Frustration, confusion, and feeling misunderstood by others compounds existing issues of feeling "different" and "not fitting in." People who do not conform to cultural norms and those who become highly acculturated are especially susceptible to this type of stressor. Being gay is often viewed as a "white" problem and is the result of "hanging around with gabachos."

From Diaz' (in press) perspective, acculturated men are highly identified with and integrated into non-Hispanic white gay culture and seldom participate in the affairs of the Latino community. He further notes that this choice is often motivated by homophobic abuse/rejection from the Latino community. Because these men feel more gay than Latino and feel more comfortable in the general gay community, they often experience internal conflicts when presented with issues of real or perceived ethnic discrimination. These men, Diaz suggests, may be trying to escape Latino homophobia by rejecting their own culture of origin and adopting a nonethnically defined gay culture that may not exist.

On the other side of the spectrum, Diaz discussed nonacculturated men who are highly identified as Latinos, preferring to primarily speak Spanish and socializing primarily in Latino-identified groups and establishments. These men tend to behave within the bounds of traditional gender roles for homosexuals in Latin-American countries, where being gay is defined in terms of gender identity (man=active; woman=receptive). For this group, the issue is to develop an identity based on two men loving one another, not just two men having sex with one another.

In both cases, men need to know that there are more options available to them beyond the "more gay than Latino" and "more Latino than gay" perspectives. Integration of gay and latino aspects of identity is another possibility and will be discussed in more detail in the section on socializing in multiple worlds.

Language

> And the worst thing about it is in Spanish, I find that there's no good word; at least I don't know of any good word for "gay." Here, gay is applied as not the fag; not the effeminate; and less scientific than homosexual. It has a comfortable medium. And in Spanish, I don't find that. It's either *homosexual*, you know, maricon, you know, a derogatory, uhm . . . there's no comfortable medium, you know. And so that . . . that made it also hard to come out to my parents.

The power that words and language possess cannot be overemphasized. Content, meaning, and affect are all mediated by the words one uses. The language of one culture may or may not easily translate into the culture of another. It has been previously noted that there is no equivalent in the Spanish language for the term *gay*. Bilingual/bicultural men often feel frustrated because they believe the Spanish term *homosexual,* carries a negative connotation and wish there were a term that depicts a more balanced picture of who they are.

In addition to translation, the choice (conscious or unconscious) of language that bilingual clients use to discuss certain issues is important. Several authors have pointed out that often there is a splitting of verbalized experience from emotional experience, depending upon which language the client is utilizing. Bilingual people may spontaneously switch to the primary language in order to better express what they are experiencing, and sometimes they may choose to speak in the secondary language in order to avoid the stress provoked by emotionally charged material (Atkinson, Morten, and Sue, 1989; Falicov, 1982; Parés-Avila and Montano-López, 1994).

In presenting preliminary data from her research on Latina lesbian immigrants, Espín (1994) reported that in individual interviews and focus groups, participants were choosing to speak about their lesbian identities in English rather than Spanish, even though Spanish was their primary language. When asked, participants reported that it was more comfortable to speak in English because sexuality was a taboo topic in their home countries; using English provided a safe emotional distance from culturally stigmatized, potentially shameful material. Again, it is important to note not only the content and the language, but the language *associated with* the content. This is also an important concept to guide bilingual/bicultural therapists as to which language may be more appropriate to use at a given point in time.

Familismo, *Family Dynamics, and Coming Out*

> My Mom, well, she said one day, "Are you, kind of like this?" [wiggles wrist back and forth] I said, "Well, whatever, you want me to be–whatever." Uh, my father, I just couldn't tell him. I've never told him. My Mom told me that she told him and that he said "okay." Well, that was great . . . so my Dad knows. My mother took it very well. She told me, "As long as you're happy."

> But, it never became real until my lover moved in with me and my parents found out. And that was about 4 years ago and my father did not take it well at all. He hasn't really spoken to me ever since. We've had maybe a brief period where we've talked, maybe for a couple of months, he tried to make an effort to talk to us. But it didn't work out. And, the last time I tried to communicate with him was about a month ago. And he said shit to me, like, uh, "I regret having anything to do with your birth," and, "I regret that you were born."

Coming out to family is considered a significant event in lesbian/gay identity development, from both a personal and political perspective. Not being out to one's family is often linked to an early stage of identity development. Pressures come from internal sources (i.e., "I should be out to the ones I love,") and from external sources ("You're not helping your community [gay] if you're not out completely."). For some, the fear of coming out may indeed be a developmental issue. For others, Latino values may be operating that need to be considered.

Familismo describes the heavy emphasis on the family as the primary source of emotional, cultural, and financial support. Extended family includes *compadres/comadres* (co-parents) and often close friends of the parents are called *tios/tias* (uncles/aunts). Corollary values include interdependence, affiliation, and cooperation (Marín, 1989). Strong expectations exist on the reliance on the family for both daily needs and emergency issues, which creates a strong sense of obligation. Given this emphasis, it is no wonder that a gay Latino man would fear risking the loss of his family if he were to come out publicly. In a society where real or perceived racism may affect his daily life, why would someone risk losing the people to whom he would automatically go to for support?

Personalismo refers to a preference for having personal relationships with people over and above procedural rules and regulations. *Simpatía* refers to the primary importance of "smooth relations" and social politeness within the family (Bernal, 1982). To a non-Latino observer, this value could easily be interpreted as conflict avoidance and judged as therapeutic resistance. *Respeto* emphasizes the need for respect, especially for authority figures. A phrase that incorporates several of the concepts noted above is *bien educado.* The direct translation, well-educated, is misleading. The phrase formally refers to how well socially educated the person is in terms of interaction and communication with elders, authority figures, and family members, as well as how the person presents himself in society.

Given all of the above, how does a therapist work with a gay Latino male with regard to coming-out issues? It is not so much the content, but the process of how one approaches the issue that is critical. Empathizing with a man struggling to maintain strong, Latino family-focused values and beliefs, understanding the importance of "protecting the family against shame (*Que dirán?*–What will people say?), and maintaining a nonjudgmental attitude toward coming-out decisions will help alleviate tension and anxiety as a client weighs the potential benefits and risks of coming out. Considering the following questions is critical: "Is this resistance to coming out a developmental issue?" and "What cultural values are operating in his decision-making process?"

Socializing in Multiple Worlds

> *Spending time in Latino community.* Very little . . . I think that if they, you know, had more gay issues, then I would, more. But the problem is . . . there's this feeling of . . . they're homophobic; they don't want any gay people. I reject anything that's homophobic. . . . My sister's husband, you know, is about the closest that I get to Mexican–straight, you know, heterosexual . . . That's as close as I get.

> *Spending time in gay community.* I find myself extremely involved in social, religious activities. . . . I belong to so many groups. And I try to attend all the meetings. And I try to do a little bit of the functions of each group. Uhm, and I know quite a bit of people in each little group.

> *Spending time in gay Latino community.* I would say, a lot . . . being a part of GLLU (Gay and Lesbian Latinos Unidos); just that one thing has really changed my life in a lot of ways, because it educates you a lot, you know, on what's going on in the community–the Latino community and the gay community. And we see the common goals that you have, and you're invited and encouraged to participate in as many events and things as possible.

In addition to the cultural context in which a person develops an identity, of equal importance is an examination of the multiple communities in which a person socializes. Morales (1990a) noted that gays and lesbians of color are faced with managing life in three different worlds: the ethnic community, the gay/lesbian community, and the predominantly white, heterosexual community. Each setting carries with it an emotional either-or, zero-sum "pull," which creates both internal conflict and conflict with the community. Racism exists in the lesbian/gay community just as it does in the heterosexual community. Homophobia exists in the communities of color just as it does in the white community. In today's "check only one box" society, many people from multicultural backgrounds end up as "other."

A fourth "world" is becoming more and more apparent that acknowledges all aspects of a person's life: the lesbian/gay community of color. The majority of the men in the Rodriguez (1991) study reported that socializing in the gay Latino community was one of the main support systems that helped them deal with the "missing" or overlooked cultural parts of themselves. Several noted initial fears, such as "Well, I thought that I'd go to this meeting and there'd be a bunch of Latinos speaking Spanish and that I wouldn't fit in. But when I finally went, I found I was just like them." Depending upon where a client is in his identity development, encouraging participation in the gay Latino community could prove very beneficial.

Dating Partners

> I have a lover and we've been together for 14 years. And it hasn't been easy. It's been like a roller coaster, but, man, you just hold on there. I would say, he's Mexican. So he's taught me a lot about my culture.

> Yeah, I don't even know what that is . . . I'm not attracted to men of my own race and culture. But I'm attracted to white Anglo men–especially, I mean, the very Aryan looking. I don't understand it. I know a lot of white men that are very attracted to Latino men. And I know the same interplays between, uhm, blacks and whites. I don't know why . . . .

In Rodriguez (1991), of the six respondents who reported that they were currently dating, three were dating Anglo men, two were dating Chicano men, and one was dating people from both cultures. Of the nine respondents who reported that they were currently in a relationship, six had Chicano/Latino partners and three had Anglo partners. Several respondents noted a decided preference for Anglo men and reported sometimes feeling "hassled" by other members of the gay Chicano community for dating outside the culture. In addition, most respondents noted cultural differences when their partner was Anglo (e.g., sex, family, dating, manner of dress, food, and displays of affection).

These findings fit with previous research on interracial dating for people of color. Sometimes this phenomenon suggests internalized racism (fears and/or negative reactions toward Latino men). As noted earlier, a man might recall the behavior of his father, negatively label it macho, and then generalize this concept to all Latino men (including himself) with accompanying internalized conflict and racism. Focus of treatment is on racial/ethnic identity. In other cases, dating outside the culture is an attraction, pure and simple, without influence on a person's identity.

The issue may also present itself in the form of relationship problems in couples counseling. Differences in cultural values, communication styles, and behavior often become interpreted as, "He refuses to understand me," or "If I do it his way, I'm giving up who I am." Helping the couple acknowledge the influences of cultural differences on their relationship and developing strategies to find commonalities and increase mutual understanding is an important intervention strategy.

Survivors of Childhood Sexual Abuse

> It was very confusing; very, very confusing . . . When I was eight or so, I really don't remember, I was molested by my cousin, who was like 15 or 16. . . . I was always labeled as a little faggot and a sissy, and whatever. But, uh, when he molested me, I really didn't know if I wanted him . . . I know I didn't like it . . . it was just sort of really weird, but I didn't know how I felt . . . and being labeled in school that I was gay and so on, I was sort of confused if I was gay because everyone has, you know, drilled it into me . . . or if I was gay because I had been molested, or was it a mixture of both . . . or was it because just that I was, you know.

Men abused as children by men and who identify as heterosexual, tend to ask the question, "Will this make me gay?" while men who identify as gay tend to ask, "Is this why I'm gay?" It is important for the clinician to help the client differentiate between the effects of trauma and sexual orientation. These types of questions can result from trauma, internalized homophobia, and/or the combination of the two. A clinical example is offered.

A 29-year-old Latino client presented for counseling with coming-out issues. Early sessions focused on the definition and meaning of sexual orientation, Latino identity issues, and internalized homophobia. In the third session, the client kept shifting between English and Spanish in an attempt to express himself congruently and disclosed that he had been molested at the age of nine or ten by a boy who was a neighbor. Subsequent sessions were devoted to processing trauma/shame/blame/guilt. "I feel so ashamed of telling my mother what happened. I'm still having trouble asking for forgiveness—*me da verguenza.*" A visualization gestalt technique was utilized in which he was able to tell his mother in Spanish about the molestation.

The feelings of shame and guilt were originally interpreted as internalized homophobia. Until his disclosure of the molestation, the focus was on identity development in general. What was talked about in English led to a tearful, emotional abreaction in Spanish. Espín's (1994) comments apply here, in that what the client talked about in English represented an attempt to distance himself from shameful material and possible familial/cultural ostracization. After breaking the silence of the trauma, the client reported feeling significantly better, and treatment was refocused on identity formation issues.

HIV/AIDS

Issues of HIV/AIDS have not previously been discussed as "aspects" of identity development; however, given the impact of HIV/AIDS on the community, its effects on how people view themselves, their friends, and their future are clear. Diaz (1995) reviewed the behavioral research on HIV risk in gay/bisexual Latino men. He noted, "It is painfully obvious that, with few exceptions, HIV risk-reduction interventions to date have not been successful in significantly decreasing—much less stopping—the spread of HIV in our communities." Diaz' review concluded that many gay Latino men engage in high-risk sexual behavior in spite of substantial knowledge of HIV transmission, high perceived risk, and strong intentions to practice safer sex.

In examining correlates of risk behavior, Carballo-Diéguez and

Dolezal (1995) investigated whether homosexually active men who were sexually abused in childhood were more likely to engage in HIV-risk sexual behavior than were men who were not sexually abused. Participants were 182 adult men of Puerto Rican ancestry living in New York City who had sex with either just men or men and women. Three groups were identified: Abuse group (men who before 13 had sex with a partner at least four years older and who felt hurt by the experience and/or were unwilling to participate); Willing/Not-hurt group (same age criteria, but did not feel hurt by experience); No-older-partner group. Results showed that men in the Abuse group were significantly more likely than men in No-older-partner group to engage in unprotected receptive anal intercourse. Incidence of risk behavior for the Willing/Not-hurt group lay between the other two groups.

Further investigation into the social and psychological correlates and predictors of safer sex behavior among gay Latino men is needed. Of particular importance to the present chapter is perceived risk and vulnerability. As reviewed in Diaz (1995), two recent studies of Latino gay/bisexual men (National Task Force on AIDS Prevention, 1993; Diaz et al., in preparation) measured participants' perceived vulnerability/risk to HIV infection. In both, participants showed a great deal of concern and daily preoccupation with AIDS. Forty percent of the men in one study and 26 percent in the other indicated that their chances of becoming HIV-infected were medium or high. Adding the percentage of men who know they are HIV positive, Diaz further stated as follows:

> Of special concern is the fact that very few men in both samples regarded their risk as zero or none. In fact, very large numbers of men believe that there is a considerable (medium to high) chance that they are now or will become infected with HIV in the future. (p. 21)

Racism, homophobia, posttraumatic stress from childhood sexual abuse, multiple losses to HIV/AIDS, identity confusion, economic insecurity, multiple worlds–are all issues (whether alone or any combination thereof) that may produce feelings of hopelessness, helplessness, anxiety, and/or depression. We must be sensitive to the sometimes subtle/sometimes blatant impact of these issues on both sense of self and sense of community. A solid sense of identity coupled with increased control over one's life–empowerment–may be powerful influences on risk-behavior decisions.

Redefinition of Familia

> But I've made my own family bonds. What I've done is–because I didn't get the support from my blood family–I went out and found some very close friends. Extremely close–where we know each other. And we'll always be friends. And we've learned to accept each other for the people we are, the person we are and we're very supportive of each other. We made our own family and I'm part of that family. And I do get my support from that.

In response to the question, "Who or what would you say has been the most helpful or supportive to you in developing and maintaining your identity?," participants in Rodriguez (1991) identified the following sources of support: family, gay and lesbian Latino social organizations, and faith in God. As previously noted, extended family is of major importance in Latino culture.

What we find today in terms of support for gay Latino men is a redefinition of the term *familia,* in terms of the addition of supportive people and not blanket replacement/rejection of family of origin. *Hermanos/hermanas* (brothers/sisters) are familiar terms in the community and include people from all races/ethnicities: men, women, gay, lesbian, transgender, and heterosexual. What matters is that they acknowledge, accept, and value the person for who he is. People in the *familia* become significant sources of support, community affiliation, and affirmation of identity. Supporting a client's redefinition of *familia* and reinforcing the importance of connection with a community can be one of the most therapeutic interventions in facilitating a client's identity development process.

IMPLICATIONS FOR CLINICAL PRACTICE

When examining all of the issues reviewed in this chapter, it would be very easy to make generalizations about the identity development experiences of gay Latino men; however, it must be kept in mind that there are individual differences in the process. Normative beliefs and behaviors may differ according to national origin. Generational level may also account for differences. Social, political, and historical experiences of first-generation immigrant, gay Latino men may be different from those of second- and third-generation men born in the United States. Rodriguez (1989) also found age-cohort differences in experiencing significant events in identity development for a sample of 251 men in Utah. Men coming out in the 1940s, 1950s, and 1960s have developed their identities with different sets of political and social influences than men coming out in the 1970s, 1980s, and 1990s.

Even when considering individual differences, cultural identity development appears to be a process and not a single event. Sometimes the process is linear, sometimes not. Each aspect of cultural identity may occur independently or concurrently with another. Men raised in Anglicized backgrounds may not develop a need or interest to reclaim Latino identity until after a gay identity has emerged. Likewise, a person may have achieved a high level of Latino identity prior to beginning his process of gay identity development. Still others may experience the processes simultaneously.

"Shoulds" become an added stress and source of guilt, embarrassment, and frustration: "I should have learned Spanish growing up," "I really should know more about my heritage," "I should have told my parents I was gay." Therapists can be extremely helpful to clients in supporting them in their process and accepting the limits of cultural identity over which they had no control, as well as acknowledging the client's potential for cultural identity development. It was commonly reported that a primary reason parents brought their children up in English was to protect them from being teased, harassed, or discriminated against for speaking Spanish. Yet in today's society, being bilingual is viewed as an asset more than as a hindrance.

It is important for the therapist to note the potential negative transference feelings a gay Latino client may have for a Latino, gay, or gay Latino therapist. Clients in the beginning stages of cultural identity development may fear homophobia from a Latino therapist or racism from a gay Anglo therapist. As noted in Helms (1993), counseling impasses often occur in situations when the counselor and the client are at significantly different stages of racial identity development. A client in a devaluation stage of ethnicity and/or sexual orientation may not trust or have interest seeing an identified Latino, gay, or gay Latino therapist.

As Atkinson, Morten, and Sue (1989) concluded, counselor/client cultural differences alone do not create barriers to counseling. A therapist's sensitivity to and knowledge of critical aspects of multicultural issues in identity development will influence his/her ability to work effectively with a gay Latino.

Knowledge of community resources is extremely important. Given the emotional and moral support available from identified gay Latino individuals and organizations, it is important for the therapist to introduce these sources of support when the client indicates he is ready to investigate this realm. Finally, once the client begins to develop a support system and establishes his new familia, it would be helpful for the therapist to affirm and validate the function of redefined family in the process of identity development.

CONCLUSION

Given all of the barriers to identity development and maintenance—racism, homophobia, heterosexism, antigay religious sentiments, cultural differences, HIV/AIDS—gay Latino men must have sources of support in order to survive and succeed. Each man brings with him his own personal tenacity and will to survive, in spite of all the challenges he faces. The richness of a multicultural identity can be developed and nurtured through exploration of the process.

The issues discussed in this chapter are offered as clinical questions, assessment markers of identity development, and considerations for therapeutic interventions with this population. Listening to a gay Latino man tell his story, validating his reality and perceptions of his identity, demonstrating awareness of the complexity of identity development, providing emotional support, and sometimes being a consultant/guide throughout the hardships and joys of the process are critical elements to psychotherapy with gay Latino men.

REFERENCES

Atkinson, D. R., Morten, G., and Sue, D. W. (1989). *Counseling American Minorities: A Cross Cultural Perspective.* Dubuque, IA: Wm. C. Brown Publishers.

Bernal, G. (1982). Cuban families. In M. McGoldrick, J. Pearce, and J. Giordano (eds.) *Ethnicity and Family Therapy.* New York: The Guilford Press.

Berry, J. W. (1993). Ethnic identity in plural societies. In M. E. Bernal and G. P. Knight (eds.). *Ethnic Identity: Formation and Transmission Among Hispanics and Other Minorities,* (pp. 271-296). Albany: State University of New York Press.

Buriel, R. and Cardoza, D. (1993). Mexican American ethnic labeling: An intrafamilial and intergenerational analysis. In M. E. Bernal and G. P. Knight (eds.). *Ethnic Identity: Formation and Transmission Among Hispanics and Other Minorities,* (pp. 197-210). Albany: State University of New York Press.

Carballo-Diéguez, A. (1989). Hispanic culture, gay male culture, and AIDS: Counseling implications. *Journal of Counseling and Development,* 68(September/October): 26-30.

Carballo-Diéguez, A., and Dolezal, C. (1995). Association between history of childhood sexual abuse and adult HIV-risk sexual behavior in Puerto Rican men who have sex with men. *Child Abuse and Neglect,* 19(5):595-605.

Carrier, J. M. (1985). Mexican male bisexuality. *Journal of Homosexuality,* 11(1/2):75-85.

Carrier, J. M. and Magaña, J. R. (1991). Use of ethnosexual data on men of Mexican origin for HIV/AIDS prevention programs. *The Journal of Sex Research,* 28(2):189-202.

Cass, V. C. (1979). Homosexual identity formation: A theoretical model. *Journal of Homosexuality,* 4(3):219-235.

Chan, C. S. (1989). Issues of identity development among Asian-American lesbians and gay men. *Journal of Counseling and Development,* 68(September/October):16-20.

Comas-Díaz, L. (1985). Culturally relevant issues and treatment implications for Hispanics. In D. R. Koslow and E. Salett (eds.). *Crossing cultures in mental health,* (pp. 31-48). Washington, DC: SIETAR International.

DeVos, G. A. (1993). A psychocultural approach to ethnic interaction in contemporary research. In M. E. Bernal and G. P. Knight (eds.). *Ethnic Identity: Formation and Transmission Among Hispanics and Other Minorities,* (pp. 235-268). Albany: State University of New York Press.

Diaz, R. M. (1995). HIV risk in Latino gay/bisexual men: A review of behavioral research. Unpublished manuscript, commissioned by the National Latino/a Lesbian and Gay Organization (LLEGO), San Francisco, CA.

Diaz, R. M. (in press). Latino gay men and the psycho-cultural barriers to AIDS prevention. In Gagnon, Nardi and Levine (eds.). *A Plague of Our Own: The Impact of the HIV Epidemic on Gay Men and Lesbians.* Chicago: University of Chicago Press.

Diaz, R. M., Morales, E., Dilán, E., and Rodriguez, R. A. (in preparation). Demographic, developmental, and psychosocial correlates of risky sexual behavior among Latino gay men in San Francisco.

Espín, O. M. (1987). Issues of identity in the psychology of Latina lesbians. In Boston Lesbians Psychologies Collective (eds.). *Lesbian psychologies*, (pp. 35-51). Urbana: University of Illinois Press.

Espín, O. (1994). Crossing borders and boundaries: The life narratives of immigrant lesbians. Symposium at the annual convention of the American Psychological Association, Los Angeles, CA.

Falicov, C. J. (1982). Mexican families. In M. McGoldrick, J. K. Pearce, and J. Giordano (eds.). *Ethnicity and Family Therapy*, (pp. 134-163). New York: The Guilford Press.

Helms, J. (ed.). (1993). *Black and White Racial Identity: Theory, Research, and Practice.* New York: Greenwood Press.

Icard, L. (1986). Black gay men and conflicting social identities: Sexual orientation versus racial identity. In J. Gripton and M. Valentich (eds.). [Special issue of the *Journal of Social Work and Human Sexuality,* 4(1/2)] *Social Work Practice in Sexual Problems,* (pp. 83-93). New York: The Haworth Press.

Keefe, S. E. and Padilla, A. M. (1987). *Chicano Ethnicity.* Albuquerque: University of New Mexico Press.

Knight, G. P., Bernal, M. E., Garza, C. A., and Cota, M. K. (1993). A social cognitive model of the development of ethnic identity and ethnically-based behaviors. In M. E. Bernal and G. P. Knight (eds.). *Ethnic Identity: Formation and Transmission Among Hispanics and Other Minorities,* (pp. 213-234). Albany: State University of New York Press.

Loiacano, D. K. (1989). Gay identity issues among Black Americans: Racism, homophobia, and the need for validation. *Journal of Counseling and Development,* 68(September/October):21-25.

Marín, G. (1989). AIDS prevention among Hispanics: Needs, risk behaviors, and cultural values. *Public Health Report,* 104, 411-415.

Morales, E. S. (1990a). Ethnic minority families and minority gays and lesbians. In F. W. Bozett and M. B. Sussman (eds.). *Homosexuality and Family Relations,* (pp. 217-239). New York: The Haworth Press.

Morales, E. S. (1990b). HIV infection and Hispanic gay and bisexual men. *Hispanic Journal of Behavioral Sciences,* 12 (2):212-222.

Morales, E. S. (1992). Counseling Latino gays and Latina lesbians. In S. H. Dworkin and F. J. Gutierrez (eds.). *Counseling Gay Men and Lesbians: Journey to the End of the Rainbow,* (pp. 125-139). Alexandria, VA: American Counseling Association.

National Task Force on AIDS Prevention (1993). *The 1991 southern states AIDS education survey: A Knowledge, attitudes and behavior study of African-American, Latino, and White men. Final Report,* San Francisco: NTFAP.

Oetting, E. R. and Beauvais, F. (1991). Orthogonal cultural identification theory: The cultural identification of minority adolescents. *International Journal of Addictions,* 25 (5A and 6A): 655-685.

Parés-Avila, J. A. and Montano-López, R. M. (1994). Issues in the psychosocial care of Latino gay men with HIV infection. In S. A. Cadwell, R. A. Burham, and M. Forstein (eds.). *Therapists on the Front Line: Psychotherapy with Gay Men in the Age of AIDS*, (pp. 339-362). Washington, DC: American Psychiatric Press.

Parham, T. (1989). Cycles of psychological nigrescence. *The Counseling Psychologist*, 17(2):187-226.

Phinney, J. S. (1993). A three-stage model of ethnic identity development in adolescence. In M. E. Bernal and G. P. Knight (eds.). *Ethnic Identity: Formation and Transmission Among Hispanics and Other Minorities,* (pp. 61-79). Albany: State University of New York Press.

Rodriguez, R. A. (1989). Significant events in gay identity development: Gay men in Utah. Unpublished master's thesis, University of Utah, Salt Lake City, Utah.

Rodriguez, R. A. (1991). A qualitative study of identity development in gay Chicano men. Unpublished doctoral dissertation, University of Utah, Salt Lake City, Utah.

Root, M. P. P. (1990). Resolving "other" status: Identity development of biracial individuals. In L. S. Brown and M. P. P. Root (eds.). *Diversity and Complexity in Feminist Therapy,* (pp. 185-205). New York: The Haworth Press.

Troiden, R. R. (1984). Self, self-concept, identity, and homosexual identity: Constructs in need of definition and differentiation. *Journal of Homosexuality*, 10(3/4):97-109.

Troiden, R. R. (1989). The formation of homosexual identities. *Journal of Homosexuality*, 17(1/2):43-73.

Warren C. (1974). *Identity and Community in the Gay World.* New York: John Wiley and Sons.

Wooden, W. S., Kawasaki, H., and Mayeda, R. (1983). Lifestyles and identity maintenance among gay Japanese-American males. *Alternative Lifestyles*, 5:236-243.

Chapter 8

Working with Parents
of Gay and Lesbian Children

Loris L. Wells-Lurie

This chapter is a composite of my own 22 years of experience raising a gay son and lesbian daughter. In anticipation of writing a chapter on this topic, I sent letters to my children's gay and lesbian friends and solicited input from parent members of two local PFLAG (Parents and Friends of Lesbians and Gays) groups. In my letters I asked for input from gay men and women about the actions of their parents, and requested that they specifically address what they wish they or their parents had done differently during the disclosure process. From parents, I asked how the experience of having a gay or lesbian child has been for them. Several of those who responded said they wished the public could understand that there is much more to being gay than just the sexual aspect of their lives. This chapter is written for both parents of gay or lesbian children and the healthcare professionals who may find themselves working with parents. Through much of this chapter, gay is used to refer to both gay men and lesbians.

SO, YOU HAVE A GAY OR LESBIAN CHILD

It is said that the most homophobic people are those who have never known or allowed themselves to know a homosexual. My first contact with gays was when my Psychology 101 professor at college brought in a group of people to talk with the class about how being gay was for them. They seemed like reasonable, stable people.

What stayed with me from that class was the advice the group said they would give to any young person: "If you're gay, be the best gay person you can be." Little did I know that I'd be giving that advice to two of my children.

Parenting is a difficult process at best, but parenting gay or lesbian children comes with additional challenges that are not necessarily there with heterosexual children. As parents of a gay child you suddenly become part of what is considered by many to be an undesirable group. You are also confronted with a lifestyle that you probably had little education about or experience with. In many respects, what the parent experiences is parallel to that of the gay child in that there are so many different feelings, fear being a common one. This is compounded by feelings of helplessness and hopelessness about this new dimension of your life that as a parent you are suddenly thrown into. In my experience, when gay children come out of the closet their parents go into the closet, practicing selective disclosure about who they tell and how much. Ultimately, however, the goal for many parents becomes one similar to that of their child: acceptance and assimilation.

Coming out as gay or lesbian is something that can occur at any age. Many gay men and women choose not to share their sexual identity with their parents at all. Often such persons feel that disclosure puts them at risk for a loss of love from others, particularly family members. Naturally, this takes a great deal of energy. It is not emotionally healthy pretending to be who you are not, and failing to disclose this information to one's parents creates a barrier between children and parents. Parents generally hope for some degree of open communication between their children and themselves, and with the secret of nondisclosure this is not possible. My own gay son, for example, tells me how much he appreciates the fact that he can talk with me about anything, especially aspects of being gay.

The reaction of parents to their children being gay is more important for younger men and women because there tends to be a greater need for parental approval in general. Older men and women are more likely to be financially secure and less dependent on family for a variety of needs. Older gay men and women are also more likely to be more desensitized to the reactions of others to their disclosure of identity. It is also not uncommon for many older gays and lesbians to feel a need to "protect" their elderly parents from this information.

Coming out as gay or lesbian to a parent can feel like a catch-22. The love of parents is extremely important, and many wonder what consequence there will be in telling the family about one's sexual orientation. Most gay men and women know either by experience or anecdotally of parents who have withheld money for college, general financial support, or even disowned their children upon learning that their child is homosexual. This awareness is with them as they consider whether to come out to parents or not. Many gay children have a greater difficulty coming out to their parents if jokes or snide remarks about homosexuals have been common in the family. Further, most parents do not know what it means to be gay, and finding out this information is something most parents are not prepared for.

Compounding the matter is the fact that many of today's parents grew up in an era where homosexuality was classified as a mental disorder. It was not until 1973 that the American Psychiatric Association decided to remove homosexuality from its official list of mental diseases. General understanding about this has been slow, and by no means is there general recognition that homosexuality is not a psychiatric illness.

Often parents find out their child is gay by other means or through other sources than from the child him/herself. One parent disclosed finding a size 12 high-heeled shoe in the garage when she was packing for a family move, only to find out later it belonged to her son. He would use the shoes when he dressed in drag. Another parent mentioned hearing a telephone message on her son's answering machine directing him to meet his friend at a gay bar in San Francisco. Yet another parent, in what has become an all-too-common scenario, was told her son was HIV positive before she even knew he was gay.

Self-identity is a major issue for all teenagers and young adults. Children frequently hear jokes about homosexuals, and television and movies typically portray gays and lesbians in unfavorable stereotypes. Rarely are there positive role models for gay children. Thus, developing and identifying what form self-image will take when growing up gay is a tremendous internal struggle. The struggle is compounded when the individual attempts to sort out personal taste from group conformity with regard to stereotypical looks and attitudes about being gay.

For example, during her high school years, when neither of us knew what was going on, my lesbian daughter's wardrobe was in a constant state of flux. There never seemed to be a "look" that pleased her. Later, when I went to Honolulu for her Masters of Social Work graduation, the clothing issue resurfaced. Have you ever tried to shop for shoes with a lesbian daughter? Finding the right kind of shoes to wear with her particular style of dress was an unending dilemma. With a tendency to reject traditionally feminine clothing, the next issue became what clothes to wear to an employment interview, pants or a skirt? For my gay son, however, any clothing with a feminine look is definitely out. Army boots are what he uses to make his statement in his Capitol-Hill world in Seattle.

Many parents live in a state of denial regarding their child's homosexuality. Gay men and lesbians I know have often said that they have tried talking with their parents, but that the parents just do not want to hear about it. Others report that their parents see it as a phase their child is going through. Though discussions about our children's sexuality can be difficult, it is not our role to explain away the fact that they are gay or lesbian. It is our responsibility, however, to listen to our children, and try to hear what it is they are trying to tell us. Too often, not listening to what our gay children have to say is nothing more than an attempt at trying to control them. Typically, when parents learn their child is gay, they ask either their child or themselves, "What did I do wrong?" Though theories abound, it does not really matter how their child "got that way."

As the parents of a gay son or daughter, you never really know how people will treat you once they learn you have a gay child. Many families have felt torn loyalties because one or more members do not accept the homosexuality of a family member. Older generations, in particular, may have a more difficult time understanding and accepting the disclosure given old-fashioned views about homosexuality. When I asked my father if he would like to visit me in San Francisco, his reply was, "I don't think I'd like to be around all those homos," even though he is fully aware that he has a gay grandson and lesbian granddaughter.

Friends, too, can surprise you. Although my friends tell me how accepting they are of homosexuality, I sometimes hear snide comments or innuendoes from them about gays. One never knows what coworkers' views are on the matter, again making it difficult to openly discuss your child's life. Be it with friends, coworkers, or even within families, it is not uncommon for parents of gay children to report that people never even mention the gay child to them. This leaves the parent feeling as if the child has died so far as others are concerned.

When the parents of a gay son or lesbian daughter find themselves discussing their feelings with a psychotherapist they often find that there is an attempt on the part of the therapist to overemphasize the *normality* of homosexuality. This is clearly an important goal, and below I address the ways in which parents can be educated about homosexuality. Yet, I would like to offer caution in this area. Though parents clearly need to have the realities of homosexuality normalized, they also need and require validation of their own feelings. In reality, some of the initial feeling of parents will include anger, resentment, and, at times, disgust. I strongly encourage helping professionals working with parents to find a balance between educating about homosexuality, and allowing for the expression of the full range of their feelings.

REGIONAL, CULTURAL, AND RELIGIOUS DIFFERENCES

Particular geographic areas of the United States are more homophobic than others. One only needs to watch the news and the political arena to gain an awareness of the particularly homophobic areas. For example, the recent video documentaries on homosexuality that come out of the Colorado Springs antigay rallies do little to encourage a feeling of safety for gays and lesbians. Because of this, many gay men and women choose to leave the communities in which they were raised in order to seek safety and a peer group in larger cities. This means that their parents may rarely see them or know even less about their lives.

Certain ethnic cultures are also more homophobic or less tolerant of gay identity than are others. At a San Francisco PFLAG meeting, a Latino mother of a gay man who is HIV positive made the statement that it is unusual to find a Latino father who can accept that his son or daughter is gay. At the same meeting, however, a Latino man reminded her that he is an accepting father of a gay son. Though her reply to him was that he was a rare exception, it points out that cultural differences can affect the disclosure process in ways that may be unfamiliar to those of us outside these groups. I have even heard parents of different cultures express hurt that their children did not come out to them sooner, given their cultural emphasis on family trust and support. I encourage health care professionals to be sensitive to cultural factors when working with families of gays and lesbians.

Perhaps a "culture" unto themselves are the right wing (typically Christian) fundamentalists. Most have an opinionated, unkind, hostile, and unapproachable stance on homosexuality that leaves little room for change. It has been this group who has made the term, *sexual preference* popular, with the thought being that if you can see homosexuality as a choice, then you can blame those who make this decision of how to live their lives. My son once said to me, "If it was a choice, few people would choose it since it is fraught with so many difficulties."

My experience is that fundamentalist parents who come to PFLAG meetings find themselves in a real bind. Often, their churches make them feel guilty and at fault for having a gay child. At a time when parents need the love and support of their church the most, many find themselves ostracized. This is when the assistance of a mental health professional can be of particular importance and value, as well as the support offered through groups such as PFLAG.

Coming out in families that have firm and rigid views regarding homosexuality (even though the biblical scripture that is often cited as condemning homosexuality is a matter of interpretation) presents added challenges, and often produces an inordinate amount of guilt for the gay or lesbian child. Many religious parents, upon learning their child is gay, will attempt to "fix" the child by seeking the services of clergy, psychiatrists, or groups that offer a remedy for change. Trying to change another's sexuality is not tackled lightly, and the consequences to the self-image and well-being of the individual are often tremendous. Most often it is unsuccessful, serving to confuse the gay person further, and results in parental disappointment with the child.

One tragic consequence of "change therapy" is that many of the people seeking change often end up either attempting or successfully committing suicide. The topic of suicide is a frequent one at PFLAG meetings, as too many gay and lesbian youth resort to suicide in their struggle. This is one reason why unconditional love and acceptance of our gay children is so important. If you have a child who is gay or lesbian, then pay particular attention to feelings of depression they may experience. Suicide is often the result of depression.

EDUCATING PARENTS

> Man is disturbed not by things but by the view he takes of them.
>
> Epictetus (60 AD)

Parents who learn their son or daughter is gay will have many questions. These will be questions about themselves, their child, society, the origins of homosexuality, etc. Let me make it clear: the problem is not with our gay children. The problem is with our misinformed society and homophobic culture. Ignorance is the real enemy. In light of this, I have found it useful to provide parents with a historical overview of homosexuality. This gives the issue a broader meaning, and it helps provide parents with a perspective of homosexuality that transcends their immediate focus.

The most valuable help with regard to understanding gay culture has been its history and how homophobia has its origins here in the United States. Many cultures in the world view homosexuality as normal. My experience is that American culture is not in the mainstream of current thinking about homosexuality. Cultural anthropologist, George P. Murdock, for example, studied 193 different cultures and found that 14 percent rejected male homosexuality and 28 percent accepted it. In 58 percent of the cultures Murdock studied, homosexuality was accepted under some circumstances and it was rejected under other circumstances. Of 225 American Indian tribes, 53 percent accept male homosexuality and 24 percent completely reject it.

A number of ancient cultures accepted homosexuality. The Greeks, for example, looked upon homosexual behavior as permissible and even desirable under certain circumstances. Plato's *Symposium* praised the virtues of male homosexuality and suggested that pairs of homosexual lovers would make the best soldiers. Many of the Greek mythological Gods and heroes, such as Zeus, Hercules, Poseidon, and Achilles, were linked with homosexual behavior. Most Greek men married, but homosexual activity was not seen as shameful or sinful in the eyes of the Greeks.

In the early days of the Roman Empire, homosexuality was unregulated by law, and homosexual behavior was common. Marriage between two men or between two females was legal and accepted among the upper classes. Several emperors, including Nero, reportedly were married to men. Many cultures currently hold this attitude, including groups in the near East and Africa (Rubin and Kirkendall, 1968).

Native Americans have traditionally had a role in their society for the group of persons we call *homosexual.* For example, the Navajo Indians recognized three distinct categories of sex and gender: male, female, and nadle. They provided females called *nadles* a high degree of autonomy, along with kinship and residence patterns that allowed for same-sex communal activities. They gave nadles an elevated political and social status role. Because nadles were in a position distinct from either sex, they had greater opportunity for personal and material gain than did other individuals.

The term, *berdache* is derived from a Persian word meaning *kept boy* or *male prostitute.* French explorers used the term to designate "passive" partners in homosexual relationships between Native American males. The *berdache* have been defined as a person of one sex who assumes the gender role of the opposite sex. A *berdache* could be also involved in cross-dressing. Prior to 1900, cross-dressing was prevalent in America; however, because the Caucasian attitude toward this was one of repugnance and condemnation, the *berdache* had to live repressed and disguised lives. Eventually, with the influence of European Christian values, Native American initiation ceremonies regarding gender roles were no longer being performed.

In the mid-1930s, George Devereux, a Freudian anthropologist, completed several studies on sexuality and berdache roles in the Mojave society of the American southwest. He focused on homosexual and lesbian cross-dressers called *alyha* (male) and *hwame* (female). During the period when children were initiated into their gender roles, usually around ten to twelve years of age, cross-gender behavior emerged. (Cross-dressing typically refers to male or female transvestitism. Cross-gender behavior refers to the assumption of the role of the other sex.) A boy wore female clothing and associated with girls. Similarly, a girl behaved as male, refusing to perform typically female tasks.

Cross-gender Mojave individuals were often shamans or married to shamans or chiefs. This suggests cultural acceptance as well as an association with status and prestige. Because they were able to combine elements of both masculine and feminine economic spheres, their productivity was high.

Instead of condemning differences in their people, the Mojave and other tribes (i.e., the Blackfeet Confederacy of Canada) gave particular honor to those they referred to as *alyha, hwame,* and *manly hearted.* Their place of honor came from their ability to achieve the characteristics and roles of femininity and masculinity in their respective cultures.

HOMOSEXUALITY AND CHRISTIANITY

Most Christians would probably say that the condemnation and persecution of homosexuality, based on Christian theology, is long-standing, with origins going as far back as the first centuries A.D. Boswell (1980), however, in his book, *Christianity, Social Tolerance, and Homosexuality* argues that for many centuries Catholic Europe showed no hostility toward homosexuality. Space does not permit me to elaborate on the extensive research of Boswell; however, I strongly encourage professionals and parents alike, who may find themselves trying to reconcile an understanding of homosexuality in light of religious belief, to read Boswell's text for a historical and insightful perspective on this issue. For example, Boswell writes the following:

> Between the beginning of the Christian era and the end of the Middle Ages, European attitudes toward a number of minorities underwent profound transformations. Many groups passed from constituting undistinguished parts of the mainstream of society to comprising segregated, despised, and sometimes severely oppressed fringe groups. (p. 3)

Boswell (1980) notes particularly that the writings of Saints Augustine and Thomas Aquinas were highly influential on Church views of homosexuality. Both said that any sexual acts that could not lead to conception were unnatural and, therefore, sinful. Saint Thomas, for example, believed that semen and its ejaculation were intended, by nature, to produce children, and that any other use of it was contrary to nature's (i.e., God's) plan. Augustine's disgust for nonprocreative sex acts was so great that he not only forbade them for married persons, but suggested that married men seek the services of a prostitute (who, Boswell notes, Augustine saw as a "natural" and necessary part of life), if need be.

The Catholic Church assumed Augustine's and Aquinas' line of reasoning, and, subsequently, became a powerful force in the regulation and punishment of sexual behavior. Homosexuals were collectively classified with traitors and heretics. The outcome was such that some homosexuals were mildly rebuked and given prayer as penitence. Others were tortured or burned at the stake. Unfortunately, our ethnocentric philosophy of homosexuality in the United States stems directly from our adaptation of these European views.

PSYCHOLOGICAL AND MEDICAL PERSPECTIVES

Parents inevitably will ask if there is some *reason* for them to be blamed because they have a gay son or daughter. Popular notions about distant fathers and overly involved mothers immediately come to mind. Though it is more important to help parents focus on acceptance and to maintain a good relationship with their child, it can be beneficial to briefly educate them about current psychological and medical perspectives on homosexuality.

Psychological theories about the origins of homosexuality can be traced back to Freud. Freud believed that homosexuality was an outgrowth of an innate polysexual predisposition. Under ordinary circumstances, the psychological development of a child would proceed from polysexual to heterosexual. Unsuccessful resolution of the Oedipal complex could result in "developmental arrest," and the outcome is homosexuality. For his part, however, Freud wrote comparatively little about homosexuality. He thought that all people have latent homosexual tendencies, and consequently, he took a fairly neutral stance on the subject. In a note from Freud to the mother of a gay son, Freud wrote the following:

> Homosexuality is assuredly no advantage but it is nothing to be ashamed of, no vice, no degradation, it cannot be classified as an illness. Many highly respected individuals of ancient and modern times have been homosexuals, several of the greatest men among them Plato, Michelangelo, Leonardo da Vinci, etc. It is a great injustice to persecute homosexuality as a crime and cruelty, too. (Masters, Johnson, and Kolodny, 1986)

Current theories regarding homosexuality are varied, and run the gamut of prenatal factors, hormonal influences, behavioral conditioning, genetics, etc. Most health care professionals are increasingly of the opinion that there are genetic factors that account for homosexuality. A 1992 *Los Angeles Times* article, for example, titled, "More Differences Found in Gay and Heterosexual Brains" summarized research conducted through The University of California. Findings from the research indicated that homosexuality is not linked to any single brain structure, but rather to changes throughout the entire brain. Researcher Simon LeVay stated, "Something unusual is clearly happening when the brain is organizing itself in fetal life." Robert Bray, spokesman for the Gay and Lesbian Task Force in Washington, DC said, "This study supports our belief that nature created us just the way we are and that there is no reason to fix anything because nothing is broken. It supports our assertion that we are born this way." (*Los Angeles Times*, August 1, 1992).

CONCLUSION

I cannot emphasize enough the need for parents of gays and lesbians to get support for themselves. It can feel so isolating trying to understand and assimilate one's feelings and reactions upon finding out about their child's homosexuality. Though support can be found through a variety of avenues, I am a strong advocate of PFLAG (Parents and Friends of Lesbians and Gays), and encourage parents and professionals to familiarize themselves with the services of this national organization.

PFLAG is a national network of self-help groups, located in most major cities in the United States (see References section for address). The mission statement of the organization is to "promote the health and well-being of gay, lesbian and bisexual persons, their families and friends, through support, to cope with an adverse society . . . . PFLAG provides education, to enlighten an ill-informed public, and advocacy, to end discrimination and to secure equal civil rights. PFLAG provides opportunity for dialogue about sexual orientation, and acts to create a society that is healthy and respectful of human diversity."

PFLAG meetings, in existence since 1974, provide a safe and supportive space for parents who have just learned that they have a gay child. Parents come and tell about their family histories and share their feelings and experiences. Emotions of parents at the meetings vary, and I have seen parents who are very accepting, and some who are despondent and even suicidal. Each parent and family member integrates the disclosure of homosexuality by their child differently. To that end, PFLAG is open and supportive to most feelings that parents will experience. Again, isolation is too common with many of the parents I have known. PFLAG helps diminish this isolation.

In closing, let me acknowledge the role and impact of AIDS on the gay community. I cannot write with any experience with regard to parenting a child who is HIV positive. My observation of friends and parents is that many are in denial as to the severity of this disease. One young man who responded to my request for input on this chapter said that his mother thinks that being gay and getting AIDS are synonymous. My hope is that through more education we can dispel such myths.

Having gay children has given me the opportunity to meet some wonderful people, their parents, and their friends. I am able to be closer to a diverse group of people which probably would not have happened unless I had my own dear gay children.

REFERENCES

Boswell, J. (1980). *Christianity, Social Tolerance, and Homosexuality.* Illinois: The University of Chicago Press.

Masters, W., Johnson, V., and Kolodny, R. (1986). Historical Notes. *The American Journal of Psychiatry,* 107(10):786-787.

"More Differences Found in Gay and Heterosexual Brains." Los Angeles Times, August 1, 1992. Calif.

Rubin, I. and Kirkendall, L. (1968). *Sex in the Adolescent Years.* New York: Associated Press.

ORGANIZATIONS

Parents and Friends of Lesbians and Gays (PFLAG). P.O. Box 24565, Los Angeles, CA 90024.

Chapter 9

Integrating a Gay, Lesbian, or Bisexual Person's Religious and Spiritual Needs and Choices into Psychotherapy

Marcia Perlstein

O God, I cried, no dark disguise
Can e'er hereafter hide from me
Thy radiant identity!
Thou canst not move across the grass
But my quick eyes will see Thee pass,
Nor speak, however silently,
But my hushed voice will answer Thee.
I know the path that tells Thy way
Through the cool eve of every day;
God, I can push the grass apart
And lay my finger on Thy heart!

The world stands out on either side
No wider than the heart is wide;
Above the world is stretched the sky,
No higher than the soul is high.

from "Renascence"
by Edna St. Vincent Millay

This article is dedicated to Nyla, for the times we touch, soul to soul, and to the memory of Judy, who modeled a complex spirituality, and Carol who is putting the pieces back together. The author also acknowledges Chris and Ginni.

As my therapy practice of 28 years has evolved, so has my own relationship to spirituality and my ability to help clients look at aspects of religion and spirituality in their own lives. The clinical issues raised through these explorations are as complex and private to clients as are those of love, sex, or money. As with the general population, gay men and lesbians seek psychotherapy for a variety of reasons. In the course of working through presenting problems, relationships with family of origin are usually explored, both historically and in the present. Issues of religion and spirituality often come up in the context of how one was raised. When it does not, I note its omission as something that may have as much importance as its presence would. Further, at times of major illness or tragedy if the client expresses anomie, isolation, or other forms of rootlessness, I raise spirituality as an option for addressing the emptiness and confusion.

All clients come with emotional scars, hence the usefulness of psychotherapy in addressing the origin of these narcissistic injuries. Many clients come with social and cultural wounds as well. Lesbians and gay men have often suffered homophobic treatment, none more virulent than the prejudices imposed by social institutions. Organized religion, for example, has housed some of the worst offenses to the sensibilities and self-esteem of gay and lesbian youth (with consequences often carried into adulthood). It is my philosophy as a psychotherapist that I must first and foremost listen carefully to each person's unique "story," to their family and social history, and to aspects of their specific relationship to religious and spiritual matters, as it emerges in context. With homophobic, racist, or sexist injuries I must first validate clients' perceptions, helping them see themselves with others similarly treated. This validation forms the foundation of our work on each person's individual responses to their options and decisions, to areas in themselves they want to develop, and to the personal learning available to themselves along with the pain.

Religion, when it meets its purposes, provides the same comforts for lesbians and gays that it does for heterosexual men and women: a sense of something greater than self or other human beings, a sense of community, answers to some universal questions, moral guidance, etc. When these needs are undermined or compromised, for anyone, it can be extremely painful. When these needs are met for lesbians and gay men, because of homophobia, a special set of betrayals and conflicts develops. In response, some choose to hide within the mainstream of their church, not letting anyone know that they are gay, some decide to fight homophobia overtly, some join alternative sects within, and some create new forms for worship and spirituality.

These struggles, decisions, and questions are sometimes a central part of someone's psychotherapy, sometimes a subset of a larger issue (such as nature of contact with family of origin), sometimes a foundation for other explorations (when someone has made conscious decisions about these questions prior to beginning psychotherapy), or occasionally, a new area for focus and consideration.

In this chapter, I present seven categories relevant to the subject of religion and spirituality in relation to gay/lesbian clients with whom I have worked. Case vignettes and discussion of the clinical issues will be used to help me accentuate my points.

SIX CATEGORIES
IN WHICH CLIENTS OFTEN BELONG

Closeted Mainstream

Jordan (as with all vignettes, names are changed to protect client identity), a 55-year-old college administrator, has quietly come out to his parents, who live in a small town in Texas. He has been with his lover for 31 years. His parents have gradually grown to accept his sexual orientation and lifestyle on some level, yet insist it remain hidden from their large family, church, and the people of the town where they live. Jordan is comfortable with their choice, feeling that they would have to fight homophobia, a fight which he feels is his and understands is not their choice. He participates, with his lover, in a mainstream church in the northern California city where he lives, not offering information about their relationship but honestly answering any questions asked. He feels that his lifestyle is common knowledge. Occasionally, he experiences discomfort in selected Bible readings or portions of some sermons, but indicates that it is no more than in other institutions of which he is part in the community where he lives. He says the benefits he receives from his religious affiliation far outweigh the drawbacks. Thus, he rarely raised the subject of his church life in therapy.

The clinical task in Jordan's case was to be to help him revisit his decisions about family of origin, their relation to him, his feelings about their choices, and an examination of his own choices in his current community vis-à-vis family and religion. The clinical challenge is to encourage a revisiting of areas Jordan may have closed off in order to clarify that current decisions are made from strength and choices rather than from fear or the belief that he does not have a choice. Proceeding slowly and respectfully was one of my goals.

Jordan was eventually able to see that while he might understand his parents' behavior, he had feelings about it and that it is alright to have feelings that he chooses not to act upon. He eventually welcomed reviewing his attitude toward his church so that he could experience himself as "rechoosing" to be part of that church in his current life rather than remaining because of inertia. His current connection with his church is both more energetic and peaceful. Just as on his job, Jordan views with open eyes the compromises that he feels he must make in order to remain part of the various institutions to which he belongs. At the same time, he has no illusions about what he gets from his religious experience and what he wishes were different. He feels more at peace with himself as he explores these choices with greater clarity.

Person Comes Out in Church or Synagogue of Origin and Joins Gay/Lesbian Religious Subgroup

Janet, a 35-year-old teacher, moved to California from a large city on the East Coast 15 years ago in order to pursue graduate studies. In her twenties she came out to her parents and relatives on the East Coast. Her parents went through a gradual process of acceptance to the point where they now work with other parents who are trying to understand their adult children's lesbian and gay lifestyles through active involvement in Parents and Friends of Lesbians and Gays (PFLAG). Janet continued attending the family synagogue when she returned East for Jewish holidays; however, when she tried joining the synagogue in the northern California community where she lived as an adult, she felt unaccepted and uncomfortable. In the mid-1980s she saw an announcement in a local lesbian weekly for a gay/lesbian seder with a group called *Sha'ar Zahav.* She attended and found that she knew a number of the other participants. She then attended a *shabbat* service sponsored by the same group. She felt that she really belonged. *Sha'ar Zahav* was a place where she could integrate her lifestyle with her religion in a way that involved an extended family. She also found religious practices emphasizing the essence and rituals of her religion in creatively revised versions.

The clinical issues for Janet were standard individuation and separation struggles with religious choices playing a role as a subset of those larger themes. Thus, she needed to find her own way as an adult to keep a connection to her very important roots and religion in a way that encouraged her to be more fully "herself." The process of coming out to her parents, educating them, and experiencing them as respectful allies enabled her to have a higher tolerance for nonacceptance. Thus, while she sought the solace of the religion in which she was raised, she found her own way as she grew in strength as an adult, separate from her parents, to an alternative form of this religion which more fully met her needs. In doing so, she revisited adolescence in her thirties, arriving at a more solid adult experience after going through a long process. In therapy, this included first hiding who she was from her parents, then gradually coming out, then trying to conform in the religious arena to win their approval, then dropping the need to win their approval, making choices for her adult life on her own terms (which included selection of a synagogue that fit) and, finally, getting closer to her parents as an adult. Janet's therapy is a wonderful example of revisiting older stages of life (in this case adolescence) and allowing a corrective, emotional experience to help her come to a stronger, happier, more integrated outcome. She was an active advocate in her own behalf, using therapy for reflection, interpretation, and encouragement. Janet was in touch with both her feelings and her simultaneous desire to actively explore options based on those finely tuned feelings and needs.

Person Joins Mainstream Religion as an Openly Gay or Lesbian Adult

Jack and John joined a Boston-area Unitarian Church because it had a lesbian minister and a large gay and lesbian congregation. Jack had been raised agnostically and John a Christian. Both had fairly good relationships with their families of origin. Jack had no pressure to follow any particular religious or nonreligious course. John's family, on the other hand, expected him to attend church. Jack, an extremely shy man, had moved to the Boston area two years before and had been steeped in his graduate studies in biochemistry leaving little time for developing new friendships with other gay men. Aside from John, he saw almost nobody and valued meeting other gays and lesbians. He thought the church might be a good place to begin forming a social network. He selected the Unitarians because he had a close heterosexual friend from the Chicago area where he had lived and worked who was a Protestant who had married a Jew and found the Unitarian fellowship most welcoming to them as an intermarried couple. The combination of knowledge of a positive and welcoming attitude among Unitarians, the lesbian minister, the fact that John missed some type of religious affiliation, and Jack needed social contact prompted them to attend.

This decision formed the basis for much work in Jack's therapy around combating the anomie, which had been his perception of the legacy of being raised in a home without religion, the strong desire for both spiritual roots and community, as well as support for developing skills in leaving the lab, picking up the telephone, and initiating social interaction. These were all subsets of the larger themes of assertion and broadening what to Jack felt like a constricted life. Additional issues included integrating his process in therapy into relationship with John. These included typical issues that arise when one member of a couple seeks therapy, while the other does not. John was an extremely supportive significant other, but did not have the same tools for introspection, interpretation, and experiencing feelings on deeper levels, which Jack was acquiring. However, he was open to have Jack serve as his "peer counselor" as John tried to grow and change in his own way alongside with his mate. All was not simple or smooth, yet the turmoil and hard work on both their parts strengthened each of them and the relationship.

Person Joins Gay/Lesbian Church

Forty-two-year-old Bill has been disowned by his family of origin who still live in the midwestern city where he was born. He came to San Francisco to, as he terms it, "be himself." Though he is out at work and maintains friendly relations with heterosexual colleagues, he spends all his social time in the gay community. He grew up attending his Lutheran church regularly and participated in many church-related activities throughout his childhood and teenage years. He joined Metropolitan Community Church (MCC) about six years ago and finds that it provides acceptance and a social as well as religious experience akin to that which he had growing up. He derives similar benefits and comforts from his family of choice as he once had in his family of origin. Every few years he "floats trial balloons" with his parents to see whether or not they are prepared to accept him. So far that has not been the case; however, several years ago, one brother brought his fiancee to San Francisco to meet Bill and they all currently maintain a warm relationship. In fact, after marrying they came for another visit and accompanied him to a Sunday morning service at MCC.

Bill's struggles with his family of origin and his desire to continue having religion in his life were an integral part of his therapeutic process. During the early stages of therapy, Bill expressed grief and anger over his parents' attitudes toward him. Because he did not want to lose all his childhood anchors, he initially tried the local mainstream version of his church at home. As he was still quite raw from the treatment he had received by his parents, he felt uncomfortable in that church, even in San Francisco. As he expressed these feelings, I asked him whether he had ever heard of MCC. He had and immediately said that the time was probably right for researching it as an option. The first time he went he felt he had "come home." He had found a place where he could get the benefits of a religious program without paying the price of not being able to be himself.

This vignette is an example in therapy of the client thinking aloud, moving himself in the direction he wanted to go, and allowing the therapist to present an option at the time he was most ready to explore it. As a clinical cautionary note, therapists should consider only making suggestions (never "shoulds") in such a way that the client feels room to explore or not explore the information provided.

Person Forms His or Her Own Relation to Higher Power

Many clients in the last decade have either come to therapy via the recovery movement (i.e., 12-step programs) or begin therapy and then are open to attending meetings of a relevant program for drug, alcohol, eating, or other addictions. Ranging from former or present members of churches or synagogues to agnostics or atheists, most of them develop a strong relationship with their own "higher power." Some relate to this being as God and simultaneously maintain or rekindle religious affiliations of some sort. Others form a spiritual connection ranging from a goddess figure to a less palpable but distinctly comforting presence that nurtures them and infuses their journey with meaning and morality. Some even substitute the term *goddess* for God in reciting the serenity prayer, saying: "Goddess, grant me the serenity to accept the things I cannot change, the courage to change the things I can, and the wisdom to know the difference." Others do not necessarily use a 12-step program for forming their own relationship with a spiritual being but feel that through self-study, reading, and the use of a variety of tools that they follow spiritual paths.

Joe is an activist for gay rights, AIDS research, and the dissemination of promising drugs for HIV-related conditions. His life is high profile and very high stress. Prior to coming to therapy he joined Alcoholics Anonymous (AA) seeking sobriety from his alcoholism. He found himself having a difficult time with the concept of a higher power, came to therapy with extreme distrust of helping professionals, yet felt he had nowhere else to turn.

The clinical tasks with Joe included helping him find a way to remain in AA while "taking what he wanted and leaving the rest." In therapy, I worked on helping him find ways to embrace his 12-step program at his own comfort level, and on not taking the concept of higher power too literally. He was in touch with a good deal of anger from being on the front lines of both gay and AIDS activism and needed help finding constructive uses for his anger without either turning it inward or acting out. In Joe's case, building on his love of nature and enjoyment of various wilderness activities, such as backpacking, river rafting, and hiking provided the key to both redirecting much angry energy and finding his own form of spirituality. He accepted the assignment of meditating and/or writing in his journal in a natural setting at least two times a week. He added another piece that was to take one weekend a month in nature where he was physically active, and could meditate and write in his journal, sometimes alone, sometimes with another person or with a small group. Joe grew to cherish the combination of active and peaceful moments in natural environments. He eventually reached for his journal instead of his wine glass. He balanced days on the picket line with time on hiking trails. He began reading daily meditations prior to writing position papers. He feared that his activism would lose its edge but found, instead, that he gained greater clarity and a more pure form of energy (with much of the frantic pace attenuated). Most important, he learned he could fight for the issues he cared about without the highly self-destructive price he had once paid. In an extremely moving moment, he revealed that while sitting at a waterfall on a recent hike he had found both his "very own higher power as well as a piece of his soul."

Joe's other issue in therapy that related to religion and spirituality was his struggle to accept his friends' decisions concerning religion, involving how they died as well as that of their significant others' and families' plans for memorial services. For a long time, rather than face his loss and grief squarely, in each instance of a lover's or close friend's death, he transferred unexplored feelings to critical attitudes about particular memorial church services, religious rituals such as last rites, and the presence of all manner of religious representatives at different friends' bedsides. As he found his own sacred moments, he discovered that he was more open to others making their own choices. At the time of this writing, he even disclosed that he had derived some solace from a Catholic service, finding himself responding in his own way, much to his own surprise, to the cadence of the Latin passages and the music.

Mary meditates on a daily basis and through finding "that quiet place within" has experienced moments of peace that she never thought possible before. She has been a lay volunteer for the last decade in a local AIDS project and finds moments over the years, where, as she puts it, "I realize why I'm on this earth." Through her relationships with the people she helps support through this epidemic, she has found a higher purpose to her own life.

Many years ago in therapy she responded to the concept of taking one small action as a first step to feeling less like a victim, less purposelessness in her own life. From that first small step, delivering meals to homebound persons with AIDS, she evolved a program for herself that has uplifted her spiritually and formed the cornerstone of her therapy program and other areas of growth. She has learned about empowerment, dignity, and caring; however, not all is rosy or simple for her. Yet even in grief and loss she is part of a community that has shared experiences that inform her own spirituality and makes inroads into her former feelings of isolation and despair. She has returned to therapy, after a long hiatus, and now is learning how to apply to herself some of the same gentleness and nurturance she offers others.

Person as Part of an Extended Family/Community Evolves a Spirituality and May Create Rituals Around Holidays and Important Events

Here are three examples of some attempts to create or join extended families and communities of a spiritual nature.

Fifty-five-year-old Rebecca came out in her forties. At the time, she was part of a large extended family that included four sets of heterosexual married couples, all with children, some of whom were her godchildren. She had spent the past 30 years with some combination of those families celebrating both secular and Jewish holidays. When Rebecca got together with her lover ten years ago, she tried to integrate her into that community with mixed results. Betty was not Jewish and did not feel comfortable either as a religious or sexual minority. In couples counseling, they experimented with different responses to the holidays from spending them alone, to having small family gatherings with Betty's family of origin, to having lesbian friends in, etc. They almost split up several times over the deeper issues raised by these conflicts including difficulty in accepting each other without trying to change each other and difficulty in negotiating differences. For the past three years, they have evolved a program that has enabled them to go from dreading the holidays to enjoying, as well as looking forward to them, from season to season. They have hosted lesbian gatherings alternating Hanukkah, Christmas, Easter, and Passover. These gatherings include women who are like extended family, and over the years Rebecca and Betty have created rituals that try to reflect the essence and meaning of each of the holidays, thereby making them meaningful to each. The women enjoy the diversity, learning about each others' religions as practiced in their families of origin, and the creative opportunities that come from applying these concepts to the persons they all have become today. In going through this process, they get to know each other in deeper and more meaningful ways, enabling their extended family to grow closer over the years. They all maintain, in addition to their chosen lesbian family, present-day relationships with their families of origin and even with other adult families including adult children, grandchildren, and nonadult children. Betty has grown somewhat more comfortable with Rebecca's heterosexual extended family and even attends some of their holiday rituals with Rebecca.

In terms of the therapy with this couple, both standard conflict resolution methods needed to be employed as well as strategies for promoting empathy. Emphasis was also required on helping each see how selected parts of childhood religious teachings (those that had brought particular comfort and meaning) could be integrated into the family they were trying to enlighten. I have found Marion Solomon's *Narcissism and Intimacy* extremely useful for this type of work. She often focuses on an individual member of a couple in the presence of the other when a narcissistic injury suffered in childhood is revisited in adulthood through a triggering event or interaction. When one member of a couple sees the pain of his or her partner, the partner is often able to empathize rather than act out or overpersonalize and, therefore, remain close in a richer, deeper way than before.

About six months after beginning long-term therapy, George began attending Buddhist meditation sittings with an alternative community built around Vipassana meditation. He found out about it from a friend who came out to him about being both gay and a practicing Buddhist. For George, the wonderful paradox of the Buddhist spiritual practice in which he participates, is that it is simultaneously a deeply private, yet comfortingly connected experience. He meditates side by side, in silence, with others who are similarly engaged in being totally present with themselves, mindful of themselves down to the finest physiological nuances. The larger Vipassana community meets in a country setting in northern California called *Spirit Rock*. It includes heterosexuals, gays, and lesbians. Several years ago, two teachers who had been active in the larger community for more than 20 years, a gay man and a lesbian, began offering semiannual meditation workshops for members of the gay and lesbian community. George attended several of the gay and lesbian workshops, as well as a Vipassana meditation retreat offered in the mountains of southern Washington, by the same team of teachers. He still attends his weekly meditations in the larger community at Spirit Rock, but finds these experiences to be even richer when he runs into, in his words, "members of the tribe" (other gays and lesbians) who are also part of the larger community.

George's therapeutic tasks work well in concert with his spiritual program. He is in a stressful business situation with his company having gone through three periods of downsizing in the last year alone. He works very hard and has difficulty stilling the anxiety and racing thoughts. In therapy, he is working out ways to reorder his priorities, sorting out his values, learning how to manage stress and slow down, accept the unknowns, and proceed proactively rather than reactively. In meditation, he is learning that he can sit still with the anxiety and come away from the experience psychically refueled and more able to face the shifting sands in his life.

Another type of community is that which Lucy found herself helping to create, based on the work of a therapist and teacher named Richard Olney. Mr. Olney traveled around the country beginning in the mid-1970s offering Self-Acceptance Training (SAT) workshops for both therapists and the general public that included the use of shamanic rituals and drumming, journeying and guided visualizations. Self-acceptance is important to all clients and takes on an added significance for gays and lesbians who have had homophobic experiences that represent a lack of acceptance from those who act out their prejudices. Participants expressed having spiritual experiences in reaching deep and peaceful places within themselves from SAT work as well as a special sense of connection with a being beyond themselves. Though the community included persons of all sexual orientation, part of the reason Lucy joined was because there was a large lesbian presence among the participants, often as high as one-quarter to one-third per workshop. She then formed special extended-family-type kinship relationships with many of those women outside the workshop. Lucy was able to continue one-to-one long-term therapy finding that her workshops with Richard Olney were a rich addition to her therapeutic process, offering new material as well as stimulating a more open look at older issues.

GENERAL THERAPEUTIC PRINCIPLES

As a therapist, I always try to work with the resources clients bring in as well as suggest avenues they might consider as an adjunct to either our one-to-one or couples work. The first client I ever saw in 1967, sent by his internist, presented with high anxiety, stress, and an ulcer. I suggested yoga as an adjunct to the work we were doing. On the one hand, I understand the pitfalls of making suggestions in a therapeutic context. Yet, on the other, I often feel that the therapy situation can become too precious and removed from the client's world. Thus, with careful framing and certain caveats when themes of alienation, isolation, rootlessness, and lack of moral rudder come up, in addition to exploring their genesis, depth, and parameters, I will often suggest consideration of specific options. The framework for the suggestion includes not taking the idea as a "should," but encouraging them to use the resource experimentally. We both focus carefully on their feelings as they try out these different possibilities. If a client comes back having been unable to try a suggestion, I never treat it as resistance. I am much more interested in the process, the meaning for the client. I want to know what did not work and why it did not, and together we can either drop the idea or modify it based on taking into account what did not work. Afterward, the client can then choose to make a commitment to him- or herself in my presence either to try the new plan or better understand their feelings on another level. I am quite careful to squarely place myself in the role of supportive witness rather than authority figure with whom the client needs to engage in a power struggle.

A THERAPIST'S SPIRITUALITY

Therapists, themselves, often participate in a religious or spiritual program. As with other private matters, this does not necessarily come up in the client's therapy; however, there are some instances where praying or meditating in the same venue as the therapist may lead the client to seek therapy with this therapist she or he has met in a such a setting. Also, in small communities, a client may hear of her or his therapist's spiritual practice and decide to try it. This is not unlike running into current or potential clients in social settings in the gay and lesbian community if the therapist is homosexual. In both instances, the clinical issues are similar. The client needs to explore her or his own preferences, as well as its meaning within the context of his or her background. If the therapist's presence in a setting outside the office poses problems for the client, then this needs to be verbalized and understood in the context of the client's clinical process. Reactions both on the part of the client and the therapist can be utilized as "grist for the therapy mill." In some instances either the therapist or client may choose not to participate in the same program at the same time.

Additionally, depending upon the school of therapy practiced by the therapist, he or she may elect, at the outset, to refer a client who comes from the same small religious or spiritual community. Other therapists may find that common spiritual experiences may enrich the clinical work. As long as both are making informed choices, keeping alert to meanings, pitfalls, and possibilities, these commonalities offer rich avenues for learning. In these types of situations, it is crucial during the therapy hour that both therapist and client remember whose hour it is and keep the focus on the client. Therapists who convey the sense of knowing that they, too, are "works in progress," with their own struggles and paths, model for their clients an important aspect of the rich possibilities in personal and spiritual exploration.

CONCLUSION

The soul appears when there is space.

from *Care of the Soul: A Guide for Cultivating Depth
and Sacredness in Everyday Life*
by Thomas Moore

The above quotation applies to helping clients slow down, allowing room for what emerges. The therapist can offer her or his clients a sense of spaciousness for their own breathing, feelings, and dreams to emerge.

For me, spirituality in a therapeutic context includes helping each client experience and believe in one's own sacredness through whatever means one requires. Moore considers a soulful moment one in which a person does not know or even try to know what happens next, but rather allows what follows next to unfold unfettered by perfectionism, a need to please others, or trying too hard. All these notions can be integrated into any therapy experience, regardless of therapeutic orientation. Options that clients may allow themselves to experience may range from participation in a mainstream or alternative church or temple to practices such as prayer, meditation, and even physical activities that promote peace and well being such as walking, jogging, yoga, tai chi, etc.

I also believe there is something sacred about the therapeutic relationship. To the extent that a person may come in and find deeper, quieter, and more thoughtful places within themselves is definitely part of the spiritual journey. Though we do not always think of one's spiritual journey in this way, this path also includes learning ways to connect with people or communities that reflect our values, accepting ourselves as well as others, developing perspective about injuries and disappointments (both real and imagined), learning to feel power, dignity, and respect for ourselves and others, working through and learning to let go of much past pain and grief, developing tools and strengths for reframing anxieties and challenges, and experiencing ourselves as part of something beyond ourselves.

Thus, through human connection, each individual, whether priest and parishioner, rabbi and congregant, teacher and student, significant other and significant other, friend and friend, and even therapist and client, connects with a level of feeling understood and inspired to the degree that each may feel the presence of an "other." Spirituality and religion, in whatever form the client chooses, can comfort grief and ultimately be a source of hope. As clients begin to appreciate sacred moments in therapy, they will be more likely to welcome these moments in other parts of their lives. The therapist, as well, will truly know why she or he is here at a particular moment in time, doing the work he or she has chosen.

REFERENCE

Solomon, M. (1992). *Narcissism and Intimacy.* New York: Norton and Company.

Chapter 10

Aging and Mental Health: Issues in the Gay and Lesbian Community

Miriam Ehrenberg

Many gays and lesbians feel that their needs as they age are no different from the needs of everyone else and that posing the question as to what mental health issues they face is heterosexist. Mental health professionals who have studied or worked with the gay and lesbian community are of several minds in this matter. Some accept the view that the mental health issues of gays and lesbians are the same as those of other aging men and women. Others see the mental health issues facing homosexuals as more troublesome. A greater number, however, feel that gays and lesbians are much better able to cope with the problems of aging than others.

The aging issue has been explored since the 1970s, and the results of the various studies conducted are contradictory. Before looking at these studies, it is helpful first to review the problems that any person in the 60-plus category can expect to encounter, regardless of his or her sexual orientation.

GENERAL DEVELOPMENTAL ISSUES
FOR THE 60-PLUS GROUP

In this youth-oriented culture, aging, which used to connote wisdom and command reverence, has negative connotations, and the boundary defining *older* has dropped significantly. There is now a negative bias against the elderly (Kite and Johnson, 1988), and a loss of respect for older people. The elderly are considered "over the hill," and the stereotypic image is of a rigid, less interesting, confused, cranky person. Special labels, such as, *senior citizen* support this image, and the *golden years* have turned to dross for many.

What actually happens as people reach their sixties? Often they experience physical changes that bring about a decline in strength, health, and memory, making them feel more vulnerable. Medication for physical ailments can also cause irritation, confusion, and depression, and because these effects are frequently unrecognized, they make people feel even worse as they attribute these states to their own failings. Another problem encountered in aging is changes in appearance, with accompanying wrinkles, jowls, stooped posture, graying hair, or balding pate, all of which create a less socially desirable look. The media and medical profession advertise ways to hide age, whether through packaged products or surgical procedures.

Many people stop working in their sixties because of either voluntary or forced retirement, and cessation of employment can have negative ramifications. It usually means a drop in income and concomitant restriction of lifestyle. Retirement also is often accompanied by a loss of one's sense of importance as one moves out of center stage while others carry on with their own work. Disengagement from the world through deteriorated health or disability, loss of employment, lack of money, and so on all add up to a loss of stimulation that makes people less interesting to themselves and others. If one cannot get out of the house much because of frailty, or lack of funds for transportation, misses out on daily interactions with others, cannot afford a movie or magazine subscription, and is not faced with challenges such as work and relationships demand, dullness easily sets in.

Another problem for the 60-plus group is that of increasing social isolation. Curtailment of activity is not the only reason for isolation. It also comes about through the illness and death of one's contemporaries, narrowing one's social world, and also limiting the support networks that these friends and relatives provided. Research has demonstrated (Day, 1991) that such supports are crucial to adjustment. People with children may experience less isolation than others, as offspring tend not only to outlive the parents but provide avenues for broadening the social chain, through their marriages, partnerships, and grandchildren. Having a connection to younger generations also enables one to fulfill the developmental task that Erikson labeled "generativity" or an enabling connection to subsequent generations. As has been demonstrated, older people not only benefit psychologically from the assistance they receive from others but also from the assistance they can provide to others (Krause, Herzog, and Baker, 1992). Children, of course, can also be a source of further pain if they reject older parents and are unwilling to make themselves available emotionally or otherwise.

On top of current problems, unaddressed problems from the past become aggravated by the new strains of life. As one ages and faces the inevitability of death, it is natural to conduct a life review. Those who feel that life has been worthwhile and that they have done the best they could are able to make peace with themselves and retain a sense of what Erikson (1950, 1968) calls *integrity.* Those who find they have not used their lives productively start blaming themselves for a life misspent and succumb to despair.

These problems of aging can be turned against oneself resulting in loss of self-esteem. In sum, as the 60-plus have less stamina and less strength to cope, they find themselves facing more stressors. Those who can cope well are those who retain a sense of control and self-determination (Rodin and Langer, 1977). Although the elderly have many challenges with which to deal, the extent of the problems they face and their ability to deal effectively with these problems varies tremendously.

RESEARCH ON MENTAL HEALTH ISSUES FOR AGING GAYS AND LESBIANS

Findings on Gay Men

The negative image pertaining to the elderly, in general, becomes markedly more negative in the popular imagination when applied to gays and lesbians. Older gay men are frequently viewed as depressed, lonely, rejected by family, spurned by younger men, oversexed, and, thereby, also disgusting. Older lesbian women are also frequently viewed as lonely and family-less, but also as emotionally cold and physically unattractive. In the 1970s, motivated in good part by the desire to dispel the negative image of older homosexuals, research attention was directed specifically toward gay populations. It was felt that negative views of gay aging were bound to create greater difficulties for young homosexuals in developing a positive gay identity and would stand in the way of acceptance of one's sexuality and one's self.

An evaluation of the results of the research on homosexual aging is difficult primarily because of the samples used. The subjects for most of the studies were recruited through gay organizations and friendship networks and seldom included subjects who were as socially isolated as many elderly are. As Bell and Weinberg (1978) point out, the questionable representativeness of most homosexual samples greatly limits the generality of findings. Some of the studies consisted solely of white, middle-, and upper middle-class urban respondents who were, moreover, very involved in organized gay activities, itself a factor to be related to mental health status. The age of the subjects also varied from study to study. Subjects in some studies were classified as *older* if over 40, and such studies did not necessarily break down responses in terms of age group. The earlier studies focused on male homosexuals, and only more recent studies have examined aging issues as related to female homosexuals. Because of these limitations, the research findings in this area offer some insight into aging issues for gays and lesbians, but do not provide any clear answers.

Kelly (1977), in a pioneering study of 241 gay men between the ages of 16 and 79, concluded that the typical aging gay man does not fit into the popular stereotype of a socially isolated, fearful person who has lost his physical attractiveness and appeal to the younger men he craves. Rather, Kelly maintained that older gays found their lives quite satisfactory, including their sex lives, and that they desired contact with men of their own age. The results presented, however, do not totally support this conclusion. Kelly's subjects were not involved at the time of the study in any lasting gay liaisons. Further, although the number of persons in emotionally gratifying liaisons initially increased with age, after age 55 these partnerships decreased to almost none.

Kimmel (1978), in a study based on a sample of only 14 men over the age of 55, also drew positive conclusions, while recognizing that they were speculative and not based on solid data. Kimmel felt that the aging gay male has advantages over his heterosexual counterpart, including greater awareness of self-responsibility, no reliance on family, more "continuity of life" because of lack of interference by children, no limiting gender roles, experience in living alone, and the ability, therefore, to cope with this state, and the possession of a friendship network for social support and sexual companionship.

Berger (1982) interviewed 112 midwestern gay men between the ages of 41 to 77 by questionnaire and selected ten of these for an extensive interview. His data, however, are not always broken down by age. He found that the men in his study had excellent psychological adjustment and that the problems they experienced were generated by social factors, not by their own attitudes. Most were highly involved in the gay rights movement and manifested self-acceptance despite the homophobia they had experienced. His subjects saw no difference in aging for heterosexuals and homosexuals. The men in Berger's study were not lonely or isolated and felt that age brought them new freedom. They maintained their earlier level of sexual activity, although with fewer partners. Almost half, however, felt that younger gay men felt an aversion to them, and those who did not socialize with younger gays had the best adjustment.

A less formal study of 17 men over 60 was conducted by Vacha (1985). His subjects had experienced considerable harassment by families, the police, and the military, had found the need to deny their homosexuality early on, were frequent users of drugs and alcohol, had difficulty achieving long-term partnerships, and had a high incidence of physical illness. Many also were wary of the gay rights movement and favored conciliation rather than militancy. Vacha's subjects accepted themselves and their aging and seemed quite sure of themselves despite very difficult lives.

Based on a longitudinal study of 54 gay men over 50, Lee (1987, 1988) disputed the previously drawn conclusion that the difficulties endured by older gays helped them to cope as they age, and related adjustment in later years to their good fortune or skill in avoiding stressful events. He also reported a generation gap between younger and older gays, leading to "invisibility" of older men who cannot accept the "hardness" of young gay lifestyles and gay liberation politics and who also fear flaunting sexual preference. Lee's older subjects avoided labeling themselves as gay, and he found no relation between disclosure of sexual orientation and life satisfaction.

Following in this vein, Grube (1990) interviewed 35 gay men, ranging in age from 40 to 92, from which he identified two different gay communities. According to Grube, older gay men identify with a traditional gay culture that tried to accommodate to the prevailing heterosexual world. Their relationships are based on mentor/protégé pairs and they come into conflict with the new gay liberationists whose relationships are modeled on organized institutional lines.

Other investigators (Friend, 1980; Francher and Henkin, 1973; Weinberg, 1970) have also reported on samples of older gay men who they describe as psychologically well adjusted, adapting to the aging process, and self-accepting.

Findings on Lesbians

Research on the mental health issues among lesbians followed in the late 1970s and 1980s. The first account was provided by Meyer (1979) who studied 20 lesbians aged 50 to 73. She found five different responses to aging among her subjects, ranging from feeling fine about it to negativity. On the whole, she found her participants to be flexible, sexually alive, and not lonely or isolated. Almvig (1982) studied 74 lesbians over 50. Her study was weighted toward white, well-educated women who lived in urban settings. The study covered respondents' self-perceptions of their mental health, thoughts about aging, family relations, support systems, preparations for the future, and connections to the gay community. Most subjects felt they were mentally healthy and were generally positive about aging. They reported "great joy and satisfaction" in their lesbianism. Their fears were related to loss of physical or mental capacities and income. Many were involved in lesbian networks.

These positive findings were duplicated in a study by Kehoe (1986) focused on lesbians over 65. Her sample of 50 lesbians was similar to Almvig's, consisting of white, well-educated women of relatively high social and economic status. According to Kehoe, the typical lesbian over 65 is "a survivor, a balanced personality, coping with aging in a satisfactory manner." A more comprehensive survey by Bradford, Ryan, and Rothblum (1994) was conducted in 1984 and 1985, and derived information from 1,925 lesbians from all 50 states. Only 3 percent of the sample consisted of women 55 or older, but responses were broken down by age group. A primary mental health risk factor was physical and sexual abuse. Slightly over one-third of those 55 or older had ever experienced abuse. Present concerns revolved around money, job, and responsibility worries, and problems with lover and/or family. Of the mental health symptoms explored, the older age group seemed relatively impervious compared to their younger compatriots. Only 4 percent indicated current problems with depression, 1 percent with anxiety, and 60 percent reported they never thought about suicide. On the negative side, however, both tobacco and alcohol use were found to increase with age. Older lesbians used other drugs less frequently, except for tranquilizers.

In an attempt to relate mental health status to lesbian identity, Bradford, Ryan, and Rothblum (1994) assessed the degree to which the lesbian identity of the sample was known to others (family, heterosexual friends, coworkers). The lowest scores were achieved by lesbians 55 years or older, leaving the authors to conclude, "the less frequent involvement among older lesbians with the lesbian and gay community and decreased openness about their sexual orientation may lead to increased reliance on alcohol to mitigate the long-term effects of isolation, lack of adequate support, and compartmentalization of their identity" (p. 240). The authors, in this connection, do not comment on the relatively low rate of depression and anxiety in this older group.

Deevey (1990) conducted a survey of 78 lesbians over the age of 50 between 1986 and 1988. Here again, the sample consisted primarily of well-educated women, all but one of whom were white. According to Deevey, most of the older women reported "excellent mental health"; however, like Bradford, Ryan, and Rothblum (1994), Deevey also found high alcohol consumption as well as extra weight in the older group.

Other Research Findings

Rather than trying to demonstrate that gays and lesbians are better adjusted than nongays and nonlesbians, some researchers have tried to study the relationship between adjustment styles of being gay. This was first done for younger gays. Berger (1982) and Lee (1987) attempted to examine the relationship among older gays, both coming to different conclusions. Berger concluded that low disclosure of gay status leads to emotional problems, whereas Lee reported that greater self-concealment is correlated with greater life satisfaction.

Adelman (1990) attempted to relate styles of being gay with adjustment patterns among both older gays and older lesbians. The data were based on a sample of 27 homosexual men and 25 lesbian women living in the San Francisco Bay Area, all of whom were white, and the majority of whom had a comfortable standard of living. The mean ages were 65.63 years for gay men, and 64.48 for lesbians. Adelman found that adjustment to aging is related to satisfaction with being gay and the developmental sequence of early gay developmental events. The latter included low disclosure at work, low involvement with other gay people, plus early age of awareness of homosexual status, but a decrease in the importance of homosexuality in later years. Adelman suggests that these results reflect a generational rather than developmental pattern. The homosexuals who were in their sixties at the time the data were collected represent a pre-Stonewall group, and their life experiences with disclosure and its ramifications must be very different from those of future generations of the 60-plus group.

The general tenor of the various research studies on aging suggests a population of sturdy people who have weathered the stresses of homophobia and discrimination and emerged better able to cope than their heterosexual agemates. These conclusions reflect the mental health status of many white, affluent, physically fit gays and lesbians who constituted the majority of the samples used, but as Cruikshank (1992) notes, these participants are quite likely to be "the most robust specimens" of their group. There are undoubtedly many unhappy and lonely gay and lesbian seniors who have not come forward to talk about their lives. As Lee (1990) points out, trying to persuade these older gays and lesbians "that they have superior capacities for adapting to old age (such as "crisis competence") does a disservice . . . . Pollyanna mythology leaves the lonely homosexual senior asking, "What's wrong with me, if the research says all those other homosexuals are so cheerful in old age?" (p. xiv). As Erwin (1993) notes, studies continue to show significantly higher rates of suicide, depression, substance abuse as well as other indicators of psychological distress among lesbians and gays of all ages than among heterosexuals.

THEORETICAL CONSIDERATIONS

Returning to the developmental problems of the 60-plus population, in general, how can these be expected to impact on those gays and lesbians who are not white, affluent, well-educated, highly involved in the gay and lesbian community with a network of friends and, moreover, not particularly sturdy physically but, perhaps, in need of a caretaker?

Gays and lesbians who must depend on others for financial help or caretaking usually have no option but to turn to general community resources. The homosexual community cannot presently provide ongoing financial grants or homophilic institutional settings for the elderly. When gays and lesbians must rely on public resources they are very likely to encounter discrimination and hostility. Most problematic is dependency on institutional care. Homophobia is rampant in many institutional settings; not only is there general disregard and contempt for older persons at large, but this is apt to be intensified in the case of gays and lesbians who may, therefore, suffer from lack of attention and friendly input, if not outright neglect.

Further, institutions tend to have little patience for partners and friends of homosexuals, particularly gay men. The staff may disregard requests of such persons for information or changes in procedures, and may actively interfere with or prevent physical interactions between homosexual residents and their guests. Displays of physical affection between gays may be considered disgusting. Heterosexual patients as well as staff may shun and isolate the homosexual patient. If it should happen that two patients are drawn to each other and seek physical affection from one another, this is difficult for staff and other patients to tolerate. It has been demonstrated (Commons, 1992) that professionals have little acceptance of sexual behavior between any institutionalized patients, but are most condemning of homosexual acts.

Ailing and financially needy homosexuals, thus, are clearly at risk for feeling rejected, isolated, and therefore, easy prey to feelings of self-doubt. There are no data available for gay men in terms of income. It is apparent, however, that despite the many high-profile wealthy gay men, particularly in the arts and entertainment fields, there are many more financially marginal gay men in these fields who can barely eke out a living while in their youth and may become destitute as they age. Data on lesbians (Bradford and Ryan, 1987) suggest that they are five times as likely as other women to have money problems and that their income level is not commensurate with their education and experience.

Social isolation, according to most gay and lesbian research studies of older people, is not a problem, but the participants whose responses led to this conclusion were primarily people active in homosexual activities or organizations. What about those gays and lesbians without such connections or in communities where such connections are not possible, that is, those living in rural areas or in fundamentalist heartland territory? First, it is not clear that older people who have access to organized homosexual activities avail themselves of these opportunities or are welcome if they do so. Younger gays and lesbians, like their heterosexual counterparts, are not immune to ageism and are not necessarily welcoming to their older brothers and sisters.

Ray Schaffer (1973) described the hypocrisy of many gay liberationists in regard to the aged in his article, "Will you still love me when I'm 64?" While being active in the gay community may be an antidote to problems in accepting aging, the gay and lesbian community itself is not accepting of the aged. As both Lee (1987) and Grube (1990) point out, liberated homosexual communities are not willing to make room for the elderly. There is a dearth of older gays in leadership positions in gay institutions and their contributions to the gay liberation movement are not generally recognized or respected.

The generation gap in the homosexual community appears to have an effect on both general social acceptance and intimate personal relationships. The gap also impacts differentially on gays and lesbians. Social isolation seems to afflict older gays more than older lesbians, probably reflecting the different social roles of men and women. Women live longer than men and are more likely to have surviving age mates within their social circle. Women are also socialized to be caretakers and, therefore, lesbians are more likely than gays to find women who will be available as part of a support network. Homosexual men have been less rigid in adhering to stereotyped sex roles than heterosexual men are, and AIDS has propelled many into the caretaker role. The continuing erosion of sex roles will probably equalize issues of isolation for future generations of gays and lesbians as they age.

Finding partners is another issue for older homosexuals that seems to be experienced differently by lesbians and gays. Older lesbians tend to feel that younger lesbians do not want them as partners, but bias against older partners is particularly marked amongst gays. From an exhaustive review of the literature, Symons (1979) concluded that there is a strong tendency among men, whether homosexual or not, to prefer younger partners, a tendency not noted among lesbians. Steinman (1990) gathered data between 1983 and 1985 on 46 gay male couples with a gap in age of at least eight years. Even though these couples did not fit the stereotype of the "sugar daddy" who "keeps" a younger man (most of his younger subjects were not financially dependent on their partners), still the older partners were drawn by the sexual excitement offered by their younger partners and the latter were attracted to the generally greater economic resources of the older partners. The older partners generally wanted more sex than their younger partners, and Steinman believes that the "refusal" of sex is one way the younger partner can counterbalance the control over financial resources exercised by the older partner. The attraction of younger men because of their intrinsic qualities and the valuation of older partners for the extrinsic rewards they can provide is a far cry from the mentor/protégé relationship that Grube (1990) found to exist traditionally.

Devaluation of older gays in terms of their intrinsic qualities is abetted by the "accelerated aging" that appears to exist among male homosexuals. Kelly (1977, 1980) found a tendency for gays to perceive "old age" starting earlier than heterosexual males, namely at around 50. In contrast, a study by Minnigerode (1976) found no difference between homosexual and heterosexual males in their perception of when old age begins, which his subjects put at around 64 years of age even though they classified themselves as "middle aged" in this age bracket. Bennett and Thompson's study (1990) offered a resolution of these seemingly contradictory results; their sample of gay men thought that other gays believe "old age" starts at 54, and that these other gays also see them as older than they see themselves.

The search for younger partners among older gays is accompanied by a concern about appearance. Interestingly, the double standard of aging that applies to the population at large seems to be reversed for homosexuals. Gays seem more concerned about their appearance than lesbians. The latter are generally free from appearance concerns and free from heterosexist male standards and fantasies that affect their heterosexual sisters. Many lesbians wear no makeup, shun high heels, and do not worry about being overweight, while many gays are much more invested in keeping up their looks and youthful appearance. This phenomenon, however, may be undergoing a generational shift and may not be applicable to younger gays and lesbians as they age.

It is possible that the search for younger partners by older gays is, in part, a search for a surrogate son. The more traditional mentor/protégé relationship and the more contemporary version of older/younger partnering may be an expression of the need for generativity. Older men may look for a son in a sexualized relationship when they do not experience having a son any other way. Similarly, "sons" may be looking for the father acceptance they were denied.

Generativity and the search for connection to the younger generation is potentially more an issue among gays than lesbians. One study (Bradford and Ryan, 1987) indicates that one-third of the older lesbian population have children, whereas most older gays do not. Although the younger generations of homosexuals are tending to build families through adoption, artificial insemination, and other means, many (like the heterosexual youth of today) do not want children. This may become problematic for them when they age as the attempt to connect to younger people through gay and lesbian community activity does not seem a viable alternative for older gays and lesbians who frequently are not welcomed. The need for connection and continuity that runs strong in all people may remain unsatisfied among gays and lesbians, leading to feelings of emptiness and reinforcing the sense of isolation that comes with age.

Although Erikson and others have focused on relationships to future generations, the importance of connection to the past has been overlooked. Many gays and lesbians not only miss a sense of continuity with the future but are also discontinuous with the past. Families have tended to suppress the homosexual chapters of family history. Because gays and lesbians often feel they have not been created in the image of their parents, the closeting of other family homosexuals denies them an important link and a place in the family history, as well as role models.

A particular area of concern that seems to pose special mental health problems for lesbians and gays is coming to terms with one's life as one approaches the inevitability of death. The extra burden placed upon gays and lesbians in this area is their relationship to their own homosexuality. Obviously gays and lesbians may stay closeted as they grow older for the same reasons they remained so while younger, fear of alienating others, losing a job, etc., but to the extent that gays and lesbians stay closeted they may experience a sense of self-betrayal. This, in turn, makes it difficult to reconcile oneself to the end of life if one feels it has not been openly lived.

The data that exist suggest that older gays and lesbians have come out less than their younger peers, and then mostly to their homosexual friends, not to family. It has been hypothesized that disclosure would be related to better adjustment. Friend (1990), for example, has developed a theory of successful aging based on different styles of identity formation and disclosure. His "stereotypic" older homosexual has internalized negative homophobic messages and remains closeted; he or she has a poor relationship to self and others and experiences loneliness and despair. Those who Friend describes as "passing" older homosexuals marginally accept their homosexuality but distance themselves from anything lesbian or gay; these people have conditional self-acceptance and spend their energies in hiding. The "affirmative" older homosexuals reconstruct homosexuality into something positive and open and thereby gain self-empowerment.

Research, however, has not borne out a relationship between openness to others and life satisfaction. As already noted, Berger (1982) found that low disclosure leads to emotional problems, whereas Lee (1987) found low disclosure is related to greater life satisfaction. Adelman (1990), in a more detailed analysis, found that low disclosure at work as well as low involvement with other gays and lesbians are related to life satisfaction. Adelman also found that high disclosure to relatives is related to high self-criticism. Adjustment to aging, however, was also highly correlated to satisfaction with being gay, but also with a decreasing importance of homosexuality in later years. These somewhat contradictory results imply that fear of stigma and ejection, at least in the current generation of older homosexuals, seems to function more as an impediment to adjustment than does inability to live openly as a gay or lesbian person. Perhaps, as Adelman's findings suggest, older gays and lesbians deal with fear of disclosure by minimizing the importance of homosexuality as they age. Adelman also attributes the decreasing importance of homosexuality in later years to the decreasing importance of sex. Another alternative explanation is that homosexuality decreases in importance as the aging person increasingly defines her- or himself in terms beyond sexual orientation.

THE ROLE OF THERAPY

There is a widespread conception that older people cannot change and they, in turn, tend to underuse professional mental health services. Little data are available about utilization of therapy resources by the gay and lesbian community and by older gays and lesbians, in particular. The assumption is that homosexuals use such services less than do heterosexuals, relying more on friends for the help they need and avoiding therapists out of fear of homophobia. Bradford, Ryan, and Rothblum (1994) found, however, that three-fourths of their sample of lesbians reported having used professional mental health service, and a high incidence of use was also reported by Morgan (1992) and Morgan and Eliason (1992). Morgan also compared therapy use of heterosexual women and lesbians and found 77.5 percent of lesbians compared to only 28.9 percent of heterosexual women in therapy. Morgan and Eliason's lesbian subjects felt that the high use of therapy by lesbians resulted from the stress they experienced because of social oppression. Another motivation for therapy attributed to lesbians was that personal growth is a positive value within the lesbian community.

According to Bradford, Ryan, and Rothblum (1994), the most common reason reported for seeking therapy is feeling sad or depressed, followed by feeling anxious, and next, feeling lonely. Many lesbians also seek treatment because of problems in personal relationships, primarily with lovers, next with family, and then with friends. In addition to high use of professional services, lesbians also use supportive resources such as friends and women's groups (Bradford and Ryan, 1987; Kurdek and Schmidt, 1987). There are scant data, however, on usage of therapy resources by older lesbians. Although they may be more likely than their heterosexual age cohorts to use therapy services, it would seem they would be less likely than younger lesbians to do so. Bradford and Ryan found that the oldest age group in their sample (55 years of age and above) saw counselors less frequently than did women between 25 and 54 years of age, but slightly more frequently than women aged 17 to 24. Greater usage of therapy among younger lesbians, except for the 17- to 24-year group, probably indicates a greater acceptance of therapy because they have been reared in a culture of therapy, and thereby feel less stigmatized by it.

Another reason older lesbians may be less likely to utilize therapy is greater fear of homophobia and self-disclosure. Older lesbian therapists, as well as their potential clients, may be out to a much lesser extent than younger lesbian therapists, thereby limiting the choices older lesbians see available to them. As most older people generally do not want younger therapists, it is assumed this would be true of lesbians and they may not be able to locate appropriate therapy resources.

There is neither published data comparing lesbians to gays in their use of therapy, nor that for comparing homosexual men to heterosexual men. At the longest established gay and lesbian counseling and psychotherapy center in New York City, the Institute for Human Identity, those seeking therapy are primarily gays, who outnumber lesbian clients ten to two; a reversal of the ratio in the heterosexual population. It is not clear whether this is an idiosyncrasy at this particular psychotherapy center or a widespread trend, nor is it clear why this divergence exists. The Institute for Human Identity also reports that lesbians who come for treatment invariably request assignment to a woman therapist. Gay clients often request a gay man as therapist but some will request a woman or have no preference. The difference here would seem to relate to fears about sexism, which many lesbians feel is just as strong among gays as it is among heterosexual men.

Often, the main quality sought in a therapist by gays and lesbians is that the therapist is also homosexual. Clients feel that shared sexual orientation is important in ensuring that the therapist will have understanding and empathy about the issues facing them, and that a homosexual therapist will be accepting. Research from the 1970s indicated that clinicians were more likely to have negative attitudes and ascribe pathology to clients whom they believed to be gay or lesbian. Research in the 1980s showed some change in a positive direction, but not enough. Wisniewski and Toomey (1987), for example, found that one-third of the social workers in their study earned scores within the homophobic range on an Index of Attitudes Towards Homosexuals. The survey, conducted by the Committee on Lesbian and Gay Concerns of the American Psychological Association (1990), found that "adherence to a standard of unbiased practice with gay men and lesbians is variable. Respondents reported substantial numbers of negative incidents involving biased or inappropriate care for lesbians and gay men" (p. iv). A basic ingredient in providing productive therapy is that the therapist be able to actively affirm gay and lesbian lifestyles.

Unfortunately, homophobia does not only exist among heterosexual therapists but can burden homosexual therapists as well. Therefore, sexual orientation alone is not an adequate basis for selecting a therapist. In addition to the usual components of good training–grounding in psychotherapy theory, supervised clinical experience, the therapist's own course of therapy–specific education and training in working with gays and lesbians is important. To date, only one user-oriented book on psychotherapy has been published that deals specifically with guidelines for gays and lesbians on how to select a therapist and evaluate him or her (Ehrenberg and Ehrenberg, 1994). Very few graduate schools in the mental health professions offer courses on gay or lesbian issues. Buhrke (1989) reported that almost one-third of the female counseling psychology students in an APA-approved doctoral program stated that lesbian or gay issues were not discussed in any of their courses.

Murphy (1992) has proposed a curriculum for training mental health workers, which has three main components. The first is information about lesbian and gay issues, the second is sensitizing clinicians to the interplay between the gay or lesbian client's presenting problems and how these are affected by sexual orientation and living in a homophobic, heterosexist society, and the third is training the clinician to focus on the interaction between his or her sexual orientation and attitudes and those of the client.

Trippet (1994) interviewed lesbians who had been in therapy to explore changes needed in mental health care. Trippet's respondents felt that their mental health care providers did not know enough about women's or lesbian issues. They were also concerned about having supportive, nonhomophobic providers. Practical changes, such as lower fees, better insurance coverage, more lesbian and female therapists, and increased accessibility were also mentioned.

Clinicians have provided a wide range of suggestions on how to work with lesbian and gay clients, reflecting the current theoretical stances in vogue. These range from psychoanalytic (Bruno-Galanti, 1992) to humanistic encounters (Smith, 1992), from cognitive analysis of coping strategies (McDougall, 1993) to the use of pets (Kehoe, 1990).

PROSPECTS AND PROPOSALS

Most research on the mental health of older gays and lesbians has been based on relatively affluent, well-educated, and physically healthy respondents, and they have been found to be psychologically sturdy with good coping skills, and content with their lives, which include networks of supportive friends. We know very little about older gays and lesbians with limited financial resources, poor health, and few homosexual friends to whom to turn. It can only be assumed that their mental health status leaves much to be desired and this could be reflected in the relatively high rates of drug and alcohol use and suicide among gays and lesbians. The psychological resiliency of some older gays has been attributed to their affirmation of their homosexuality, and their openness about their sexual orientation. Research findings, however, do not necessarily lead to that conclusion. The data could be interpreted to indicate that education and affluence lead to a more satisfying life and make it possible for one to live according to one's own dictates rather than comply with social standards. Status and financial security also help one find and keep partners of choice.

Research indicates that older gay men gravitate toward younger, more physically attractive partners and are aided in their search if they command power and influence. Older gays and older lesbians have not usually found themselves welcomed by their younger compatriots, and tend to feel alienated. They may remain in the closet, in part, because they cannot identify with the more flamboyant and radical style of younger gays and lesbians, but they may also remain in the closet because they are not invited into the living room where their younger, supposed comrades are interacting.

What implications and applications can be drawn then? Several concepts emerge. Health care professionals are encouraged to share and discuss these concepts with their clients, as well as examine their own position on the topics.

1. It would be useful for gays and lesbians to give more attention to life issues within the gay and lesbian community as well as the struggle between it and the broader society. This is not only important for older homosexuals, but is important for younger gays and lesbians as well. If the gay and lesbian community is to be a genuine substitute for family, then it needs the role modeling and lessons of experience that older gays and lesbians can provide. A family stays alive and vibrant to the extent that it offers its older members the possibility of interacting with youth to give them a sense of generativity and continuity.
2. Older gays and lesbians might consider keeping a journal of their experiences to pass on to others. For those who feel isolated, it provides a way of feeling connected, and the journal

can be a valuable resource for younger homosexuals who need to hear from others about the different pathways life can follow. Such journals could be passed on from individual to individual, and perhaps, could some day become the nucleus of a library of homosexual life to which everyone could have recourse.

3. Mental health professionals have to reexamine their assumptions about aging, about disclosure, and about what makes for life satisfaction and stability. Individuals vary greatly in their circumstances and not everyone has the temperamental predisposition, the support system, or the financial security to place oneself in potential jeopardy. Openness with oneself is essentially more important than openness with what may be a hostile world.

4. Therapy with older gays and lesbians becomes more meaningful when it includes a life review that deals with both what has been done well and what may not have been accomplished. If not dealt with previously, then feelings about one's sexual orientation should be explored, and the older person should be encouraged to accept her or his homosexuality.

REFERENCES

Adelman, M. (1990). Stigma, gay lifestyles, and adjustment to aging: A study of later-life gay men and lesbians. *Journal of Homosexuality,* 4:7-32.

Almvig, C. (1982). *The Invisible Minority: Aging and Lesbianism.* New York: Utica College of Syracuse University.

Bell, A. P. and Weinberg, M. S. (1978). *Homosexualities.* New York: Simon and Schuster.

Bennett, K. C. and Thompson, N. L. (1990). Accelerated aging and male homosexuality: Australian evidence in a continuing debate. *Journal of Homosexuality,* 20:65-75.

Berger, R. M. (1982). *Gay and Gray: The Older Homosexual Man.* Boston: Alyson.

Bradford, J. B. and Ryan, C. (1987). *National Lesbian Health Care Survey: Mental Health Implications for Lesbians.* Maryland: National Institute of Mental Health.

Bradford, J. B., Ryan, C., and Rothblum, E. D. (1994). National lesbian health care survey: Implications for mental health care. *Journal of Consulting and Clinical Psychology,* 62:228-242.

Bruno-Galanti, C. (1992). Homosexual preoccupation in a gero-psychiatric client: A case for psychoanalytically oriented therapy. *Perspectives in Psychiatric Care,* 28:21-24.

Buhrke, R. A. (1989). Female student perspectives on training in lesbian and gay issues. *The Counseling Psychologist,* 17:629-636.

Committee on Lesbian and Gay Concerns. (1990). *Final Report of the Task Force on Bias in Psychotherapy with Lesbians and Gay Men.* Washington, DC: American Psychological Association.

Commons, M. L. (1992). Professionals' attitudes towards sex between institutionalized patients. *American Journal of Psychotherapy,* 46:571-580.

Cruikshank, M. (1990). Lavender and gray: A brief survey of lesbian and gay aging studies. *Journal of Homosexuality,* 20:77-87.

Day, A. T. (1991). *Remarkable Survivors: Insights into Successful Aging Among Women.* Washington, DC: Urban Press Institute.

Deevey, S. (1990). Older lesbian women: An invisible minority. *Journal of Gerontological Nursing,* 16:35-39.

Ehrenberg, O. and Ehrenberg, M. (1994). *The Psychotherapy Maze: A Consumer's Guide to Getting in and out of Therapy.* Northvale, NJ: Jason Aronson.

Erikson, E. (1950). *Childhood and Society.* New York: Norton.

Erikson, E. (1968). *Identity: Youth and Crisis.* New York: Norton.

Erwin, K. (1993). Interpreting the evidence: Competing paradigms and the emergence of lesbian and gay suicide as a social fact. *International Journal of Health Services,* 23:437-453.

Francher, S. J. and Henkin, J. (1973). The menopausal queen. *American Journal of Orthopsychiatry,* 43:670-674.

Friend, R. A. (1980). Gayging: Adjustment and the older gay male. *Alternative Lifestyles,* 3:231-248.

Friend, R. A. (1990). Older lesbian and gay people: A theory of successful aging. *Journal of Homosexuality,* 20:99-118.

Grube, J. (1990). Natives and settlers: An ethnographic note on early interaction of older homosexual men with younger gay liberationists. *Journal of Homosexuality,* 20:119-135.

Kehoe, M. (1986). Lesbians over 65: A triply invisible minority. *Journal of Homosexuality,* 12:139-152.

Kehoe, M. (1990). Loneliness in the aging homosexual: Is pet therapy an answer? *Journal of Homosexuality,* 20:137-142.

Kelly, J. (1977). The aging male homosexual: Myth and reality. *The Gerontologist,* 17:16-79.

Kelly, J. (1980). Homosexuality and Aging. In J. Marmor (ed.) *Homosexual Behavior: A Modern Reappraisal.* New York: Basic Books.

Kimmel, D. C. (1978). Adult development and aging: A gay perspective. *Journal of Social Issues,* 34:113-130.

Kite, M. E. and Johnson, B. T. (1988). Attitudes toward older and younger adults: A meta-analysis. *Psychology and Aging,* 233-244.

Krause, N., Herzog, A. R., and Baker, E. (1992). Providing support to others and well-being in later life. *Journal of Gerontology: Psychological Sciences*, 47:300-311.

Kurdek, L. A. and Schmidt, J. P. (1987). Perceived emotional support from family and friends in members of homosexual, married, and heterosexual cohabiting couples. *Journal of Homosexuality*, 14:57-68.

Lee, J. A. (1987). What can gay aging studies contribute to theories of aging? *Journal of Homosexuality*, 13:43-71.

Lee, J. A. (1987). Invisible lives of Canada's gray gays. In V. Marshall (ed.) *Aging in Canada*. (138-155). Toronto: Fithenry and Whiteside.

Lee, J. A. (1990). Foreword. *Journal of Homosexuality*, 20:xii-xix.

McDougall, G. H. (1993). *Clinical Gerontologist*, 14:45-57.

Meyer, M. (1979). The older lesbian. Unpublished master's thesis. Dominguez Hills, CA: California State University.

Minnigerode, F. A. (1976). Age-status labeling in homosexual men. *Journal of Homosexuality*, 1:273-276.

Morgan, K. S. (1992). Caucasian lesbians' use of psychotherapy: A matter of attitude? *Psychology of Women Quarterly*, 16:127-130.

Morgan, K. S. and Eliason, M. J. (1992). The role of therapy in Caucasian lesbians' lives. *Women and Therapy*, 13:27-52.

Murphy, B. C. (1992). Educating mental health professionals about gay and lesbian issues. *Journal of Homosexuality*, 22:229-246.

Quam, J. K. and Whitford, G. S. (1992). *Gerontologist,* 32:367-374.

Rodin, J. and Langer, E. J. (1977). Long-term effects of a control relevant intervention with institutionalized aged. *Journal of Personality and Social Psychology,* 35:897-902.

Schaffer, R. (1973). *Will you still need me when I'm 64? The Gay Liberation Book.* San Francisco: Ramparts Press.

Smith, P. P. (1992). Encounters with older lesbians in psychiatric practice. *Sexual and Marital Therapy,* 7:79-86.

Steinman, R. (1990). Social exchanges between older and younger gay male partners. *Journal of Homosexuality*, 20:179-206.

Symons, D. (1979). *The Evolution of Human Sexuality.* New York: Oxford Press.

Trippet, S. E. (1994). Lesbian's mental health concerns. *Health Care for Women International*, 15:317-323.

Vacha, L. (1985). *Quiet Fire: Memoirs of Older Gay Men.* Trumansburg, New York: The Crossing Press.

Weinberg, M. S. (1970). The male homosexual: Age-related variations in social and psychological characteristics. *Social Problems*, 17:527-537.

Wisniewski, J. J. and Toomey, B. G. (1987). Are social workers homophobic? *Social Work*, 32:454-455.

Chapter 11

Lesbian Grief and Loss Issues in the Coming-Out Process

Carol A. Thompson

As a lesbian psychotherapist, specializing in trauma and loss, I am interested in loss issues and ways to reframe loss as a normal process. In my work, I often see women in the process of coming out who are struggling with a variety of issues that contain a loss component. My belief is that lesbians are raised to value a heterosexual lifestyle, and that it is natural to grieve the loss of that value as part of the coming-out process. Additionally, lesbians lose the inherent rites and privileges of the majority position such as marriage, divorce, societal acceptance of the relationship, and the esteem of family and community. Finally, there is a broader loss that lesbians experience by virtue of often being isolated from the heterosexual community. It is these aspects of loss that I will address in this chapter.

LOSS

In our society loss is linked with death or oftentimes divorce and is often seen as tragic. Society's response to loss is often to deny or ignore that the loss has occurred (Rando, 1984). There are losses throughout our infancy and childhood, the first being birth when we lose the warm, comfortable existence of the womb. We lose mother's breast as we are given solid food. We give up being held in order to walk. Each time we change or begin something new we shed some of the old. Loss, therefore, is not something tragic, but rather a normal part of living. Life is a series of transitions and giving up the past for the present happens constantly.

Bowlby (1969, 1973, 1980) offers a theory of attachment and loss suggesting that people establish strong, emotional bonds to others from a need for security and safety, and that there is a strong, counteremotional reaction when that bond is threatened or broken. The reaction is one of loss and grief for the lost object or ideal (Bowlby, 1980; Klass, 1987; Weenolsen, 1988). Grieving refers to the feelings, thoughts, physical symptoms, or behavioral changes that may result from loss (Worden, 1991).

Numerous authors have described the mourning process (Linde-mann, 1944; Klass, 1987; Parkes, 1972; Rando, 1984; Weenolsen, 1988; Worden, 1991). Of note is the work of William Worden and Patricia Weenolsen. Worden (1991), a grief theorist, describes four tasks of mourning: (1) to accept the reality of the loss, (2) to experience the pain of grief, (3) to adjust to an environment where the deceased is missing, and (4) to emotionally relocate the deceased and move on with life. Weenolsen (1988) discusses what she calls loss and transcendence in four phases: (1) grieving, (2) searching for the lost object or ideal, (3) replacement, and (4) integration. I will rely upon a combination of these stage models in describing a clinical model for working with lesbians around issues specific to the loss of the majority position of heterosexuality during the coming-out process.

COMING OUT

Most of us were raised by heterosexual parents with the values of the heterosexual majority, including marriage and children. We grew up knowing that our families had an expectation that we would marry, and most of us also held that expectation. For many lesbians, the dream of marriage, or the reality of it if we were married, came into conflict with what we were beginning to learn about ourselves. There have been many articles describing the coming-out process (Cass, 1979; Coleman, 1982; Dank, 1971; Hanley-Hackenbruck, 1989; Hencken and O'Dowd, 1977; Lewis, 1984; Sophie, 1986; Troiden, 1989). What each of these models has in common is an attempt to put into understandable linear form the complicated nonlinear process of identifying as lesbian and acting on that awareness. Also described in each is the way in which the individual who is coming out deals with society. Cass (1979), for example, describes a period of social isolation, whereas the woman compares her behavior to society, in general, and finds that she is different. Coleman (1982) places the feeling of difference in the pre-coming-out stage and self-acceptance in the coming-out stage. In a society where the majority of the population still defines homosexuality as wrong (Hyde and Rosenburg, 1980), coming out involves dealing with both internal and external homophobia, the institutionalized prejudices around homosexuality (Forstein, 1988). In addition, lesbians and gay men make up 10 percent of the population (Reinisch and Beasley, 1990) and we are, therefore, demographically, a minority.

Somewhere in the coming-out process, lesbians must deal with the fact that they are identifying with a segment of society that is stigmatized (Fein and Nuehring, 1981). By choosing to identify as lesbians, we are not entitled to marry lesbian partners, divorce, carry joint health insurance with our partners, or publish pictures in the newspaper to signify intentions to legalize our relationships. Public display of affection brings the risk of public censure and/or possible loss of job. Finally, coming out to families and friends brings the risk of being rejected or even disowned. Despite the many losses in the coming-out process, lesbians have proven to be every bit as well-adjusted as their heterosexual counterparts (Rothblum, 1988). Regardless, one of the ways to deal with the loss of the inherent privileges is to recognize, acknowledge, and grieve that loss.

Betty Berzon (1988) addresses the issue of loss in her book *Permanent Partners*:

> With the letting go of a perception of self that is clearly heterosexual one can experience a profound feeling of loss. As with any loss the way to move beyond grief is to acknowledge and express it. Expressing grief over the loss of one's heterosexual status, and all the fantasies about the future that went with it, has not been too popular a topic for dialogue in the gay and lesbian community. But, at this stage of identity development, grieving the loss of the heterosexual blueprint for life is an inescapable part of what is going on. The more it is acknowl-

edged and talked about, the sooner it can be worked through and prevented from becoming a chronic, underlying theme in the person's relationships. (pp. 48-49)

In the five-stage model I am proposing, I am suggesting that loss is an additional aspect of the coming-out process and that the stages of loss happen in conjunction with various stages of the coming-out process.

Stage One: *To accept the reality of the loss of heterosexual identity and its privileges.*

Clients coping with stage-one issues experience many conflicting feelings. Often women are clear at this point that they are lesbians but are sad or angry at the injustices they see inflicted on lesbians by a heterosexual society. It is important that therapists not rush clients through the process of acceptance of the loss of the heterosexual identity. Peggy Hanley-Hackenbruck (1989), for example, in her article about coming out, describes grieving as "necessary for the formation of the new ego ideal through the giving up of the previous heterosexual ideal" (p. 29). It can be tempting to point out the many positive aspects of being lesbian; however, it is not useful to clients at this juncture to hear these positive aspects from the therapist. Otherwise, the client must then defend her feelings of anger or sadness to the therapist or it is possible she will feel guilty for having negative feelings about being lesbian. Clients need to work through these feelings in their own time.

We can help clients by asking them to describe the dreams and expectations they had for a heterosexual life or describe for us those ideals that were handed down to them from their families. Encouraging detailed descriptions of weddings, wedding showers, engagement photos, and so on, helps clients to recognize the dreams they probably had since childhood.

Rituals, too, are often helpful in the letting-go process. Richard Whiting (1988) discusses the idea of a ritual for letting go as follows:

The symbolic actions described within the letting-go category are commonly, yet not exclusively, utilized in healing and identity rituals. The letting-go action facilitates a cleansing and healing process. Over the years we have asked people to burn, freeze, bury, flush, or send up in balloons a variety of symbolic items such as photographs, rings, letters, written memories, psychiatric records, and clothes. Such ritual actions have assisted people in moving beyond traumatic events and meanings that have interfered with their living in the present. (p. 93)

Letter writing is oftentimes a useful ritual. The clients write a good-bye letter to their heterosexual identity. Composing a wedding invitation for the dreamed-of weddings and then burning or burying it helps with those dreams which are especially painful to let go of.

Stage Two: *Acknowledge specifics of the loss and look for ways to "fit in."*

Weenolsen (1988) describes a process that she calls searching. In grieving, searching is an almost unconscious wish for the return of the lost object or person. When someone dies there is a period of time during the grief process when the bereaved feel restless and anxious. They often find themselves wandering from room to room as if in search of something (Parkes, 1982). I often see this same searching behavior in lesbians as they are looking for ways to fit into the lesbian community and are letting go of their heterosexual identity. This is the point at which women begin to join social organizations or go to bars. They begin to test out their degree of comfort in these settings within the gay and lesbian community. At the same time they often begin to discover some discomfort at events where they may have been comfortable before, such as office parties or showers. Peggy Hanley-Hackenbruch (1989) describes the process as practicing or exploring within the new community. It is often a time mixed with fear and ambivalence for the emerging lesbian.

Anger at the loss of privileges, such as marriage or divorce, often surfaces at this point, as well as discomfort about coming out to people. Recently, a client of mine blurted out in a group that she hated being a lesbian. She was angry at always having to come out to people or guarding her conversation if she did not come out. She resented the fact that people assumed she was heterosexual unless she told them otherwise. It was important for this woman to verbalize her feelings and obtain support for them. Only by resolving her negative feelings can she find her positive feelings. It can be helpful to ask clients to make a list of both positive and negative aspects of being lesbian. This list can be redone periodically as a check to see if the clients' thoughts and feelings are changing.

Stage Three: *To feel the pain of the loss and to grieve.*

As stated earlier, our socialized response to loss is often denial, whereas sadness would be the more natural response (Rando, 1984). We cannot resolve a loss unless we acknowledge it and grieve. The process of grieving and letting go allows an internalization of the lost object or ideal so that the client is not constantly preoccupied with the loss. The therapist can ask clients such questions as: How does it feel to think of giving up this dream? The therapist can help the clients access whatever loss, anger, or guilt feelings they may have. In grieving, it is important to experience these feelings even though painful. Avoiding them only allows the feelings to accumulate and interfere at a later date. Unresolved feelings of grief often translate into patterns of behavior that will ensure a continued avoidance of feeling pain (Bowlby, 1980). This can interfere with intimacy in relationships. Resolution of the painful feelings will allow clients to move to an experience of their lesbianism as positive.

Stage Four: *To adjust to life as a lesbian.*

Once clients have grieved the loss of their heterosexual identity, they are free to celebrate being lesbian. I must note that while this process has been described in a linear fashion, it rarely happens so neatly, and often the clients are grieving, raging, and celebrating all at the same time. Helping clients create rituals to celebrate coming out emphasizes the importance of their lesbian identity and marks a demarcation of giving up a heterosexual identity. The clients could be encouraged to give parties celebrating coming out, send announcements to friends, attend lesbian support groups, or march in a Gay Pride parade.

Stage Five: *To integrate lesbian life into the lesbian community and broader society.*

This is also a stage that overlaps other parts of the coming-out process. Sometimes lesbians have already found the lesbian community by the time they are out. Unfortunately, not all women will complete this stage. I see many women who are isolated from the lesbian community and do not want to become a part of it. Some women tell me they have chosen to socialize with heterosexuals because it keeps their love relationship safe. Other women have such internalized homophobia that they do not want to be identified with "those" types.

For those women who can integrate into the lesbian community, the therapist can be helpful as a resource. I keep lists of activities and organizations that I offer to clients. Clients also need to be able to process their experiences the first time they attend all lesbian events. If there are any parts of the events that make them uncomfortable they may feel some guilt and need some assistance in working this through.

In addition, the therapist can assist clients with integrating their lesbian experience into a broader heterosexual community. This is often a very difficult time for clients who struggle with how to be lesbians in a "straight" world or how to deal with family and friends. Some women choose to isolate themselves from any social functions that will have heterosexuals at them and others cut themselves off from any people from their "former life." Both of these positions are an extreme way to cope with the discomfort of trying to integrate into the heterosexual society. The therapist can encourage clients in their struggle, allow for the processing of feelings, and aid with reality checks concerning external homophobia.

OTHER CONSIDERATIONS IN COMING OUT

Not all lesbians experience loss issues when coming out. For some women coming out is an exciting experience. For women who come out in the context of a relationship, falling in love often takes focus over any potential difficulties, and the question of societal acceptance or self-labeling is only thought about later. If women are in their thirties or older, and not married, coming out often gives them a sense of identity and power they had not experienced as heterosexuals. Clients will tell me that they often felt like failures in the heterosexual world having never married or had children, and in coming out as lesbians they felt as if they had found themselves and now fit into the lesbian community. In this instance, there is no grieving of the heterosexual identity. That grieving happened as the women were trying unsuccessfully to live as heterosexuals.

This grief model is also slightly different for women who have been married. These women have to let go of both their view of the sanctity of marriage and their sense of selves as being derived from their role as wives (Charbonneau and Lander, 1991). These women may be trying to grieve the loss of their marriage, and role as wives, as they are fighting for custody of their children, perhaps simultaneously trying to convince a judge of their suitability as a parent. This will often delay the grief process until a later date when lesbians can safely feel any sadness they have about leaving the heterosexual identity.

Women of color may also have a different experience in coming out. Their grief is often in feeling that in order to come out they must give up their racial communities and the support that they traditionally have received from them. One young woman told me that it took her two years longer to come out because of the shame she felt at turning her back on her community. Anita Cornwall, in her book, *Black Lesbian in White America*, states that, "Not the least of many problems that the black lesbian has to contend with is the extreme conservatism that prevails in the black community" (p. 9). She then goes on to say that the religious beliefs of the black community, and their reliance on the Bible, contribute to many black lesbians feeling guilty for being lesbian. For these women, it is not only the heterosexual community that feels judgmental but their own racial or ethnic community.

My choice as a white therapist is to help these women find black or Hispanic therapists who will support them and give them ways to also stay within their own community if that is their choosing. If that is not possible, then I will suggest ways for these women to connect, such as attending functions in their ethnic community together so that they can establish a new network of support.

Jewish lesbians may also have a somewhat different experience closer to that of women of color. Some Jewish lesbians cut themselves off from their Jewish communities in favor of lesbian communities, convinced they were unwanted (Balka and Rose, 1989). Christie Balka (1989) writes of her experience in the book she coedited, *Twice Blessed: On Being Lesbian or Gay and Jewish.*

> We made love for the first time shortly before Rosh Hashanah. I remember walking into services at an egalitarian minyan that fall, my face flushed, feeling that the ground had shifted (and perhaps was still shifting) underneath me. I had marched in my first lesbian and gay pride parade that summer, publicly affirming my love for a woman. I remember looking around at familiar faces in the minyan, davenning a familiar service, and thinking that Judaism contained no road maps for my experience that year. (p.2)

ROLE OF THE THERAPIST

Although I have given some therapeutic interventions throughout this chapter, I would like to comment about the overall role of the therapist. In grief work, it is imperative for the therapist to have done her own work. If I have not dealt with my own loss issues, then each time a client speaks with sadness about losing her heterosexual privileges or heterosexual identity, I will not be able to hear it. Additionally, I will be so uncomfortable that I might discourage her from voicing these feelings or worse yet try to convince her that she does not feel bad.

It is very difficult work to sit with those who are truly grieving, because we can only be there as the witness. We cannot "fix it" or make it better as it is exactly the experience of grieving that ultimately eases the pain. I also think that as lesbian therapists we need to examine our own social and political views as well as our internalized homophobia. It is too easy for those of us who believe in being out to not respect the safety of passing for lesbians who are still not sure they like being lesbian, or to subtly imply that lesbians need to be political.

It is incumbent upon the therapist to be as nonjudgmental as possible, allowing clients the freedom to choose their own pace in coming out and how, or even if, she grieves any part of the life she is leaving behind. Further, I think as therapists we need to examine our own stereotypes around lesbianism. Because I almost never go to bars I have to remember to list local bars as places where my clients can go and be aware of the events that local bars may be sponsoring. Finally, I believe it is our responsibility as therapists to examine our own issues concerning coming out and loss whether through therapy, a supervision group, or via peer support.

CONCLUSION

Clients of mine who have grieved, either during the coming-out process or at a later date, have responded with great relief at feeling permission to express feelings they had often felt were unacceptable or politically incorrect. One woman responded with tears when I asked if there were anything she would miss of her heterosexual lifestyle. She said she felt sad that she would never have the family approval her brother had because he was married. She also said that it felt good to finally cry about not going to her high school prom. She had felt like such a failure for not having a date even though she knew that she was not attracted to men. Clients also have expressed that, after grieving, they are much less angry at their families and straight friends. As one woman put it, "I'm not jealous of what they have anymore." Experiencing the loss allows women the opportunity to experience the full joy and celebration of being lesbian.

REFERENCES

Balka, C. and Rose, A. (Eds.) 1989. *Twice blessed: On being lesbian or gay and Jewish*. Boston: Beacon Press.

Berzon, B. (1988). *Permanent partners*. New York: E. P. Dutton.

Bridges, K. L. and Croteau, J. M. (1994). Once-married lesbians: Facilitating changing life patterns. *Journal of Counseling and Development*, 73:132-140.

Bowlby, J. (1969). *Attachment and loss: Attachment*. (Vol. 1). New York: Basic Books.

Bowlby, J. (1973). *Attachment and loss: Separation, anxiety, and anger*. (Vol. 2). New York: Basic Books.

Bowlby, J. (1980). *Attachment and loss: Loss, sadness, and depression.* (Vol. 3). New York: Basic Books.

Cass, V. (1979). Homosexual identity formation: A theoretical model. *Journal of Homosexuality,* 4:219-235.

Charbonneau, C. and Lander, P. (1991). Redefining sexuality: Women becoming lesbian at mid-life. In Sang, B., Warshaw, J., and Smith, A. (eds.). *Lesbians at mid-life: The creative transition,* (pp. 35-43). San Francisco: Spinsters Book Co.

Coleman, E. (1982). Developmental stages of the coming out process. *Journal of Homosexuality,* 7:31-43.

Cornwall, A. (1983). *Black lesbian in white America.* Tallahassee, FL: Naiad Press.

Dank, B. (1971). Coming out in the gay world. *Psychiatry,* 34:180-197.

Fein, S. B. and Nuehring, E. M. (1981). Intrapsychic effects of stigma: A process of breakdown and reconstruction of social reality. *Journal of Homosexuality,* 7(1):313.

Forstein, M. (1988). Homophobia in gay men and lesbians in psychotherapy. Paper presented at Clinical Issues with Gay Men and Lesbians, A Workshop for Harvard Medical School.

Hanley-Hackenbruck, P. (1989). Psychotherapy and the "coming out" process. *Journal of Gay and Lesbian Psychotherapy,* 1(1):21-39.

Hencken, J. and O'Dowd, W. (1977). Coming out as an aspect of identity formation. *Gay Academic Union Journal: Gai Saber,* 1:18-22.

Hyde, J. and Rosenberg, B. (1980). *Half the human experience* (2nd ed.). Lexington, MA: D. C. Heath.

Klass, D. (1987). John Bowlby's model of grief and the problem of identification. *Omega,* 18(1):13-22.

Lewis, L. (1984). The coming out process for lesbians: Integrating a stable identity. *Social Work,* 29:464-469.

Lindemann, E. (1944). Symptomology and management of acute grief. *American Journal of Psychiatry,* 101:141-148.

Markowitz, L. M. (1991). Homosexuality: Are we still in the dark? *Family Therapy Networker.* Jan-Feb:27-35.

Moses, A. and Hawkins, R. (1982). *Counseling lesbian women and gay men: A life issues approach.* St. Louis: C. V. Mosby.

Parkes, C. M. (1972). *Bereavement: Studies of grief in adult life.* Madison, CT: International Universities Press.

Reinisch, J. M. and Beasley, R. (1990). *The Kinsey institute new report on sex: What you must know to be sexually literate.* London: Penguin Books.

Rando, T. (1984). *Grief, dying, and death.* Champaign, IL: Research Press.

Rothblum, E. D. (1988). Introduction: Lesbianism as a model of a positive lifestyle for women. In Rothblum, E. D. and Cole, E. (eds.). *Loving boldly: Issues facing lesbians.* New York: Harrington Park Press.

Sophie, J. (1986). A critical examination of stage theories of lesbian identity development. *Journal of Homosexuality,* 12:39-51.

Troiden, R. (1989). The formation of homosexual identities. *Journal of Homosexuality.* 17:43-73.

Weenolsen, P. (1988). *Transcendence of loss over the life span.* New York: Hemisphere Publishing.

Whiting, R. (1988). Guidelines to designing therapeutic rituals in E. Imber-Black, J. Roberts, and E. R. Whiting (eds.). *Rituals in families and family therapy,* (pp. 84-109). New York: W. W. Norton and Co.

Worden, W. (1991). *Grief counseling and grief therapy: A handbook for the mental health practitioner* (2nd ed.). New York: Springer.

Chapter 12

The Perils of Sexual Objectification: Sexual Orientation, Gender, and Socioculturally Acquired Vulnerability to Body Dissatisfaction and Eating Disorders

Michael D. Siever

"Anorexia Nervosa: The Starving Disease Epidemic"–*U.S. News and World Report* (1982)
"My Daughter Was Starving Herself to Death"–*Good Housekeeping* (1982)
"A Deadly Feast and Famine"–*Newsweek* (Seligmann, 1983)
"Is the Binge/Purge Cycle Catching?"–*Ms.* (Squire, 1983)
"Bulimia: A Woman's Terror"–*People* (Bernstein, 1986)
"The Nightmare of Disturbed Eating"–*Teen* (Barbera-Hogan, 1986)

As these headlines from articles in the popular press indicate, the eating disorders, anorexia nervosa and bulimia, have captured the attention of the media and, by extension, the public. A recent tally of the number of articles relating to these disorders listed in the *Reader's Guide to Periodical Literature* revealed over 75 articles on eating disorders in the popular press during a five-year period. Television has presented several docudramas on the subject, and various celebrities have publicly confessed their battles with eating disorders to the eager public. Karen Carpenter's death from anorexia nervosa was widely reported in the media, and Jane Fonda has publicly revealed her struggles with both anorexia and bulimia. The frequency and prominence with which reports on both of these disorders have appeared in the mass media reflect the widespread nature of these problems.

Although some have speculated that the media, by sensationalizing and even glamorizing these illnesses, have contributed to this new "epidemic," there is no question that there has been a dramatic increase in the incidence and prevalence of eating disorders. Anorexia nervosa and bulimia have changed from being rare, obscure diseases to common, widespread problems frequently encountered by both medical and mental health professionals. Although some of this increase in the prevalence of eating disorders is attributable to the increased awareness of eating disorders in both the public and the medical and mental health professions, it is clear that the growth in the incidence and prevalence of these disorders is real rather than merely an artifact of increased awareness and more accurate diagnosis.

EPIDEMIOLOGY OF EATING DISORDERS

Although there are indications that eating disorders have occurred for centuries, anorexia nervosa was previously considered a rare and unusual disease, and bulimia has been recognized and described as a disorder unto itself only in the past two decades. Numerous epidemiological studies have demonstrated a dramatic increase in the incidence and prevalence of these disorders (Duddle, 1973; Jones et al., 1980; Kendell et al., 1973; Theander, 1970). A seemingly ever-increasing number of young people, out of a morbid fear of being fat, either voluntarily starve themselves into an emaciated state or regularly engage in eating binges and then attempt to purge themselves. Frequently, both types of disordered eating behavior are found in the same person, either sequentially in her or his history or concurrently.

The serious consequences of these disorders make this trend a matter of great concern. In addition to the emotional distress evident in these disorders, it has been well documented that both anorexia nervosa and bulimia can have significant consequences for the physical health of those afflicted. Both illnesses can result in grave and sometimes irreparable health problems including but not limited to electrolyte disturbances, cardiac irregularities, renal dysfunction, neurological abnormalities, and gastrointestinal damage. Without treatment or remission, both anorexia and bulimia can be fatal.

The incidence of these eating disorders has not, however, been distributed evenly throughout the population. Most estimates are that 90 percent of those suffering from these disorders are women. Young women appear to be particularly vulnerable; the average age at onset for both these disorders is during the adolescent years. Various studies have indicated also that these young women tend to come from the middle to upper socioeconomic strata of society.

SOCIOCULTURALLY ACQUIRED VULNERABILITY

Anorexia nervosa and bulimia nervosa are clearly multideter-mined disorders. To understand the origins of these illnesses, one must look at sociocultural, developmental, psychological, and biological factors. Despite the obvious importance of individual intra-psychic and interpersonal variables involved in the development of an eating disorder, the highly uneven gender distribution of eating disorders and the rise in incidence and prevalence make it particularly crucial to examine the sociocultural factors.

Zubin and his colleagues (Zubin, Magaziner, and Steinhauer, 1983; Zubin and Spring, 1977; Zubin and Steinhauer, 1981) have proposed a vulnerability model for the development of schizophre-nia, which I believe is applicable to other mental disorders, including eating disorders. In this paradigm, psychopathology is seen as resulting from an interaction between (1) an individual's vulnerabil-ity, both inborn in terms of genetic, neurophysiolological, and biochemical elements and what the individual acquires in terms of developmental, environmental, and learning histories; (2) stressful life events; and (3) moderator variables, such as social support and learned coping style. This chapter will examine what Zubin and his colleagues refer to as "acquired" vulnerability, that is, vulnerability to eating disorders acquired via socialization and continually rein-forced by our culture.

A strong case has been made for the importance of sociocultural influences in the development of a vulnerability to eating disorders in women. Many observers have pointed out the enormous pressure placed on women in our culture to be physically attractive and thin, in particular, which puts them at increased risk for developing eating disorders (Boskind-Lodahl, 1976; Bruch, 1973, 1978; Chemin, 1981; Garfinkel and Garner, 1982; Orbach, 1978; Rodin, Silberstein, and Striegel-Moore, 1985; Striegel-Moore, Silberstein, and Rodin, 1986). Our society places enormous value on being physically attractive, in general, and on being thin, in particular. Extreme stigmatization, in fact, confronts those who are regarded as obese. Studies have shown that, although these attitudes affect people of all ages and both genders, these social norms are applied much more rigorously to women than men (Canning and Meyer, 1966; Goldblatt, Moore, and Stunkard, 1965). Consequently, most women in our society are dissatisfied with their bodies, are constantly monitoring their weight and engaging in some form of dieting, and perceive themselves overweight, regardless of the accuracy of this assessment (Rodin, Silberstein, and Striegel-Moore, 1985; Wooley and Wooley, 1984).

Several studies have also indicated that this pressure on women to be thin has increased significantly over the past 35 years, the same period in which there has been a dramatic increase in cases of eating disorders (Gagnard, 1986; Garner et al., 1980; Snow and Harris, 1986). Like fashions in attire, fashions in the ideal body shape change with the times. An illustration of the change in ideal female form that has transpired in recent years can be found in the study by Garner et al., which showed that, over the 20-year period from 1958 to 1978, the average weight of women in both *Playboy* centerfolds and the Miss America Pageants had declined steadily. In yet another illustration of the growing obsession with weight loss in women, Garner et al. also found that there were over 70 percent more diet articles in six women's magazines in the years 1969 to 1978 than in the preceding ten-year period.

Ironically, while the ideal held up to women has become increasingly thin, the average woman has actually been getting heavier (Metropolitan Life Insurance Company, 1983; Society of Actuaries, 1980). Thus, it is clear that our culture places a high value on slenderness that is applied, particularly strongly to women, and that the standards for what is an acceptably slim body for women have become increasingly stringent and unrealistic over the past 30 years.

These two factors provide the basis for the paradigm of socioculturally acquired vulnerability to eating disorders.

EATING DISORDERS AND MEN

But what of men? Where do they fit into this paradigm? In order to have a more complete understanding of sociocultural factors in the creation of a vulnerability to eating disorders, it is necessary to account for males with eating disorders. Although several proponents of socioculturally acquired vulnerability have extensively examined the sociocultural factors that appear to be important in explaining both the disproportionate incidence of eating disorders among women and the recent rise in prevalence, little attention has been paid to males that are afflicted with anorexia nervosa and/or bulimia.

Despite the fact that some of the earliest descriptions of anorexia nervosa included case histories of males (Gull, 1874; Morton, 1689), very little mention has been made of males in the psychological or psychiatric literature on eating disorders during most of this century. In fact, many authors completely eliminated the possibility of anorexia nervosa in males by the use of amenorrhea as a diagnostic criteria (Cobb, 1943; Kidd and Wood, 1966; Nemiah, 1950), or because they felt that anorexia nervosa was the result of a "fear of oral impregnation" (Kessler, 1966). Even though amenorrhea is no longer necessary for the diagnosis of anorexia nervosa and few adhere to the psychodynamic notion of "fear of oral impregnation," most people, both within and without the medical and mental health professions, think of anorexia nervosa and bulimia as "women's diseases" and thus are unlikely to look for or think of eating disorders in males. Because of all these reasons, it has been suggested that eating disorders are significantly underdiagnosed in males (Anderson and Mickalide, 1983).

The little research that has been done on the sociocultural factors that might create a vulnerability to eating disorders in men has been primarily with those whose career choice dictates that they must maintain a certain weight, such as professional athletes, dancers, and models. These studies have shown that such pressures do, in fact, produce disordered eating attitudes and behaviors, although not always sufficiently severe as to warrant a diagnosis of anorexia nervosa or bulimia nervosa (Enns, Drewnowski, and Grinker, 1987; King and Mezey, 1987; Rodin, Silberstein, and Striegel-Moore, 1985).

Recently, however, the possibility and existence of males with eating disorders has been acknowledged, and several studies of anorexic and bulimic males have been conducted. Although the results of these studies are not consistent, several have found that a disproportionately high number of these men are gay or experiencing conflict over their sexual orientation (Crisp, 1967; Crisp and Toms, 1972; Dally, 1969; Herzog et al., 1984; Schneider and Agras, 1987).

SEXUAL ORIENTATION AS A FACTOR IN ACQUIRED VULNERABILITY

In addition, several proponents of the paradigm of socioculturally acquired vulnerability to eating disorders have commented that it seems probable that, because of similarities in the sociocultural context for gay men and heterosexual females, gay men are likely also to be particularly vulnerable to eating disorders (Herzog et al., 1984; Striegel-Moore, Silberstein, and Rodin, 1986). The gay male subculture, it is suggested, imposes similarly strong pressures on gay men to be physically attractive and thin, in particular. Gay men, like women, experience extreme pressure to be eternally slim and youthful looking and are, therefore, also likely to be dissatisfied with their bodies and at increased risk for the development of eating disorders. Despite the frequency with which this observation has been made by social and political commentators (Altman, 1982; Clark, 1977; Kleinberg, 1980; Lakoff and Scherr, 1984; Millman, 1980), empirical investigation of this phenomenon had occurred only recently. Several researchers (Berscheid, Walster, and Bohrnstedt, 1972, 1973; Herzog, Newman, and Warshaw, 1991; Sergios and Cody, 1985, 1986; Silberstein et al., 1989; Yager et al., 1988) have conducted empirically based studies that investigated the importance of physical appearance for gay men and confirmed the impression that physical attractiveness is highly valued by gay men.

This emphasis on being physically attractive in the gay male subculture and the consequent body dissatisfaction experienced by gay men seems likely to result in a vulnerability to anorexia nervosa and bulimia nervosa (Herzog et al., 1984; Striegel-Moore, Silberstein, and Rodin, 1986). Recent empirical research comparing non-clinical samples of gay and heterosexual men have concluded that this heightened emphasis on appearance in the gay male subculture does indeed increase the vulnerability of gay men to both body dissatisfaction and the attitudes and behaviors associated with eating disorders (Herzog, Newman, and Warshaw, 1991; Silberstein et al., 1989; Yager et al., 1988).

PERILS OF SEXUAL OBJECTIFICATION

Little attempt has been made, however, to explain the reasons for this heightened emphasis on physical appearance in the gay male subculture or explore what common elements might produce this emphasis on being physically attractive for both gay men and heterosexual women. One explanation is the desire of both groups to attract and please men (Hatfield and Sprecher, 1986). Numerous studies have shown that men are more concerned than women with the physical attractiveness of a potential partner (Coombs and Kendell, 1966; Stroebe et al., 1971; Vail and Staudt, 1950). The concern of men for looks and their tendency to sexually objectify their partners is well known in our culture. Thus, both gay men and heterosexual women strive to be physically attractive in order to attract a desirable mate and, in this culture, an essential component of being physically attractive is a slender, youthful body.

If this shared desire to be physically attractive in order to attract or please men is the basis of a vulnerability to eating disorders, then one would predict that lesbians and heterosexual men would be unlikely to show this increased vulnerability. Physical attractiveness is of primary importance to men in their assessment of a potential partner, whereas women place a higher value on other features, such as status, power, income, and personality (Hatfield and Sprecher, 1986). Because physical attractiveness is less essential in attracting a female partner, heterosexual men and lesbians are subject to less pressure to be physically attractive.

Previous Research

Although there has been extensive research comparing body satisfaction and its correlates between heterosexual women and men and some recent studies comparing gay and heterosexual men, there have been few empirical investigations that examined lesbians and their attitudes toward physical attractiveness, their body satisfaction, or the prevalence of eating disorders. The lesbian subculture has been described as downplaying, even actively resisting, the dominant cultural value placed on beauty for women (Blumstein and Schwarz, 1983; Brown, 1987). Dworkin (1988), on the other hand, argues that lesbians, like all women in this society, are socialized to consider their appearance a primary aspect of their lives and must conform to traditional standards of beauty for social acceptance.

Striegel-Moore, Tucker, and Hsu (1990) measured body satisfaction, disordered eating, and self-esteem in small samples of lesbian and heterosexual female college students and found statistically significant differences in general psychological distress but not in body satisfaction or eating disorders. The higher level of psychological distress found in the lesbian sample did not reach a clinical level and was, the authors suggested, more likely attributable to living in a homophobic, heterosexist society than to emotional disturbance associated with eating disorders. Concerns about physical condition and weight as assessed by a measure of body esteem were equally related to self-esteem in the lesbian sample, whereas only weight concerns were related to self-esteem in the heterosexual female sample. The author did find a nonsignificant trend indicating lesbians diet less and binge more than heterosexual women, but the incidence of purging was too infrequent in their sample for analysis. They did not directly measure attitudes toward the importance of appearance and physical attractiveness.

Brand, Rothblum, and Solomon (1992) assessed weight concerns and disordered eating in a sample of lesbians, gay men, and heterosexual women and men, and concluded that body dissatisfaction and the attitudes and behaviors associated with eating disorders appeared to be more related to gender than sexual orientation. Unfortunately, their samples were so highly disparate that it is difficult to evaluate the validity and reliability of the conclusions. The sample sizes ranged from 133 heterosexual women to 13 gay men; the lesbian and gay male subjects mostly were in their thirties and no longer in school, and the heterosexual female and male subjects were college students in their late teens. Although gender effects were more frequent and of greater magnitude than were effects of sexual orientation, significant interactions between gender and sexual orientation were found with the difference between subjects' self-reported ideal weights and life insurance normed weights and with a single-item measure of preoccupation with weight.

CURRENT STUDY

In an attempt to more thoroughly explore gender and sexual orientation as factors in an acquired vulnerability to body dissatisfaction and eating disorders, Siever (1988, 1990, 1994) compared beliefs about the importance of physical attractiveness, body satisfaction, and eating attitudes and behaviors in equivalent samples of lesbians, gay men, heterosexual women, and heterosexual men. The hypothesis was that heterosexual women, because of sexual objectification by men, would show the strongest belief in the importance of their own physical attractiveness, the greatest dissatisfaction with their bodies, and the highest frequency of attitudes and behaviors that typify eating disorders. It was predicted that gay men, because of a similar experience of sexual objectification, would resemble heterosexual women more than heterosexual men in the importance they place on their own physical attractiveness, their dissatisfaction with their bodies, and their eating attitudes and behavior. In contrast, because both lesbians and heterosexual men experience less sexual objectification, it was predicted that lesbians would resemble heterosexual men more than heterosexual women, with less emphasis on being physically attractive, less body dissatisfaction, and fewer attitudes and behaviors associated with eating disorders.

Two-hundred fifty college students participated in this study. The sample included roughly equal numbers of lesbians, gay men, heterosexual women, and heterosexual men. The majority were white, middle-class young women and men attending either a university or community college. All subjects completed a packet of self-report questionnaires that included the Body Esteem Scale (BES), (Franzoi and Herzog, 1986, 1987; Franzoi and Shields, 1984); a Physical Attractiveness Questionnaire (PAQ), (Siever, 1990); the Body Shape Questionnaire (BSQ), (Cooper et al., 1987); the Body Size Drawings (BSD), (Stunkard, Sorensen, and Schulsinger, 1972); the Eating Attitudes Test (EAT), (Garner and Garfinkel, 1979; Garner et al., 1982); the Eating Disorders Inventory (EDI), (Garner et al., 1982); and the Reasons for Exercise Inventory (REI), (Silberstein et al., 1989).

In this chapter, I will discuss the results of this study and the implications for further research and clinical practice. Greater detail on the specific characteristics of the sample, methods and measures, and the results of the study with statistical analyses have been reported elsewhere and can be found in Siever (1988, 1990, 1994).

Importance of Physical Attractiveness

There were clear differences in the importance that the groups placed on physical attractiveness that were consistent with the hypothesis that sexual objectification results in a heightened concern for physical attractiveness. Lesbians, who tend to neither sexually objectify their female partners nor be sexually objectified by them, were the least concerned about physical attractiveness. Relative to the other groups, they said it was neither important to them in their evaluations of their partners nor did they think it important to their partners.

Gay men and heterosexual women, on the other hand, showed a much higher concern for physical attractiveness. They were more concerned with the physical appearance of their partners than lesbians and thought that their own physical appearance was more important to their male partners. Both gay men and heterosexual women indicated that improving their physical attractiveness was a more significant motivator for exercising, lending further confirmation to the hypothesis that gay men and heterosexual women place greater importance on physical attractiveness.

The results for heterosexual men were less clear and perhaps reflect changing cultural standards. Heterosexual men placed the greatest importance on the physical appearance of their female partners, yet their perceptions of how important physical appearance is to their female partners were somewhat inconsistent. This may reflect the recent trend toward increased pressure on men to be more physically attractive (Mishkind et al., 1986). This increasing sexual objectification of men is apparent from an observation of popular culture. One now sees products being sold with images of lean, muscular, scantily clad young men almost as often as with slender, scantily clad young women. Cash, Winstead, and Janda (1985, 1986) found that, although women still face greater pressure than men to be physically attractive and continue to be more dissatisfied with their bodies, this pressure for the "perfect" body is increasing for both genders.

Despite this growing pressure on men to be physically attractive, heterosexual men still appear to be less concerned with their appearance than gay men. Although the measures of the importance of physical attractiveness did not clearly differentiate gay and heterosexual men, the greater importance gay men placed on physical attractiveness as a motivator for exercising suggests that physical appearances are still more important to gay men. Silberstein et al. (1989) also found that gay men reported physical appearance more important to their sense of self compared to heterosexual men, whereas heterosexual men considered being physically active more important to their sense of self.

Body Satisfaction

The data on body satisfaction appear also to confirm the hypothesis that sexual objectification results in body dissatisfaction. Heterosexual men are clearly the least plagued by doubts and complaints about their bodies. In research conducted with presumably heterosexual populations, it has been found that men are likely to evaluate their bodies in terms of effectiveness, and that women evaluate their bodies in terms of appearance (Lerner and Karabenick, 1974; Lerner, Orlos, and Knapp, 1976). Thus, whereas heterosexual men are most likely to view their bodies as tools with which to compete with each other through strength and athletic prowess, heterosexual women are more likely to view their bodies as objects for aesthetic evaluation and are constantly forced to compare their bodies with the sylph-like models, actresses, and beauty pageant contestants presented regularly in the media.

Gay men, who are also likely to view their bodies as sex objects with which to attract men, are like heterosexual women, more prone to body dissatisfaction. The finding that gay men are significantly more dissatisfied with their bodies than are heterosexual men corroborates previous research (Herzog , Newman, and Warshaw, 1991; Silberstein et al., 1989; Yager et al., 1988). In fact, in this study, it appears that gay men may be even more unhappy with their bodies than are heterosexual women. Perhaps this is due to the potential for gay men to be dissatisfied with their bodies on two dimensions. Like heterosexual men, they may worry that their bodies are inadequate in terms of strength and athletic prowess and, like heterosexual women, they may doubt their physical attractiveness. This also may be related to the fact that the gay men in this sample were older and may be holding on to an unrealistically youthful ideal for their bodies.

The lesbians in this sample had a significantly higher mean Body Mass Index (BMI). The BMI, weight divided by the square of height, is a measure commonly used for the evaluation of weight status, which, unlike the Metropolitan Life Insurance Height and Weight Tables, does not require knowledge of frame size (Metropolitan Life Insurance Company, 1954, 1983). The significantly higher mean BMI of the lesbians in this sample may have contributed to the lack of statistically significant differences between lesbians and heterosexual women on most of the body dissatisfaction measures. There was, however, a consistent trend on almost all the body dissatisfaction measures for lesbians to be, despite their higher mean body mass, less dissatisfied with their bodies than heterosexual women.

Acquired Vulnerability to Eating Disorders

The prediction that heightened concern for physical attractiveness and consequent body dissatisfaction would lead to increased vulnerability to eating disorders was also confirmed in this study. As predicted, heterosexual women generally scored the highest on the eating disorders scales and heterosexual men scored the lowest. Lesbians generally reported a lower frequency of the attitudes and behaviors associated with eating disorders than heterosexual women, with the differences reaching statistical significance on two-thirds of the scales. Gay men consistently reported a higher frequency of these attitudes and behaviors than did heterosexual men. This confirmation of predicted differences is especially noteworthy considering that the lesbians in this sample were significantly heavier than the heterosexual women. It appears that the lesbians in this sample, despite being larger and dissatisfied with their weight, were less likely to express their weight concerns with the dysfunctional attitudes and behaviors associated with eating disorders.

The numbers and proportions of subjects in each group that fell above the clinical cutoff on the Eating Attitudes Test also provide confirmation of the predicted group differences. Whereas only two lesbians and two heterosexual men scored above the cutoff, nine gay men and eight heterosexual women scored in the clinical range. This represents 4.2 percent of the lesbian sample, 3.4 percent of the heterosexual male sample, 13.8 percent of the heterosexual female sample, and 16.7 percent of the gay male sample. With heterosexual women and men, these figures are consistent with those found in other studies that used the Eating Attitudes Test with school-age populations. The percentages of presumably heterosexual women who scored above the cutoff have ranged from a high of 22 percent (Leichner et al., 1986) to a low of 6 percent (Button and Whitehouse, 1981), with most falling around 11 to 12 percent. There are fewer studies that have included male subjects, but the percentage of men, again presumably heterosexual, whose scores were above the cutoff in those few studies ranged from 6 percent in Leichner et al.'s study to 0 percent in Button and Whitehouse's study.

Direction of Body Dissatisfaction

One striking result of this study was the differences in the direction of body dissatisfaction among the groups. These differences appear to be purely a function of gender. While the women in this sample, be they lesbian or heterosexual, rarely wished to be larger, nearly a third of the men, regardless of their sexual orientation, wished to gain weight. These gender differences are likely to be a product of a combination of biological and social factors. Girls, who even before puberty have 10 to 15 percent more body fat then boys, tend to start gaining body fat at puberty. Boys, on the other hand, tend to enter the "gangly" phase of their development at puberty, gaining mostly muscle and lean tissue, and do not generally start gaining additional body fat until a later stage in their physical development (Striegel-Moore, Silberstein, and Rodin, 1986).

This biological reality contrasts sharply with the cultural ideals for physical attractiveness. While women are held to an ideal of almost prepubertal slenderness, the model for the ideal masculine body in recent times has been the mesomorphic figures of muscle men like that of Sylvester Stallone or Arnold Schwarzenegger. In light of this, it is worth noting that many of the men who reported that they wished to gain weight specifically commented that their desire was for increased muscle mass, not fat.

Although some have pointed to the tendency for men in their late adolescence and early adulthood to wish to gain weight as a factor in the extremely low incidence of anorexia and bulimia in men (Garner and Garfinkel, 1980; Striegel-Moore, Silberstein, and Rodin, 1986), the results of this study suggest that the heightened emphasis on a youthful, physical appearance in the gay male subculture counteracts this phenomenon. While the same proportion of gay men as heterosexual men wished to be bigger, twice as many gay men as heterosexual men wished to lose weight. Given that the gay men in this sample had a slightly lower mean Body Mass Index, this result is particularly striking.

Examination of the within-group differences among subgroups based on direction of body dissatisfaction also lends further confirmation to the research hypotheses. Although desire to lose or gain weight seems not to be a significant factor in the value placed on physical attractiveness for any of the groups, it appears to be a meaningful factor in the level of body satisfaction and frequency of eating disorders symptoms. It seems that the desire to lose or gain weight has less effect on how heterosexual men feel about their bodies than it does for the other groups. The direction of body dissatisfaction appears to have a stronger effect on the frequency of dysfunctional eating attitudes and behaviors for gay men and heterosexual women than it does for lesbians and heterosexual men.

The results of this study lend further weight to the growing body of research that points to sociocultural variables as significant risk factors for the development of anorexia nervosa and bulimia nervosa. Substantial literature already exists on the sociocultural variables that put heterosexual women at particular risk for eating disorders (Boskind-Lodahl, 1976; Bruch, 1973; Garfinkel and Garner, 1982; Striegel-Moore, Silberstein, and Rodin, 1986). Several recent studies have shown that men who must remain a certain weight, such as athletes, dancers, and models, have a higher frequency of the attitudes and behaviors associated with eating disorders (Enns, Drewnowski, and Grinker, 1987; King and Mezey, 1987; Rodin, Silberstein, and Striegel-Moore, 1985). This study, along with that of Yager et al. (1988), confirms previous speculation that the heightened emphasis on physical attractiveness in the gay male community places gay men at increased risk for the development of disordered eating attitudes and behaviors. Further, it appears from the lesbian sample in this study that sociocultural factors can have an immunizing effect; lesbians, because of a decreased emphasis on physical appearance in their community, appear less vulnerable to the attitudes and behaviors that typify eating disorders.

Methodological Problems

Although the results of this study appear to strongly confirm the research hypotheses, some methodological problems must be mentioned. There are often problems encountered when using questionnaires developed with clinical populations and designed as clinical screening tools. When conducting epidemiological research with nonclinical samples using such instruments, one can get surprising and confusing results. For example, in this study, on the Oral Control subscale of the Eating Attitudes Test, lesbians, gay men, and heterosexual men who wished that they were thinner scored lower than those who were content with their shape or who wished to be heavier. An examination of the individual items of this subscale revealed that this pattern reversal was due primarily to items such as "Others would prefer if I ate more" and "Other people think I am too thin." With this nonclinical population, these items were being endorsed by subjects who were content with their size or wanted to gain weight, rather than persons who wanted to lose weight as would often be the case in the clinical populations with and for whom these scales were developed. The unusual results on the Oral Control subscale should remind us that items developed with a clinical population may be answered similarly by a nonclinical population, but for very different reasons.

The scoring method developed for the Eating Attitudes Test and the Eating Disorders Inventory is another example. The original scoring method gives the most pathological response a score of three, the second most extreme response a two, the next response a one, and zero to the remaining three responses. As noted by Ollendick and Hart (1986), while this scoring method may be logical for a screening instrument, it is not appropriate for epidemiological studies as it collapses the three responses most likely to be endorsed in a nonclinical population. It also creates a skewed distribution that makes the validity of any statistical analysis questionable. The necessity of devising a different scoring method for the EAT and the EDI call into question the statistical validity of much of the previous epidemiological research that has been done with these measures.

Gender Bias

In addition, the almost exclusive use of female populations for the development and validation of the EAT, EDI, and BSQ raises the question of the validity of their use in any samples including men. Although the wording of some items were changed in this study for this specific reason, it is difficult to determine to what extent gender bias remained. Turnbull, Freeman, and Annandale (1987) found that their sample of bulimic men would have been missed if the EAT or EDI had been used for screening. None of the men in their sample scored above the cutoff on the EAT, and their EDI scores were more similar to those of normal women than women with eating disorders. They attributed the relatively low scores of their male bulimic subjects to the gender bias of these instruments. If gender bias in these scales tends to depress scores for men, further research is needed to determine if and why gay men are less effected by this gender bias.

Another problem that must be noted is the inevitable difficulty of self-report measures. It is entirely possible that much of the difference between groups is the result of response sets on the part of the groups. Heterosexual men may have scored lower on many of the scales because of a tendency to downplay negative feelings or greater reluctance to admit to dysfunctional attitudes. The results of the Mood Subscale of the REI may represent this phenomenon.

Women, be they lesbian or heterosexual, indicated mood improvement as a more significant reason for exercising than men, regardless of their sexual orientation. The extent to which the group differences represent response sets rather than true differences is also a question for further investigation.

Political Context

The scores of the lesbian group may, to an unknown extent, reflect a political stance in the lesbian community rather than indicate true attitudes and behaviors. The feminist political perspective on resisting sexual objectification and the oppression of the obese may have colored the responses of many of the lesbians in this sample. Many of the comments written in the margins of the questionnaire by lesbian subjects suggest that this may have played a role in the way that they answered items.

In their study of lesbian college students, Striegel-Moore, Tucker, and Hsu (1990) used two comparison groups of heterosexual women: one recruited from women's studies courses, the other recruited from the psychology department's subject pool. The authors assumed that the group drawn from women's studies classes were more feminist than the group drawn from the subject pool and shared a feminist perspective with the lesbian students, but, unfortunately, did not attempt to empirically verify this assumption. With this rudimentary attempt to control for degree of feminist thinking, all the differences found were an effect of sexual orientation, not presumed degree of feminism. Future research should more effectively address response sets based on feminism as well as gender-based response styles.

Some of these problems and methodological differences may contribute to the discrepancy between the findings in the present study and the results in other similar studies. Striegel-Moore, Tucker, and Hsu (1990) found no statistically significant difference between small samples of lesbian and heterosexual female college students on body esteem, but it is difficult to make direct comparisons since they used BES subscale scores rather than the total score. The BES subscales were not used in the present study since Franzoi and Shields (1984) used separate factor analyses to create different subscales for women and men. These subscales, therefore, could not be used to compare across all four groups. It is noteworthy, however, that, in Striegel-Moore, Tucker, and Hsu the Weight Concern and Physical Condition subscales of the BES were equally related to a measure of self-esteem for the lesbian sample, whereas only the Weight Concern Subscale was related to self-esteem for the heterosexual female sample.

Striegel-Moore, Tucker, and Hsu (1990) also found no statistically significant difference between lesbians and heterosexual women on disordered eating. They, however, grouped the Drive for Thinness and Body Dissatisfaction Scales of the EDI with the BES subscale scores in a MANOVA (Multiple Analysis of Variance) and, because the MANOVA was nonsignificant, did not report any univariate statistics. They grouped the Bulimia Scale of EDI with two, single-item measures of the frequency of dieting and binge eating in a MANOVA and, again, because of nonsignificance, did not report univariate statistics. As previously mentioned, their sample sizes were so small that the incidence of purging did not allow for analysis. They did not directly measure attitudes toward the importance of appearance and physical attractiveness, nor did they assess subjects' weight status or the difference between subjects' actual and ideal weights.

Brand, Rothblum, and Solomon (1992) compared lesbians, gay men, and heterosexual women and men on weight concerns and disordered eating and found a greater magnitude and frequency of gender main effects than sexual orientation main effects. Again, direct comparisons are difficult because Brand, Rothblum, and Solomon measured weight concerns rather than body esteem and used different statistical techniques to analyze their data. They performed a two (gender) by two (sexual orientation) analysis of covariance and reported main and interaction effects but not group means. Additionally, as previously discussed, their samples were so different in terms of size, origin, age, and educational status that it is difficult to evaluate the generalizibilty of the results.

CONCLUSIONS

Although the findings in the present study that gay men indicate a heightened concern with physical attractiveness and greater body dissatisfaction are consistent with previous research comparing gay and heterosexual men (Herzog , Newman, and Warshaw, 1991; Silberstein et al., 1989; Yager et al., 1988), there have not been consistent results indicating a greater frequency of attitudes and behaviors associated with eating disorders among gay men. Silberstein et al. found that gay men did not score significantly higher than heterosexual men on the EAT and that the same number of gay men as heterosexual men scored in the clinical range on the EAT. They did, however, report that gay men who wished to be thinner had higher scores on the EAT. While Yager et al. (1988) found significant differences between gay and heterosexual male college students on several of the EDI scales, Herzog, Newman, and Warshaw (1991) did not find significant differences between gay and heterosexual men on EDI scales.

More research is necessary to obtain a clearer, more consistent picture of the differences or lack thereof between lesbians and heterosexual women and between gay and heterosexual men. Future research needs to examine to what extent these discrepant findings are the result of the previously discussed scoring method problem with the EAT and the EDI, the most commonly used measures of the attitudes and behaviors associated with eating disorders, but other issues also need to be addressed. None of the research thus far has looked at possible relationships between the value placed on appearance, body satisfaction, dysfunctional eating attitudes and behaviors, and stages of coming out, self-acceptance, internalized homophobia and heterosexism, and assimilation into the lesbian and gay communities in samples of lesbians and gay men. Some of the differences in the findings in this research literature may be the result of differences on these variables among the lesbian and gay male samples. Many of the lesbians in this study, for example, made comments in the margins of the questionnaires indicating that they had experienced greater difficulty with body satisfaction and dysfunctional eating before they had come out. It is possible that lesbians and gay men begin to look more different from their heterosexual counterparts as they become more assimilated into the lesbian and gay subcultures and gain a greater acceptance of themselves as lesbians and gay men. This study suggests that this assimilation process may produce different results for lesbians and gay men with lesbians becoming less dissatisfied with their bodies and gay men becoming more obsessed with their appearance.

All of the research cited in this chapter treats sexual orientation as a dichotomous variable. Subjects were classified as heterosexual or homosexual. This may also affect the results. In reality, sexual orientation is a continuous variable from homosexuality through bisexuality to heterosexuality. Further research is needed to determine whether the treatment of sexual orientation as a dichotomous variable distorts the results obtained. It is quite possible that the use of sexual orientation as a continuous variable would provide a much richer understanding of the phenomena discussed in this chapter.

Although these and other methodological problems need to be addressed in further research in this area, the results of this study were dramatic enough to provide substantial support for the hypothesis that sexual objectification results in an increased emphasis on physical attractiveness, greater body dissatisfaction, and increased vulnerability to eating disorders. The results of this study enhance our understanding of the individual psychological ramifications of our culture's obsession with youth and beauty. They elucidate the ways in which sexual objectification operates within the lesbian and gay subcultures and the dominant heterosexual culture. They point to the need for attempts to reduce the emphasis on appearance and beauty in our culture which appears, if anything, to be increasing and may be causing emotional distress in ever greater numbers of people.

These results are also important specifically in the prevention and treatment of eating disorders. Although there are undeniably many important individual psychological factors in the development of eating disorders, these occur in a sociocultural context that places inflated value on youth and beauty and encourages the obsession with dieting and weight loss that is the hallmark of anorexia and bulimia. Failure to acknowledge the sociocultural context of these disorders leading to disproportionate or exclusive emphasis on emotional aspects may be actually detrimental to the treatment of these disorders. Changes in our cultural values will be important in counteracting both the "normative discontent" (Rodin, Silberstein, and Striegel-Moore, 1985, p. 267) that most heterosexual women and gay men feel about their bodies and the growing incidence and prevalence of eating disorders in these two groups.

REFERENCES

Altman, D. (1982). *The homosexualization of America, the Americanization of the homosexual.* New York: St. Martins Press.

Anderson, A. E. and Mickalide, A. D. (1983). Anorexia nervosa in the male: An underdiagnosed disorder. *Psychosomatics*, 24, 1066-1075.

Berscheid, E., Walster, E., and Bohrnstedt, G. (1972, July). A *Psychology Today* questionnaire: Body image. *Psychology Today*, 6, 57-66.

Berscheid, E., Walster, E., and Bohrnstedt, G. (1973, November). The happy American body: A survey report. *Psychology Today*, 7, 119-131.

Blumstein, P. and Schwarz, P. (1983). *American couples: Money, work, and sex.* New York: William Morrow.

Boskind-Lodahl, M. (1976). Cinderella's stepsisters: A feminist perspective on anorexia nervosa and bulimia. *Signs: Journal of Women in Culture and Society*, 2, 342-356.

Brand, P. A., Rothblum, E. D., and Solomon, L. J. (1992). A comparison of lesbians, gay men, and heterosexuals on weight and restrained eating. *International Journal of Eating Disorders*, 11, 253-259.

Brown, L. (1987). Lesbians, weight, and eating: New analyses and perspectives. In *Boston Lesbian Psychologies Collective* (Eds.), *Lesbian Psychologies*, (pp. 294-309). Urbana: University of Illinois Press.

Bruch, H. (1973). *Eating disorders: Obesity, anorexia nervosa, and the person within.* New York: Basic Books.

Bruch, H. (1978). *The golden cage: The enigma of anorexia nervosa.* Cambridge, MA: Harvard University Press.

Button, E. J. and Whitehouse, A. (1981). Subclinical anorexia nervosa. *Psychological Medicine*, 11, 509-516.

Canning, H. and Meyer, J. (1966). Obesity—Its possible effects on college acceptance. *New England Journal of Medicine*, 275, 1172-1174.

Cash, T. F., Winstead, B. A., and Janda, L. H. (1985, July). Your body, yourself: A *Psychology Today* reader survey. *Psychology Today*, 22-26.

Cash, T. F., Winstead, B. A., and Janda, L. H. (1986, April). The great American shape up: Body image survey report. *Psychology Today*, 30-37.

Chernin, K. (1981). *The obsession: Reflections on the tyranny of slenderness.* New York: Harper and Row.

Clark, D. (1977). *Loving someone gay.* Millbrae, CA: Celestial Arts.

Cobb, S. (1943). *Borderlands of psychiatry.* (Harvard University Monograph in Medicine and Public Health No. 4). Cambridge, MA: Harvard University Press.

Coombs, R. H. and Kendell, W. F. (1966). Sex differences in dating aspirations and satisfaction with computer-selected partners. *Journal of Marriage and the Family*, 28, 62-66.

Cooper, P. J., Taylor, M. J., Cooper, Z., and Fairburn, C. G. (1987). The development and validation of the Body Shape Questionnaire. *International Journal of Eating Disorders*, 6, 485-494.

Crisp, A. H. (1967). Anorexia nervosa. *Hospital Medicine*, 1, 713-718.

Crisp, A. H. and Toms, D. A. (1972). Primary anorexia nervosa or weight phobia in the male: Report on 13 cases. *British Medical Journal*, 1, 334-338.

Dally, P. (1969). *Anorexia nervosa.* London: Heinemann.

Duddle, M. (1973). An increase in anorexia nervosa in a university population. *British Journal of Psychiatry*, 123, 711-712.

Dworkin, S. H. (1988). Not in man's image: Lesbians and the cultural oppression of body image. *Women and Therapy*, 8, 27-39.

Enns, M. P., Drewnowski, A., and Grinker, J. A. (1987). Body composition, body size estimation, and attitudes towards eating in male college athletes. *Psychosomatic Medicine*, 49, 56-64.

Franzoi, S. E. and Herzog, M. E. (1986). The Body Esteem Scale: A convergent and discriminant validity study. *Journal of Personality Assessment*, 50, 2431.

Franzoi, S. E. and Herzog, M.E. (1987). Judging physical attractiveness: What body aspects do we use? *Personality and Social Psychology Bulletin*, 13, 19-33.

Franzoi, S. E. and Shields, S. A. (1984). The Body Esteem Scale: Multidimensional structure and sex differences in a college population. *Journal of Personality Assessment*, 48, 173-178.

Gagnard, A. (1986). From feast to famine: Depiction of ideal body type in magazine advertising: 1950-1954. In E. F. Larkin (Ed.), *Proceedings of the 1986 Conference of the American Academy of Advertising.* Norman, Oklahoma.

Garfinkel, P. E. and Garner, D. M. (1982). *Anorexia nervosa: A multidimensional perspective.* New York: Brunner/Mazel.

Garner, D. M. and Garfinkel, P. E. (1979). The Eating Attitudes Test: An index of the symptoms of anorexia nervosa. *Psychological Medicine*, 9, 273-279.

Garner, D. M. and Garfinkel, P. E. (1980). Sociocultural factors in the development of anorexia nervosa. *Psychological Medicine*, 10, 647-656.

Garner, D. M., Garfinkel, P. E., Schwartz, D., and Thompson, M. (1980). Cultural expectations of thinness in women. *Psychological Reports*, 47, 483-491.

Garner, D. M., Olmstead, M. P., Bohr, Y., and Garfinkel, P. E. (1982). The Eating Attitudes Test: Psychometric features and clinical correlates. *Psychological Medicine*, 12, 871-878.

Garner, D. M., Olmstead, M. P., and Polivy, J. (1983). Development and validation of multidimensional eating disorder inventory for anorexia nervosa and bulimia. *International Journal of Eating Disorders*, 2, 15-35.

Goldblatt, P. B., Moore, M. E., and Stunkard, A. J. (1965). Social factors in obesity. *Journal of the American Medical Association*, 192, 1039-1044.

Gull, W. W. (1874). Anorexia nervosa (Apepsia hysterica, anorexia hysterica). *Transactions of the Clinical Society of Medicine*, 7, 22-28.

Hatfield, E. and Sprecher, S. (1986). *Mirror, mirror: The importance of looks in everyday life.* New York: SUNY Press.

Herzog, D. B., Newman, K. L., and Warshaw, M. (1991). Body image dissatisfaction in homosexual and heterosexual males. *Journal of Nervous and Mental Disease,* 179, 356-359.

Herzog, D. B., Norman, D. K., Gordon, C., and Pepose, M. (1984). Sexual conflict and eating disorders in 27 males. *American Journal of Psychiatry,* 141, 989-990.

Jones, D. J., Fox, M. M., Babigian, H. M., and Hutton, H. E. (1980). Epidemiology of anorexia nervosa in Monroe County, New York: 1960-1978. *Psychosomatic Medicine,* 42, 551-558.

Kendell, R. E., Hall, D. J., Hailey, A., and Babigian, H. M. (1973). The epidemiology of anorexia nervosa. *Psychological Medicine,* 3, 200-203.

Kessler, J. (1966). *Psychopathology of childhood.* Engelwood Cliffs, NJ: Prentice Hall.

Kidd, C. B. and Wood, J. F. (1966). Some observations on anorexia nervosa. *Postgraduate Medical Journal,* 42, 443-448.

King, M. B. and Mezey, G. (1987). Eating behavior in male race jockeys. *Psychological Medicine,* 17, 249-253.

Kleinberg, S. (1980). *Alienated affections: Being gay in America.* New York: St. Martin's Press.

Lakoff, R. T. and Scherr, R. L. (1954). *Face value: The politics of beauty.* Boston: Routledge and Kegan Paul.

Leichner, P., Arnett, J. Rallo, J. S., Srikameswaran, S., and Vulcano, B. (1986). An epidemiologic study of maladaptive eating attitudes in a Canadian school age population. *International Journal of Eating Disorders,* 5, 969-982.

Lerner, R. M. and Karabenick, S. A. (1974). Physical attractiveness, body attitudes, and self-concept in late adolescents. *Journal of Youth and Adolescence,* 3, 307-316.

Lerner, R. M., Orlos, J. B., and Knapp, J. R. (1976). Physical attractiveness, physical effectiveness, and self-concept in late adolescents. *Adolescence,* 11, 313-326.

Metropolitan Life Insurance Company. (1954). Measurement of overweight. *Statistical Bulletin,* 65, 20-23.

Metropolitan Life Insurance Company. (1983). 1983 Metropolitan height and weight tables. *Statistical Bulletin,* 64, 2-9.

Millman, M. (1980). *Such a pretty face: Being fat in America.* New York: W. W. Norton.

Mishkind, M. E., Rodin, J., Silberstein, L. R., and Striegel-Moore, R. H. (1986). The embodiment of masculinity: Cultural, psychological, and behavioral dimensions. *American Behavioral Scientist,* 29, 545-562.

Morton, R. R. (1689). *Phthisiologia–Or a treatise of consumptions wherein the difference, nature, causes, signs, and cure of all sorts of consumptions are explained.* London: Sam Smith and Benjamin Walford.

Nemiah, J. C. (1950). Anorexia nervosa: A clinical psychiatric study. *Medicine,* 29, 255-268.

Ollendick, T. H. and Hart, K. J. (1986). Drs. Ollendick and Hart reply [letter]. *American Journal of Psychiatry,* 143, 680-681.

Orbach, S. (1978). *Fat is a feminist issue.* New York: Berkeley Press.

Rodin, J., Silberstein, L. R., and Striegel-Moore, R. H. (1985). Women and weight: A normative discontent. In T. B. Sonderegger (Ed.), *Nebraska symposium on motivation: Psychology and gender,* Vol. 32, (pp. 267-307). Lincoln: University of Nebraska Press.

Schneider, J. A. and Agras, W. S. (1987). Bulimia in males: A matched comparison with females. *International Journal of Eating Disorders,* 6, 235-242.

Sergios, P. and Cody, J. (1985/86). Importance of physical attractiveness and social assertiveness skills in male homosexual dating behavior and partner selection. *Journal of Homosexuality,* 12, 71-54.

Siever, M. D. (1988, August). Sexual orientation, gender, and the perils of sexual objectification. Paper presented at the 96th Annual Convention of the American Psychological Association, Atlanta, Georgia.

Siever, M. D. (1990). Sexual orientation, gender, and socioculturally acquired vulnerability to eating disorders (Doctoral dissertation, University of Washington, 1989). Dissertation Abstracts International, 50, 5335B.

Siever, M. D. (1994). Sexual orientation and gender as factors in socioculturally acquired vulnerability to body dissatisfaction and eating disorders. *Journal of Consulting and Clinical Psychology,* 62, 252-260.

Silberstein, L. R., Mishkind, M. E., Striegel-Moore, R. H., Timko, C., and Rodin, J. (1989). Men and their bodies: A comparison of homosexual and heterosexual men. *Psychosomatic Medicine,* 51, 337-346.

Silberstein, L. R., Striegel-Moore, R. H., Timko, C., and Rodin, J. (1988). Behavioral and psychological implications of body dissatisfaction: Do men and women differ? *Sex Roles,* 19, 219-232.

Snow, J. T. and Harris, M. B. (1986). An analysis of weight and diet content in five women's interest magazines. *Journal of Obesity and Weight Regulation,* 5, 194-214.

Society of Actuaries and Association of Life Insurance Medical Directors of America. (1980). *Build and blood pressure study, 1979.* Chicago: Author.

Striegel-Moore, R. H., Silberstein, L. R., and Rodin, J. (1986). Toward an understanding of risk factors for bulimia. *American Psychologist,* 41, 246-263.

Striegel-Moore, R. H., Tucker, N., and Hsu, J. (1990). Body image dissatisfaction and disordered eating in lesbian college students. *International Journal of Eating Disorders,* 9, 493-500.

Stroebe, W., Insko, C. A., Thompson, V. D., and Layton, B. D. (1971). Effects of physical attractiveness, attitude similarity, and sex on various aspects of interpersonal attraction. *Journal of Personality and Social Psychology,* 18, 79-91.

Stunkard, A., Sorensen, T., and Schulsinger, F. (1980). Use of the Danish Adoption Register for the study of obesity and thinness. In S. Kety (Ed.), *The genetics of neurological and psychiatric disorders,* (pp. 115-120). New York: Raven Press.

Theander, S. (1970). Anorexia nervosa: A psychiatric investigation of 94 female patients. *Acta Psychiatrica Scandinavica,* (Suppl. 214), 1-194.

Turnbull, J. D., Freeman, C. P. L., and Annandale, A. (1987). Physical and psychological characteristics of five male bulimics. *British Journal of Psychiatry,* 150, 25-29.

Vail, J. P. and Staudt, V. M. (1950). Attitudes of college students toward marriage and related problems: I. Dating and marriage selection. *Journal of Psychology,* 30, 171-182.

Wooley, S. C., and Wooley, O. W. (1984, February). Feeling fat in a thin society. *Glamour,* pp. 198-252.

Yager, J., Kurtzman, F., Landsverk, J., and Wiesmeier. (1988). Behaviors and attitudes related to eating disorders in homosexual male college students. *American Journal of Psychiatry,* 145, 495-497.

Zubin, J., Magaziner, J., and Steinhauer, S. (1983). The metamorphosis of schizophrenia: From chronicity to vulnerability. *Psychological Medicine,* 13, 551-571.

Zubin, J. and Spring, B. (1977). Vulnerability–A new view of schizophrenia. *Journal of Abnormal Psychology,* 86, 103-126.

Zubin, J. and Steinhauer, S. (1981). How to break the logjam in schizophrenia. *Journal of Nervous and Mental Diseases,* 169, 477-492.

Index